Joomla! 3 Beginner's Guide

A clear, hands-on guide to creating perfect content managed websites with the free Joomla! CMS

Eric Tiggeler

[PACKT] open source *
PUBLISHING   community experience distilled

BIRMINGHAM - MUMBAI

Joomla! 3 Beginner's Guide

First published: March 2013

3 9547 00384 1256

Production Reference: 1130313

Published by Packt Publishing Ltd.
Livery Place
35 Livery Street
Birmingham B3 2PB, UK.

ISBN 978-1-78216-434-0

www.packtpub.com

Cover Image by Brian D. McStotts (mcshots@earthlink.net)

Credits

Author
Eric Tiggeler

Reviewers
Peter Martin

Sanjeev Shrestha

Acquisition Editor
Robin de Jongh

Lead Technical Editor
Mayur Hule

Technical Editors
Dominic Pereira

Dennis John

Project Coordinator
Anish Ramchandani

Proofreader
Katherine Tarr

Indexer
Tejal R. Soni

Graphics
Aditi Gajjar

Production Coordinator
Manu Joseph

Cover Work
Manu Joseph

About the Author

Eric Tiggeler is an author of several books on Joomla!, such as the highly successful *Joomla! 2.5 Beginner's Guide*. He has written several Dutch Joomla! guides. His book got excellent reader reviews. Eric also writes tutorials for several computer magazines and for the Dutch Joomla! community website. Over the last ten years, Eric has developed numerous websites, big and small—many of them using Joomla!

Eric is fascinated by the Web as a powerful, creative, and ever-changing means of communication—and by revolutionary software such as Joomla!, enabling anybody to create beautiful and user-friendly websites.

On a daily basis, Eric works as a consultant and copywriter at a communication consultancy company affiliated with the Free University of Amsterdam. Over the last few years, he has written more than twenty Dutch books on writing and communication. His passion is making complex things easy to understand.

Eric Tiggeler is married and has two daughters. He lives and works in Hilversum (The Netherlands). On the Web, you'll find him on www.joomla.erictiggeler.nl (in Dutch) and www.joomm.net (in English).

Any book is a team effort, so I'd like to thank everyone at Packt for their encouraging commitment to this project. Thanks also to the reviewers—for testing the alpha version of this book and helping me create a thoroughly reliable final release!

About the Reviewers

Peter Martin has a keen interest in computers, programming, sharing knowledge, and how people use information technology. He has a bachelor's degree in Economics (International Marketing Management) and a master's degree in Mass Communication.

He discovered PHP/MySQL in 2003 and Joomla's predecessor, Mambo CMS, a year later. Peter has his own business www.db8.nl (founded in 2005) and he supports companies and organizations with Joomla implementations, support, and Joomla extension development.

Peter is actively involved in the Joomla community where he is a member of the Community Leadership Team and Global Moderator at the Joomla forum.

Furthermore, Peter has reviewed the following Packt Publishing books:

- *Joomla! Search Engine Optimization* by Ric Shreves
- *Joomla! 2.5 Beginner's Guide* by Eric Tiggeler
- *Joomla! 1.6 First Look* by Eric Tiggeler
- *Joomla! 1.5 Templates Cookbook* by Richard Carter

His other interests are open source software, Linux (Debian, Arch Linux), Raspberry Pi, music (collecting vinyl records), art house movies, and trivia. Peter lives in Nijmegen, The Netherlands.

Sanjeev Shrestha works for a company based in Nepal as a Director of Technology and Innovation. He started his career as a web developer using PHP, MySQL nearly 10 years ago. Sanjeev holds a Engineering degree in IT from Pokhara University, Nepal. His main interests are web development, Linux administration, Cloud Computing and distributed systems.

He is an avid Joomla! lover and has been working with Joomla! since 2007. He has developed numerous popular Joomla extensions.

He loves open source and leaves no stone unturned to promote open source technologies in the local market. He is a proud founding member of PHP Developers Nepal and MongoDB users Nepal which promotes knowledge sharing among the developers.

I would like to thank my family and friends who let me sit alone for hours to read the book and review. I would also like to thank Packt Publishing for providing me with this opportunity to review the book.

www.PacktPub.com

Support files, eBooks, discount offers and more

You might want to visit www.PacktPub.com for support files and downloads related to your book.

Did you know that Packt offers eBook versions of every book published, with PDF and ePub files available? You can upgrade to the eBook version at www.PacktPub.com and as a print book customer, you are entitled to a discount on the eBook copy. Get in touch with us at service@packtpub.com for more details.

At www.PacktPub.com, you can also read a collection of free technical articles, sign up for a range of free newsletters and receive exclusive discounts and offers on Packt books and eBooks.

http://PacktLib.PacktPub.com

Do you need instant solutions to your IT questions? PacktLib is Packt's online digital book library. Here, you can access, read and search across Packt's entire library of books.

Why Subscribe?

- Fully searchable across every book published by Packt
- Copy and paste, print and bookmark content
- On demand and accessible via web browser

Free Access for Packt account holders

If you have an account with Packt at www.PacktPub.com, you can use this to access PacktLib today and view nine entirely free books. Simply use your login credentials for immediate access.

Table of Contents

Preface

Joomla is one of the most popular open-source Content Management Systems, actively developed and supported by a world-wide user community. It's a free, fun, and feature-rich tool for anyone who wants to create dynamic, interactive websites. Even beginners can deploy Joomla to build professional websites, although it can be challenging to get beyond the basics and build the site that completely meets your needs. This book will help you to start building websites with Joomla quickly, learning step-by-step to get the most out of its advanced features.

What this book covers

Chapter 1, Introduction: A New and Easy Way to Build Websites, in this chapter you'll learn why you want to use Joomla to create an advanced, cool-looking site that's easy to expand, customize, and maintain.

Chapter 2, Installation: Getting Joomla Up and Running, helps you learn how to install Joomla on your own computer or on a web server, and how to create a sample site.

Chapter 3, First Steps: Getting to Know Joomla, here, you'll get familiar with the basic concepts of Joomla, the administrative interface, and the principles of a website constructed out of 'building blocks'.

Chapter 4, Web Building Basics: Creating a Site in an Hour, here, you'll face a real-life challenge of using Joomla to build a basic but expandable website fast. You'll customize Joomla's default sample site to fit your needs, adding content, menu links, and change the site's look and feel.

Chapter 5, Small Sites, Big Sites: Organizing your Content Effectively, makes it easy to add and find information on your site by designing a clear, expandable, and manageable structure for your content.

Chapter 6, Creating Killer Content: Adding and Editing Articles, will teach you to create content pages that are attractive and easy to read, and you'll learn about different ways to add images and to to tweak the page layout.

Chapter 7, Welcoming Your Visitors: Creating Attractive Home Pages and Overview Pages, here, you'll create a home page and overview pages to entice visitors to actually read all your valuable content.

Chapter 8, Helping Your Visitors Find What They Want: Managing Menus, will teach you how you can help the visitor to find what they want easily by designing clear and easy navigation through menus.

Chapter 9, Opening Up the Site: Enabling Users to Log In and Contribute, shows how to enable users to log in and allow them to create content and manage the website.

Chapter 10, Getting the Most out of Your Site: Extending Joomla, teaches you on how to extend Joomla's capabilities using all sorts of extensions—using an image gallery to attractively display pictures, automatically showing article teasers on the home page, or enhancing your workspace by installing an easier content editor.

Chapter 11, Creating an Attractive Design: Working with Templates, explains how templates will give your site a fresh look and feel, and make it easy to create an individual look, different from a "typical" Joomla site. You'll also learn to install and customize templates.

Chapter 12, Attracting Search Engine Traffic: SEO Tips and Techniques, will show you how to increase your site's visibility for search engines by applying Search Engine Optimization (SEO) techniques, such as creating friendly URLs.

Appendix A, Keeping the Site Secure, will show you some simple, common-sense steps you can take to keep your site safe from hackers or data loss.

Appendix B, Creating a Multilingual Site, here, you'll find a walkthrough of the steps involved in creating a bilingual website, using the multilingual capabilities built into Joomla.

Appendix C, Pop Quiz Answers, contains answers to the multiple choice pop quizzes you will find throughout the book.

What you need for this book

To follow the tutorials and exercises in this book, you'll need a computer with Internet access. It's recommended to have a web hosting account so that you can install Joomla online.

Who this book is for

The *Joomla! 3 Beginner's Guide* is aimed at anyone who wants to build and maintain a great website and get the most out of Joomla. It helps you build on the skills and knowledge you may already have of creating websites—but if you're new to this subject, you won't have any difficulty understanding the instructions. Of course, we'll touch upon basic terms and concepts (such as HTML and CSS), but if you're not familiar with these, you'll also find references to some web resources.

Conventions

In this book, you will find several headings appearing frequently.

To give clear instructions of how to complete a procedure or task, we use:

Time for action – heading

1. Action 1
2. Action 2
3. Action 3

Instructions often need some extra explanation so that they make sense, so they are followed with:

What just happened?

This heading explains the working of tasks or instructions that you have just completed.

You will also find some other learning aids in the book, including:

Pop quiz – heading

These are short multiple-choice questions intended to help you test your own understanding.

Have a go hero – heading

These are practical challenges and give you ideas for experimenting with what you have learned.

You will also find a number of styles of text that distinguish between different kinds of information. Here are some examples of these styles, and an explanation of their meaning.

Code words in text are shown as follows: "Change the `width` and `height` values to reflect the size of the new image. To shift the image a little to the left-hand side, decrease the `margin-left` value."

A block of code is set as follows:

```
#logo {
    float:left;
    background:#e5e5e5;
    display:inline-block;
    padding:0 20px;
    font-size:18px;}
```

When we wish to draw your attention to a particular part of a code block, the relevant lines or items are set in bold:

```
#logo {
    float:left;
    background:#e5e5e5;
    display:inline-block;
    padding:0 20px;
    font-size:18px;}
```

New terms and **important words** are shown in bold. Words that you see on the screen, in menus or dialog boxes for example, appear in the text like this: "In the **Menu Manager: Edit Menu Item** screen, click on the **Page Display Options** panel name on the right-hand side of the screen to open this panel."

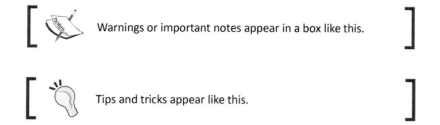

Warnings or important notes appear in a box like this.

Tips and tricks appear like this.

Reader feedback

Feedback from our readers is always welcome. Let us know what you think about this book—what you liked or may have disliked. Reader feedback is important for us to develop titles that you really get the most out of.

To send us general feedback, simply send an e-mail to `feedback@packtpub.com`, and mention the book title through the subject of your message.

If there is a topic that you have expertise in and you are interested in either writing or contributing to a book, see our author guide on `www.packtpub.com/authors`.

Customer support

Now that you are the proud owner of a Packt book, we have a number of things to help you to get the most from your purchase.

Errata

Although we have taken every care to ensure the accuracy of our content, mistakes do happen. If you find a mistake in one of our books—maybe a mistake in the text or the code—we would be grateful if you would report this to us. By doing so, you can save other readers from frustration and help us improve subsequent versions of this book. If you find any errata, please report them by visiting `http://www.packtpub.com/submit-errata`, selecting your book, clicking on the **errata submission form** link, and entering the details of your errata. Once your errata are verified, your submission will be accepted and the errata will be uploaded to our website, or added to any list of existing errata, under the Errata section of that title.

Piracy

Piracy of copyright material on the Internet is an ongoing problem across all media. At Packt, we take the protection of our copyright and licenses very seriously. If you come across any illegal copies of our works, in any form, on the Internet, please provide us with the location address or website name immediately so that we can pursue a remedy.

Please contact us at copyright@packtpub.com with a link to the suspected pirated material.

We appreciate your help in protecting our authors, and our ability to bring you valuable content.

Questions

You can contact us at questions@packtpub.com if you are having a problem with any aspect of the book, and we will do our best to address it.

1

Introduction: A New and Easy Way to Build Websites

You want to build a website. It should look great, and it should be easy to use and maintain. Keeping it up-to-date should be effortless. Changing the appearance of your site should take minutes, not hours. You don't want to manage it all by yourself, but you want to enable other people to log in and write new content without having to understand HTML or other coding languages. And when your site grows, it should be easy to extend it with new functionality—maybe adding a forum, or a newsletter. If that's what you're looking for, welcome to Joomla.

When it comes to creating a great, professional-looking website that's easy to use, you really can't beat the power of a **Content Management System** (**CMS**) such as Joomla. Without writing a single line of code, you can create any kind of site, boasting a variety of cool and advanced features.

Join the CMS revolution

Maybe you have already built websites the traditional way. That basically meant creating HTML documents—web pages—one by one. As the site grew, you'd end up with a bunch of HTML documents, trying to keep all of them organized and making sure all menu links stay up-to-date. You'd probably maintain the site by yourself, because it was hard for other people to find their way around the structure of your particular site, or be proficient in the web editing software you use.

Enter the Holy Grail of web building: the Content Management System! A CMS is an application that runs on a web server. It allows you to develop and maintain a website online. It comes packed with features, ranging from basic features to add and modify content to advanced functionality such as user registration or site search capability. In short, a CMS makes it possible to build sites that would normally involve a full team of web professionals with a massive amount of time, money, and expertise at their disposal.

All that magic is made possible because a CMS is really an advanced set of scripts (written in a scripting language, such as PHP) that uses a database to store the content of your website. From that database, it retrieves bits and pieces of content and presents them as web pages.

This dynamic way of storing and presenting content makes a CMS very flexible. Do you want to show only a selection of articles from a specific category on a page? Do you want to display only the intro texts of the most recent articles on the home page? Do you want to add a list of links to the most popular contents? Do you want to limit access to registered users? It's all possible—just pick the right settings. Additionally, a CMS allows you to integrate all sorts of extra features, such as contact forms, picture galleries, and much more.

The best part is that CMSes like these are yours to download and deploy today. You can pick your CMS of choice from a range of freely available open source products. Your new CMS-powered site can be online tomorrow. Now how's that for a great deal?

 What's open source software? The source code of this type of software is "unlocked", unlike software developed commercially. Everyone has access to the Joomla source code and software developers are encouraged to modify and to help improve the software. The name Joomla stands for "all together". It's as much a software product as it is an international community of people working together voluntarily to expand and improve that product. Most open source software is distributed free of charge, as is the case with Joomla. However, some Joomla extensions are commercial—you have to pay for them, but it's still open software (that is, you get access to the source code).

Why would you choose Joomla?

There are many open source CMSes around. They're all great tools, each with its own typical uses and benefits. Why would you want to choose Joomla?

- People tend to choose Joomla because they find it easy to use. It has a clear and friendly user interface that keeps on getting better over the years. The redesigned Joomla 3 interface makes it easy to create and publish articles to keep your site current. You can manage content anytime, anywhere, whether you're using a web browser on a PC, a tablet computer, or a smartphone.

◆ Adding new features to your site takes just a few clicks. There are thousands of extensions available for Joomla, ranging from menu systems to commenting systems and forums.

◆ It's very easy to change the site's appearance—templates for Joomla are abundant and can be installed within minutes, giving your site a fresh look and feel.

◆ The current Joomla release, version 3, adds many improvements and new features. It's easier to install the CMS, the HTML output is based upon the latest standards, and dozens of little changes—such as an improved text editor screen for creating content—make the CMS easier to work with and more powerful.

Apart from these typical Joomla benefits, it comes with all of the advantages of a state-of-the-art CMS. To name just a few:

◆ It's really easy to add or edit content and to keep it organized (even if there's lots of it). Joomla allows you to categorize content using an unlimited number of multilevel categories.

◆ Keeping hyperlinks up-to-date is greatly automated. For example, you can add category overview pages without ever having to manually update them—on a category overview page, Joomla will automatically add links to all new pages you'll put in that category.

◆ You don't have to maintain the website all by yourself. Other users can add content, add new menu items, and much more.

The numbers seem to indicate that Joomla is the open source CMS of choice for web builders worldwide. It's the engine behind some 20 million websites worldwide and this number is still growing rapidly day by day. It's is one of the biggest open source software projects around, supported by a huge user community and constantly being developed further by an international team of volunteers.

What kind of sites can you build with Joomla?

Let's have a look at some great real-world examples of sites built using Joomla. If you're anything like me, seeing inspirational examples is what makes you want to get started right away, creating something equally cool (or preferably something even better). These are just a few examples from the Web and from the Joomla site showcase (`http://community.joomla.org/showcase`). They are very diverse sites from very different organizations, each with their own goals and target groups. What they have in common is that they deploy Joomla in a way that you could too. They adapt the CMS to their specific needs, making it perfectly suited for the content they present and the impression they want to make.

Here's an example from the Alliance for Catholic Education in the United States (`ace.nd.edu`). The home page uses various ways to present highlights from the site's impressive amount of contents.

The following example is a website of a M+H Architects, providing a clear and attractive overview of their services and projects (`mharch.com`):

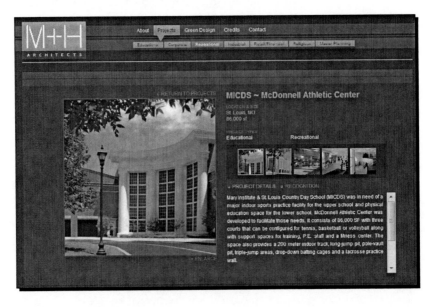

Joomla can handle complex sites with thousands of pages. Here's an illustration of a content-rich site with a made-to-measure design—the Guggenheim Museum website (guggenheim.org):

One final example demonstrates that Joomla sites don't have to look anything like a typical CMS-powered site. You can use quite a different design—and still take advantage of Joomla's default functionality to power the site. This site presents a Dutch events company (puurspecialevents.nl):

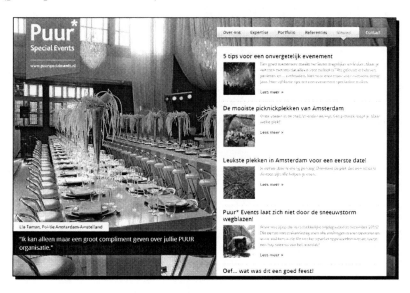

If you're looking for some more inspiration, browse the official Joomla showcase at `http://community.joomla.org/showcase` or go to `www.bestofjoomla.com` and have a look around the **Best of Sites** section.

Learning to use Joomla

It may sound too good to be true. Does Joomla really make creating state-of-the-art websites easy as ABC. Let's be honest—it will make it reasonably easy, but of course it does require you to invest some time and effort. After all, working with Joomla (or any CMS) is very different from building websites the traditional way. You'll notice this as soon as you start installing the system. Compared to setting up a simple static website consisting of a few HTML pages, building a Joomla-powered site takes a bit more preparation. You'll need hosting space that meets specific requirements and you'll need to set up a database. It's very doable, and this book will guide you through the process step by step.

Once you've got Joomla set up, you'll soon get the hang of creating a basic site. The next challenge is to get things just right for your particular goals. After all, you don't want "just any Joomla-powered site"—you want to build a specific site, aimed at your specific target audience. The *Joomla Beginner's Guide* will help you to go beyond a basic site and make the choices that fit your goals.

Even using a CMS, it will take time and effort to create and maintain great websites. However, Joomla will make it much easier and much more fun for you (and your web team members) to get your site started and keep it evolving.

What you'll learn using this book

The *Joomla Beginner's Guide* isn't just about Joomla—it's about making websites, and it shows you how to use Joomla to make the best website you can. After all, if you're interested in all Joomla features and capabilities, you can get a reasonable impression by exploring the interface by yourself and trying out the menus and options. However, even a user-friendly interface doesn't tell you how to deploy it in the best way in real-life circumstances. What's the best and fastest way to get started, what features and options are particularly useful, what are the ones you probably don't have to bother using at all? I want to help you to tame the beast that's called Joomla, to find your own way around and to get things done—with a great-looking, user-friendly website as the output. That's what the *Joomla Beginner's Guide* is all about.

The *Joomla Beginner's Guide* is focused on learning by doing—the structure of the book reflects the process of building a website. In the first few chapters, you learn how to install Joomla, take a tour of the system, and get a feel for what it's like. After that, you'll learn all that's needed to build and maintain your own site, such as:

- mastering the fundamentals by creating a basic website in one hour
- adapt and expand the site to meet your changing needs. You'll set up a site structure and learn how to add different types of pages
- how to make content easy to find through well-designed menus and design an attractive home page
- how to engage your web visitors and turn them into active users who can register and add content
- extend Joomla's capabilities and add special features (such as a picture gallery) to the site
- change the site layout and make it more attractive
- how to tweak the site to attract search engine traffic and to keep the site safe

Feel free to skip chapters!

Don't worry, to learn using Joomla you don't have to follow all the book chapters and the exercises in them step by step. After you've gone through the introductory chapters, maybe you feel comfortable to skip to changing the design of your site or adding extensions. That's okay—you can jump straight into most of the further chapters and follow the exercises there as long as you have a working version of Joomla and some dummy content available.

What's the current version of Joomla?

On the Joomla website, two versions are available for download: 2.5 and 3.x. Joomla 2.5 will be supported until 2014. It's still commonly used, especially by experienced web developers, who need a matured CMS and want to be able to choose from thousands of extensions, developed specifically for 2.5. Joomla 3.0 is the first release of the next generation. It's stable and reliable, but the Joomla developers will keep on improving it until the new long-term release, 3.5, is finished. When you start using Joomla now, your best choice is version 3; you'll benefit from the latest improvements and features straight away, and the number of extensions you can choose from is growing rapidly, day by day.

As Joomla 3 is still being actively developed, new features may become available. An example is the Tags component, which is planned to be added in version 3.1. For updates on these additions, consult the website accompanying this book, www.joomm.net.

About the example site

In the course of this book, you'll learn how to build a realistic example site step-by-step. Instead of just learning about Joomla's capabilities in general terms, you'll meet real-world web building challenges. Throughout the book, you'll achieve all of your fictitious client's goals (that is '*I want a website that my web team members can update themselves*' or '*I want a website that makes it easy to navigate through a large amount of content*').

Now who's that client of yours? It's CORBA, a club of Collectors Of Really Bad Art. They just love bad paintings and ugly sculpture. They argue it can be valuable art—in its own, ugly way. The CORBA people need a website to inform the public about their goals, informing the public about all sorts of bad art, showcasing fine examples of ugly art, and encouraging people to join and participate.

You'll take the CORBA site through different stages of development. First you'll base the site on Joomla's default design and layout:

Later on, you'll add advanced features and shape the site's contents and design to meet the changing needs of your client:

The CORBA site is a good example of what you can accomplish with Joomla. You start out with a basic website and add sophisticated features as you go. Of course, you can follow along in this book without having to actually perform all of the actions described—but you'll find it's a good and fun way to learn building a site and honing your skills step-by-step.

Summary

In this chapter, you've been introduced to the wonderful world of the Joomla CMS. You've learned about the difference between building a website the traditional way and using a CMS. You don't have to create HTML documents (web pages) one by one. Instead you use a web application to develop and maintain your site.

Using a CMS such as Joomla, you can create more powerful sites that are easier to maintain. You've also been introduced to the benefits of using Joomla, such as its ease of use, the ability to add extra features, and the ability to quickly change the look and feel of the site. In the rest of this book, you'll learn how to build a realistic example site with Joomla step-by-step.

However, that's enough background information for now—let's get started! In the next chapter, you'll get the Joomla software up and running. After that, you'll get familiar with the way Joomla works and start building.

2

Installation: Getting Joomla Up and Running

Joomla isn't just an ordinary software package that you can install on your own computer, it needs a Web server to run. If you're new to Joomla, installing a web application may seem daunting. And, let's be honest, running the installation procedure is probably the least exciting part of working with Joomla. However, if you just follow the required steps, it's pretty straightforward. It does take a little preparation, but if you've got everything ready, you can walk through Joomla's user-friendly setup wizard that takes most of the hassle out of the installation.

In this chapter, you'll install Joomla on a web server, allowing you or anyone else with Internet access to immediately see and visit your Joomla-powered site. Your site will be accessible via your own web address (URL), such as `http://www.example.com`. When you build and customize the site, you'll access the site through your browser.

Don't fear the technical mumbo jumbo

Joomla will make it really easy for you to build a state-of-the art website, but installing the program will inevitably introduce you to some technical names and acronyms. Don't let this intimidate you. If you've never heard of PHP, MySQL, and the like, you may be tempted to call in your computer geek nephew to carry out the installation for you, allowing you to jump ahead to the fun and creative part—creating a beautiful site. But rest assured, you can pull this off yourself. It's like following directions to a destination in a city you're new to. If you keep to the instructions, you're certain to get there. Moreover, the more often you do this, you'll get to know the city map better and better. It will take you less and less time to get a new Joomla site up and running.

In this chapter you'll learn about:

- What you need to install Joomla
- How to get Joomla up and running
- What's in the box: what do you get when you install Joomla?
- Where to find further help if you get stuck

So let's get started!

What do you need to start?

To be able to install and run Joomla, you'll need hosting space and a few tools. Here's a full shopping list.

Hosting space

First of all, you'll need hosting space—a place on a web server where you can set up your site, making it accessible for anyone with Internet access. Your hosting account should support the PHP scripting language (as Joomla is written in PHP), it should support the type of database that Joomla uses, called MySQL, and it has to run the Apache server software. Specifically, these are the system requirements for Joomla 3.x:

- **PHP 5.3.1 or higher**: PHP is the scripting language that Joomla is written in.
- **MySQL 5.1 or higher**: The MySQL database is where Joomla stores its data (the contents of your site).
- **Apache 2. x or higher**: Apache is the web server software that processes the PHP instructions for how to pull in contents from the database and display a web page.
- **XML and Zlib support**: Your host's PHP installation should support XML and Zlib functionality. Moreover, the PHP **Magic Quotes GPC** setting should be off. If this setting currently isn't okay, your web host should be able to correct this.

You shouldn't have any difficulty finding hosting accounts that meet these system requirements. If you're not sure, any hosting provider should be able to tell you if they support Joomla.

You can find detailed system requirements at the Joomla official help site: `http://www.joomla.org/technical-requirements.html`.

What if you don't have hosting space?

If you don't have a hosting account yet, you can install Joomla on your computer. This does involve installing web server software first. This means you'll make Joomla run on your computer as if it were a real, "live" web server.

- ◆ The quickest way to do this is to use an all-in-one installation package. Go to http://bitnami.org to download the free, open source **BitNami Joomla Stack** that will automatically install both the web server software and Joomla in one go.

- ◆ Another option is to first install the web server software, and then install the Joomla software on your computer. There are several free web server software packages available, such as XAMPP for Windows, Linux and Apple computers, WampServer for Windows, and MAMP for Apple. See www.wampserver.com, www.apachefriends.org/en/xampp.html, or www.mamp.info.

This approach is OK for testing purposes and it makes it easy to develop a site without having access to a web server. However, there are also a couple of drawbacks. You'll have access to your Joomla site from just one computer, and when your site is ready for the world, you'll have to install it on a real web server anyway. In this book, we'll focus on installing and running Joomla on a web server.

FTP software

To transfer files from your computer to a web server, you need special FTP software. **FTP** is short for **File Transfer Protocol**. An FTP program is comparable to the Windows File Explorer or the Mac Finder. You use it to manage files and move them from one place to another—the only difference being that the FTP program allows you to move files from your computer to your hosting space on a web server (and vice versa).

If you are new to FTP, do a web search for FTP Tutorial to get familiar with the basic procedures. See, for example, http://www.freewebmasterhelp.com/tutorials/ftp.

Looking for FTP software? Check out the free (open source) **FileZilla** software, available for computers running Windows, Apple, and Linux. You can download it from http://filezilla-project.org. And if you're using Firefox, you might be interested in **FireFTP**, an FTP plugin for your browser.

More than one browser

If you're perfectly happy with whatever your current browser may be, you won't have any trouble managing your Joomla site with it. However, people creating websites often install more than one browser on their computer. Apart from the ever-popular Microsoft Internet Explorer (`http://windows.microsoft.com/en-US/internet-explorer/download-ie`), you might want to install Google Chrome (`www.google.com/chrome`), and Mozilla Firefox (`www.mozilla.org`). Having more than one browser allows you to check if your site looks okay in all major browsers. Do make sure that you have the current version of these browsers. Older browsers may not render current websites as they should (especially older versions of Microsoft Internet Explorer are notorious in this respect).

A special benefit of having Chrome or Firefox at your disposal is that these browsers offer a couple of features that make your web-developing life much easier. Google Chrome comes with built-in Developer Tools; right-click on a web page and select the **Inspect Element** functionality to get a look under the hood and analyze the HTML and CSS source code of a page. This can be of great help when you want to customize the style and layout of your website. In Firefox, you have access to similar functionality by installing the Firebug browser add-on (more about using web development tools in *Chapter 11, Creating an Attractive Design: Working with Templates*).

Upgrading from previous versions of Joomla

If you've already built websites with Joomla 1.5 or Joomla 2.5, you can upgrade your existing site to Joomla 3.0 or higher. However, this isn't an automated process. How much effort this takes, depends on what Joomla version your current site is running on and what extensions and templates you're using. What can you do if you want to keep your existing content and the existing structure of your website when upgrading to Joomla 3.x? Here's an overview of the possibilities.

 When you decide to upgrade your site, make sure to create a backup of your current site. This way, if anything goes wrong, you can always revert to the old situation. A great (and free) tool to back up Joomla sites is **Akeeba Backup**, which is available for all Joomla versions from 1.5 up. Visit `www.akeebabackup.com` for more details. To get an impression of the way Akeeba works, see the *Creating a backup with Akeeba Backup* section in *Appendix A, Keeping the Site Secure*.

Updating Joomla 1.5 to 3.x

If your old site is still running on Joomla 1.5, the switch to Joomla 3.x will involve a serious migration process. There's no built-in functionality that takes care of the upgrading. The main reason is that the structure of the content database has changed substantially since Joomla 2.5. However, there are a few tools available to help you migrate your site to the most recent version.

You may want to try out a free extension for Joomla, a component called **jUpgrade**. This will move your entire site, including its database, from 1.5 to 2.5. At the time of writing, jUpgrade doesn't support migrating to Joomla 3.x. After migrating to Joomla 2.5, you'll have to update Joomla 2.5 following the procedure described later in this chapter (see *Updating Joomla 2.5 to 3.x*).

Using jUpgrade, you will still have to update a few things yourself. For example, a template used in Joomla 1.5 won't work in higher versions, so you'll have to use a new template or update the old one. The same holds for extensions used in your old site.

All in all, this means that jUpgrade will be very useful if you want to migrate the CMS itself and its main content (articles and default Joomla extensions). You can find a detailed tutorial on upgrading Joomla 1.5 using jUpgrade on the website accompanying this book:

```
http://www.joomm.net/index.php/joomla-tips-and-tutorials/upgrading-
joomla-1-5-to-2-5
```

You can read more about upgrading on the Joomla documentation pages. See `http://docs.joomla.org/Migrating_from_Joomla_1.5_to_Joomla_2.5`.

 At the time of writing, there's one commercial extension available that takes care of migrating Joomla 1.5 sites to 3.0 in one step—**SP Upgrade**. However, keep in mind that templates and extensions will still have to be upgraded manually. See `http://extensions.joomla.org/extensions/ migration-a-conversion/joomla-migration/15609`.

Updating Joomla 2.5 to 3.x

Since Joomla 2.5, the CMS supports "one click" updates to keep it up-to-date. You can use the built-in Update component of Joomla 2.5 to upgrade to version 3.0 or higher. However, there are a few things to keep in mind:

- The template system of Joomla 3.x has changed, which means you can't just use your old Joomla 2.5 template in Joomla 3.x. You'll have to find out whether the template builder has created a new version that's compatible with Joomla 3.x, or you'll have to convert the old template. Another option is to use the switch to Joomla 3.x as an occasion to change the look of your website and use a new 3.0-ready template.

- Most third-party extensions developed for Joomla 2.5 will have to be converted by their developers to make them Joomla 3.x compatible. If you need to use an extension that's not yet ready for Joomla 3.x, you may need to look for a 3.x-ready extension by another developer that offers similar functionality.

In the previous chapter, you've read about the Joomla release cycle: there will be updates for Joomla 3.x until the next major release, Joomla 3.5, is published.

By default, in Joomla 2.5 you'll only receive updates for Joomla 2.5 (for example, 2.5.1 and so on). To enable automatic updating from Joomla 2.5 to Joomla 3.x, go to **Components | Joomla Update**. Click on **Options** and select **Update server: Short Term Support**.

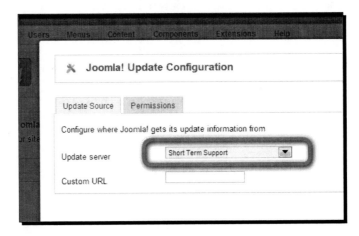

After you've saved this setting, Joomla will notify you as soon as updates are available and it will let you update Joomla 2.5 to 3.x and higher.

Installing Joomla in four steps

If you have set up a web hosting account and got the tools you need, you're set to go. Installing Joomla takes these steps:

1. Download the Joomla files from `www.joomla org`.
2. Place the files on the web server.
3. Create a database.
4. Install Joomla itself, using an installation wizard.

The rest of this chapter will give you a detailed walkthrough of this procedure.

Time for action – downloading the Joomla files

Let's begin and download the current version of Joomla.

1. Point your browser to www.joomla.org. On the home page, click the **Joomla 3** button:

2. You'll be taken to the download page. Select the latest release (at the time of writing this is 3.0.2):

3. Make sure to download the Full Package (the other versions are upgrades for existing Joomla installations).

4. The default download file is a ZIP file. Download this file to your hard drive.

5. Unpack the compressed file to a folder on your hard drive. If you don't have a software program for unpacking files, check out http://www.7-zip.org for an open source file extraction program.

What just happened?

You've downloaded and extracted the Joomla software files. All files required to install Joomla are now stored in a folder on your computer.

Time for action – placing the files on the web server

Next, start up your FTP program (see *What do you need to start?* earlier in this chapter) and upload all the unzipped files in the folder to the web server. This is how you do it:

1. In your FTP program, browse to the folder containing the unzipped Joomla files. Select all files (do not select the folder, only its contents).

2. Select the target directory, the root directory of the web server. The root directory is often called `httpdocs`, `htdocs`, `httpd`, `public_html`, or www. If you can't find that folder, your web hosting company should be able to help you out.

> Don't worry about the name of the root folder (`httpdocs` or any of the other names listed previously). This name won't show up in the web address of your site. Visitors don't have to type www.`example`.`com/httpdocs`, just www.`example`.`com` will take them to your site. However, if you create a folder within `httpdocs`, this folder name will show up in your web address. If you create a folder named `httpdocs/joomla` and install Joomla there, your site will be accessible only through www.`example`. `com/joomla` This means you should only create such a subfolder if this is what you want (for example, when you're just testing Joomla and you want to keep using the root directory for your existing site).

3. In your FTP program, select all files in the Joomla folder. The list of files should resemble the one in the left half of the screen shown in the following screenshot. The following illustration shows the FileZilla screen, but if you're using another FTP program, this shouldn't look much different:

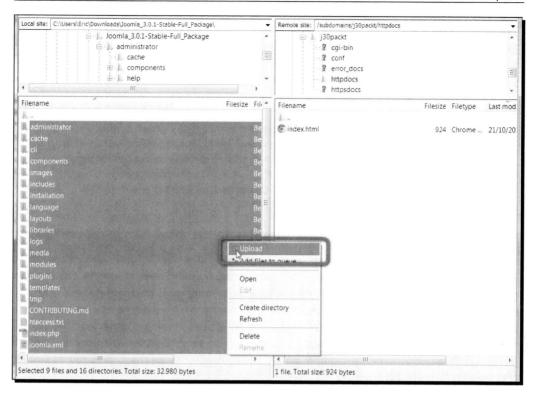

4. On the web server (the right-hand side of the FTP program screen), select the destination folder (httpdocs).

5. On your computer (the left-hand side of the FTP program screen), select all files in the folder containing the Joomla files you unzipped previously. Right-click in the list with selected files and choose **Upload** to copy the Joomla files to the web server root directory.

What just happened?

You've just got your FTP program to copy all Joomla files from your computer to the web server. Don't worry if this takes some time, as uploading thousands of Joomla files can take 10 minutes or more, depending on the speed of your Internet connection.

Some web hosting companies support a feature that allows for faster uploading: they allow you to upload the zipped Joomla file and extract it on the web server, using the file manager tool of the web server control panel. If your hosting provider supports this feature, it's much faster than extracting the ZIP file on your computer and uploading thousands of separate files.

Time for action – creating a database

The next step is creating an empty database for Joomla. If you're new to Joomla, the concept of a web application using a database may take some getting used to. The database isn't a regular file that you can create (or copy, move, or delete) on the web server. To create and manage a database, you use special software. Most web hosting companies offer you database access through a web interface (usually called a **control panel**). Popular control panels are **Plesk** and **CPanel**. You'll find details on the control panel that's available to you in your hosting account information.

In the following example, we'll use **Plesk 8** to create a new database. If your hosting company provides another control panel, the basic procedure won't be very different. However, if you're not sure how to access your web server control panel, your host should be able to provide you with the details. You'll also find online documentation for common web hosting control panels; for CPanel, search for `MySQL Database Wizard` on `http://docs.cpanel.net` to find information this subject.

Sometimes web hosting providers don't allow their users to create their own database. Instead, they provide a pre-installed database. If this is the case, you can go on to step 4, running the Joomla installation wizard. You will need some database details for this: the database name, the database username, and a password for this user. Check the account information you received from your host.

1. Log in to the Plesk control panel with the account information you have received from your hosting provider. To add a new database, click **Databases** and click **Add New Database**.

2. Enter a name for the new database, for example, **joomladatabase**. Click **OK**.

3. Create a new user for the database. Click **Add New Database User** and enter a database username and database password for the new database user:

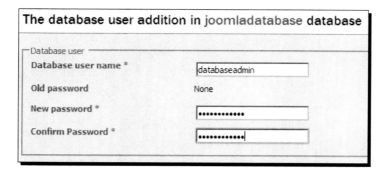

4. Make a note of the data you need to install Joomla later on: the database name, the database username and database password.

What just happened?

Using a web control panel, you've set up an empty database and created a database user. You're almost there; this is the last step in preparing the Joomla installation.

Time for action – running the Joomla installation wizard

You've got all Joomla files copied to the web server, you've got a database ready to be filled. Let's finally install Joomla:

1. Enter the URL for your site (for example, `http://www.example.com`) in your browser. The installation screen will come up:

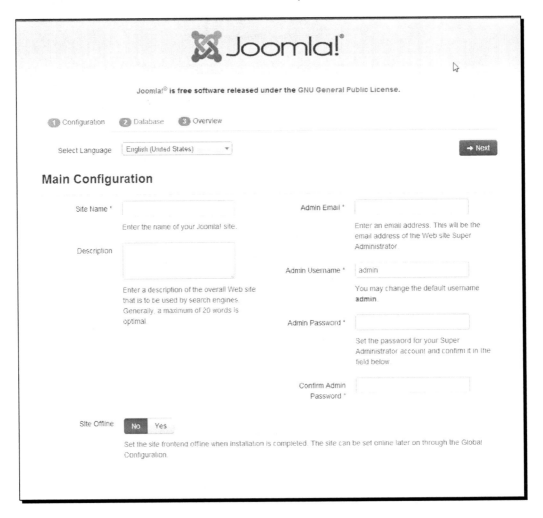

The Joomla installer will check if your web server setup meets the installation requirements. If it does, you'll be taken to the **Main Configuration** screen. However, if any of the required web server settings isn't met, you won't be able to install Joomla. In that case, Joomla will display a screen of required settings and mark the ones that require attention. If there are any problems, get in touch with your web hosting company to have them correct the web server settings for you.

2. In the **Main Configuration** screen, change the settings and enter information as follows:

   ❑ **Select Language**: You can select the language you want to use during the installation, if you need to change the default setting.

   ❑ **Site Name**: Enter the name for the website; this will be displayed in the browser title bar (and in some cases in the site header). In this example, we've entered Corba—you'll learn more about this esteemed client for your example site in later chapters.

   ❑ **Description**: It's okay to leave this blank for now. Here you can enter one or two sentences explaining what your site has to offer. The information is important for search engines, but you can add this in a later stage through Joomla's configuration settings.

   ❑ **Admin Email**: Enter a valid e-mail address. Joomla will use this to send system messages and it will be used as the e-mail address for the default administrator user account.

   ❑ **Admin Username**: Your default username is `admin`. For security reasons, you'll want to choose a username that's not too easy to guess (preferably something more original than `admin`). However, in this example we'll keep to the default setting for convenience.

   ❑ **Admin Password**: Enter the site administrator password. This is a different password from the one you've entered previously for the database user. This new password is created here and now; you'll use this to login to Joomla after the installation. Make a note of the username and the password!

   ❑ **Site Offline**: This is set to **No** by default. After installation the (empty) site will be immediately online. Select **Yes** if you want to keep it inaccessible for visitors, and make it visible only for yourself after logging in. In that case, after installation of Joomla visitors will see a message that the site is temporarily offline.

3. Click on the **Next** button. You'll be taken to the **Database Configuration** screen.:

4. In this screen, enter the following details:

- ❏ **Database Type**: You can probably leave this set to **MySQLi**. Currently, most web hosts support MySQLi (MySQL Improved), which allows for faster and more secure communication with the database than the traditional MySQL database type.

- ❏ **Host Name**: Usually this is local host (unless your web hosting company has provided you with another name).

- ❏ **Username**: Enter the username for the database you created earlier. If you haven't created the database yourself, your hosting provider should be able to provide you with the database and user details. In our example, the username is `databaseadmin`.

- ❏ **Password**: Enter the database user password you created when setting up the database. Again, if the hosting provider has created the database, they should be able to provide you with the user password for the database.

- ❏ **Database Name**: Enter the database name you chose when you created the database. If you haven't created the database yourself, you can enter the name you have received from your webhost.

- ❏ **Table Prefix**: You can leave this field unchanged. A Table Prefix is relevant only when one database is shared by several Joomla installations. This way, each of them can look up the appropriate data in the database by checking for the correct prefix.

- ❏ **Old Database process**: This option is only relevant when you've installed Joomla before, and need to empty the tables (the contents) of a previous database. Select **Backup** to back up existing database contents from a previous Joomla installation, or select **Remove** to remove them.

5. Once the **Database Configuration** screen is complete, click **Next**. Joomla will now check if it can connect to the database.

6. If you see an error message, you've probably made a typo when entering the database details. Make sure you have typed the password correctly. You can go back to the database details screen, enter the correct data and click **Next** again.

7. If all goes well, you are taken to the **Finalisation** screen:

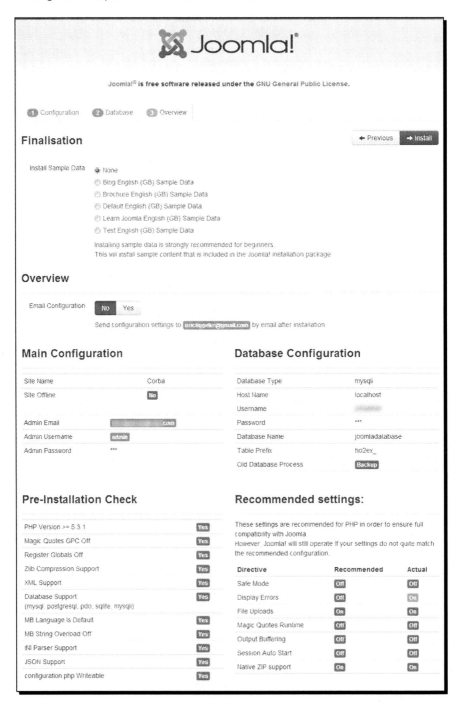

8. Although this is an impressively long screen (you'll have to scroll to see it in full), its main purpose is to give you an overview of all current settings. You'll only have to make one or two choices here.

❑ **Install Sample Data**: When you create a Joomla site for the very first time, it's a good idea to install sample data. You can choose from several sets of sample data; for example, you can select **Blog Sample Data** to install Joomla with some example blog articles, menus, and modules. In this case, select **Learn Joomla English (GB) Sample Data**. Using this sample data option, you get a ready-made sample site to build upon, already filled with example pages, menus, and extras. If you want to follow the exercises in this book, you'll need to install the **Learn Joomla English (GB) Sample Data**.

If you don't install sample data, you have to create all content from scratch. You'll prefer this option when you're Joomla-savvy and know where to start, how to add content, and how to customize things.

❑ **Email Configuration**: Select **Yes** if you want Joomla to send you an e-mail with an overview of all site settings. When you select **Yes**, you'll be presented with an extra option—whether you want to send passwords via e-mail too. For security reasons it's recommended not to send passwords via e-mail.

9. Click on the **Next** button. Joomla will now start installing and it will display the installation progress. In a few seconds, you'll be presented with the last screen:

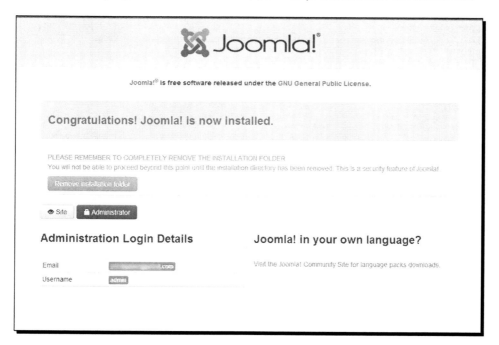

10. You're good to go now. Just one thing left to do. Before you can use Joomla, you should delete the folder named `installation` The `installation` folder contains information that's needed for the installation, but it's now no longer required (and you do not want to reveal its contents to hackers). Click the **Remove installation folder** button to do this; the button text will change to **Installation folder successfully removed.**

What just happened?

Congratulations! You've installed Joomla. In the current screen, click on the **Site** button to see what your Joomla site looks like.

But there's more to Joomla than meets the eye of the web visitor. To go to the "secret" login page of your site, enter your site URL in your browser address bar, adding the word "administrator": `www.example.com/administrator`.

You'll see this page:

Here, you can log in to the administrative interface or "backend" of the site using the username (that you chose on the **Main Configuration** page of the installation routine) and the password that you created during installation (make sure you enter the site administrator password, not the database user password). Click **Log in** to reveal the Joomla web interface:

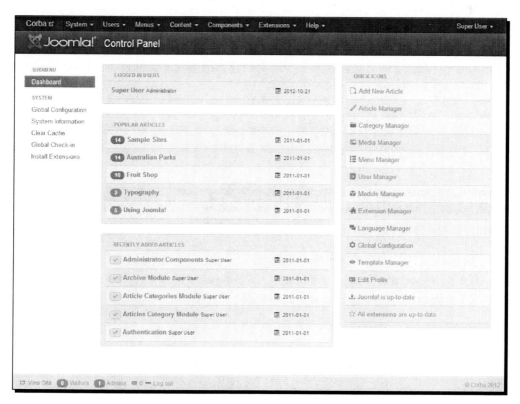

Protecting your site

You've just installed Joomla, so you probably want to get to the fun stuff right away, and start creating cool sites. You're right of course, but still it's a good idea to keep an eye on security issues from the very start. As soon as you've got your site set up, it's really important to make sure you don't leave any doors open to people who like to break into other people's websites. Check *Appendix A, Keeping the Site Secure*, to learn how you can keep your site secure.

Got stuck? Get help!

Looking for more help and tips on installing Joomla?

- ◆ Visit the Joomla documentation site at `http://docs.joomla.org` and check the *Getting Started with Joomla* pages at `http://www.joomla.org/about-joomla/getting-started.html`.
- ◆ Don't forget there are many free video tutorials on YouTube. Search for `install Joomla 3.0` and you'll be presented with a truckload of installation guides.
- ◆ If you're having trouble installing Joomla, chances are your problem has already been solved on the official Joomla forum dedicated to installation issues. On `http://forum.joomla.org`, look for the *Installation* section or use the forum's search functionality.

Point your browser to `www.joomm.net`, the website accompanying this book, to find answers to frequently asked Joomla questions.

Pop quiz – test your knowledge of installing Joomla

Q1 Why do you need FTP software before you can install Joomla?

- a. To unzip the installation package.
- b. To upload files from your computer to the web server.
- c. To backup your site.

Q2 What are the main steps in installing Joomla?

- a. First upload the Joomla files, then run the web installer.

b.   Download Joomla, unpack and upload the files, create a database, then run the web installer.

c.   Download Joomla, unpack and upload the files, run the web installer, create a database.

Q3 What username and passwords do you have to enter in the Joomla web installation wizard?

a.   The username and password needed to login to the Joomla backend.

b.   The username and password needed to access the MySQL database.

c.   The username and password needed to access the MySQL database, and the username and password needed to login to the Joomla backend.

Summary

In this chapter, you've learned how to install Joomla. Specifically, we covered:

- To be able to install and run Joomla, you'll need hosting space that meets Joomla's specific server requirements. You also need an FTP software to put the required files on a web server. You might want to install a few different browsers.

- Installing Joomla takes four steps:

    - First, you get the current Joomla file package from www.joomla.org and uncompress the packaged files on your computer.

    - Then, using FTP, you place the downloaded files on your hosting space.

    - Next, you'll create a database before you can actually start installing Joomla.

    - The final step is running the Joomla web installer in your browser. This guides you through the installation process.

- The output of the Joomla installation has two faces. The Joomla frontend displays an example website that is publicly accessible, the backend is Joomla's web management interface where for now just one VIP is allowed to log in—you!

Now that you've got Joomla up and running, it's about time to find out what this great new web development tool can do.

In *Chapter 3, First Steps: Getting to Know Joomla*, you'll explore the Joomla frontend and backend, and you'll get a first taste of building websites the Joomla way.

3

First Steps: Getting to Know Joomla

Congratulations! You have just installed Joomla. This means you can now step into Joomla, and start using one of the most exciting and powerful web building tools. Before you begin building your own site in the next chapter, let's take some time to get acquainted with the way Joomla works. The system has a clean, user-friendly interface that's easy to learn and fun to work with; you'll be amazed at how fast you can perform content management magic in just a few clicks. This chapter introduces you to Joomla's basic functions.

In this chapter you will:

- ◆ Get acquainted with the Joomla way of building and maintaining websites.

- ◆ Explore the user interface; try out the main screens and toolbars.

- ◆ Examine the Joomla example website that you installed. What are the main features and special functions that Joomla offers out of the box?

- ◆ Get your feet wet and try out some of the most common administration tasks. Publish your first content, add an extension, and tweak a few settings.

This way you'll get a taste of what it's like to use Joomla as your web toolbox and get ready to build your own site in the next chapter. So let's get started!

Making the switch – building websites the Joomla way

If you're new to Joomla and to Content Management Systems (CMSes), you'll find creating sites using a CMS takes a bit of getting used to. Even if you have some experience building websites, you'll have to adapt to a different way of working. But it's certainly worth the effort, and Joomla will make it easy on you—really! Before we explore the example site you've installed in the previous chapter, we'll have a brief look at just what's so different about building websites with Joomla.

As you may know, ages ago—at least before 2005, when Joomla came to be—most websites were handcrafted. Creating a website meant creating pages. For every new web page, you had to create a separate HTML document. You would design a basic page layout and re-use that over and over again, adding new pages and adapting the layout to fit the type of content. Whatever tool you used—Adobe (then Macromedia) Dreamweaver, Microsoft FrontPage, or maybe a plain text editor—you would be designing, coding, editing, or building the same web page your visitors would see on your website.

Getting anything published on the Web meant uploading pages (HTML documents) from your computer to a web server. Adding and updating content or managing hyperlinks was basically handicraft. You'd open a page in an editor, make changes, and upload it to the web server again. Those were the bad old days of static websites.

Those days are long, long gone. Today, most websites are dynamic. They use a CMS to make it easier to create and manage content. These CMS-based sites are either built from scratch (by web programmers creating a custom CMS to meet specific client requirements) or based upon a generic CMS such as Joomla that can be customized and expanded. And it's that dynamic bit that makes working with a CMS so all-new and different.

Sorry, web pages have ceased to exist

Okay, now brace yourself for the main difference between the static old school approach and building websites using a CMS such as Joomla—there are no web pages.

Of course, a visitor browsing your site still experiences that website as—basically—a collection of pages. In Joomla, however, the page your visitor sees isn't really a page. Rather, it's a collection of little blocks of interactive data that the CMS pulls from a database. These blocks can be arranged and combined into web pages in many different ways.

As soon as your visitor clicks on a link, he actually sends a request to Joomla to assemble bits and pieces of data to present a full web page. If your site visitor clicks on Home, they'll see a page consisting of headings, images, and teaser texts. If they click on a **Read more** link, a new mix of data is displayed. This can consist of the same article heading from the home page, possibly the same teaser text and image (now combined with the full body text) links to related articles, banners, and different menu options.

When creating static websites, the HTML page you designed would be the exact same HTML page the site visitor would see. This one-to-one relationship has gone out the window. Of course, to a visitor a Joomla powered site still consists of the web pages they see in their browser. However, behind the scenes, in Joomla, you won't be editing "pages"—after all, there are no pages in Joomla. To change the output (the web page) you edit the different building blocks. These blocks can be any part of the final page: the main article, a menu entry, a banner, or a list of hyperlinks to related items.

A CMS is like a Coffee Machine system

In a way, a CMS functions just like those big multi-option coffee machines used in office environments—although the quality of the output of a CMS is incomparably better! However, the same principles apply: the user presses a button to select any of the available options; the machine invisibly fetches all of the required ingredients and mixes these to serve a cup of fresh coffee, latte, frappuccino, or decaf.

This is similar to the way a CMS serves content. As the site visitor clicks on a link, the mighty machine gathers whatever combination of content parts is needed from the database to complete this particular order and it pours the output into a coffee cup—sorry, a web page.

The benefits of the CMS approach to websites

The dynamic approach of CMSes, such as Joomla, makes creating websites flexible. You don't have to manually create dozens of rigid content pages, copying menus and other common elements from page to page as you extend your site. Instead, you'll choose a basic page layout and add any combination of building blocks you need:

- Do you want to create a home page with four headings, teaser texts, read-more links, a main menu, a random image, a login form, or a list of links to popular articles? You can do this easily, as the Joomla CMS allows you to combine different blocks of content into your home page. No programming skills needed!

- If your site has a section about digital photography, do you want all content pages about DSLR cameras to display a banner to attract attention to your special newsletter on the subject? In Joomla, it's a breeze.

- Would you like to have different items on your home page on every day of the week? Do you want to set a particular starting date and an ending date for publishing your articles? It's all possible. While you're on a holiday, you can have your home page automatically updated with the articles you prepared beforehand!

To summarize: you've got the power! You determine what "content blocks" Joomla packs together onto any specific page and you also set the order and the layout of these blocks on the browser screen.

All of this magic is made possible by Joomla's built-in PHP wizardry. It uses the powerful PHP scripting language to communicate with a database, gathering just the blocks of data you need and presenting them the way you want.

A website built of blocks

Now what does this building blocks thing look like in real life? The following is an illustration of Joomla's page building system dissected.

A web page in Joomla basically consists of the three parts displayed in the following screenshots. A base layout (**1**), the main content block (**2**), and as many function blocks as you like (**3**):

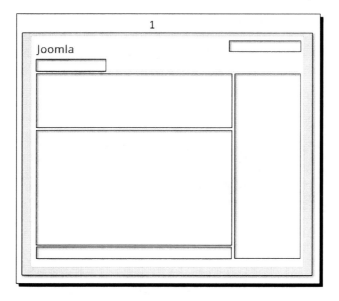

(1) The base layout: This defines the presentation of all content (the amount of columns, background colors, header graphics, and so on). This base layout also contains "positions" (spaces Joomla can fill with its content blocks). In Joomla, this base layout is defined in a template. Generally, you set the template once and forget about it. It controls the graphic design; it's not part of your daily routine of content management. You'll learn more about using templates in *Chapter 11, Creating an Attractive Design: Working with Templates*.

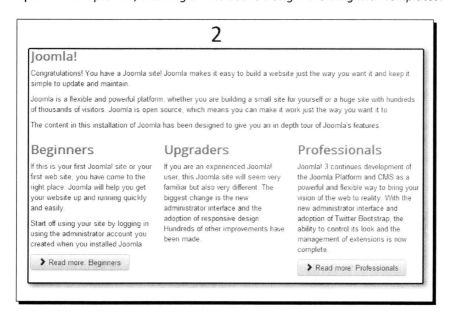

(2) The main content area: This is the essential part; it contains the cold hard content. Whether you'll publish an article, show a contact form, or a photo gallery, it will appear here. In Joomla, this area is called the **mainbody**. In most cases, the mainbody appears in the middle of the page.

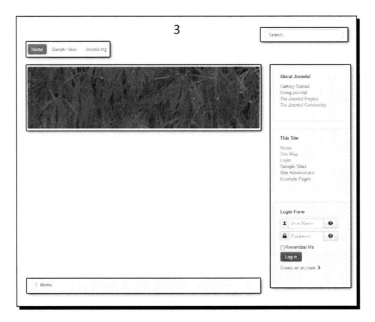

(3) The blocks around the main content area: Examples are the search box, the Main Menu in the right-hand sidebar and the Login Form. These blocks are called **modules**. Modules can contain advanced functionality: menus, dynamic lists with hyperlinks to popular content, random images, slideshows, and so on. Anything in the top, left, right, or bottom of a Joomla page is displayed using modules. The default Joomla installation comes with dozens of modules; the system is very extensible.

To summarize: the template functions as a frame; the main content area or "mainbody" is the central and essential building block that fits right in the middle; and modules are blocks that you can add and arrange around that, just the way you like, to add essential functions (or just fun and pizzazz) to your site.

Introducing frontend and backend – the Joomla interface

Okay, so how do you get to build the website you want using the Joomla set of building blocks? How do you get the main content area to show content the way you want to? How do you work with modules? To answer these questions, we'll first have a look at the Joomla interface, the workspace that contains all tools and controls you'll need for any web building magic.

The following screenshot shows the two faces of the Joomla example site you installed in the previous chapter—the frontend and the backend:

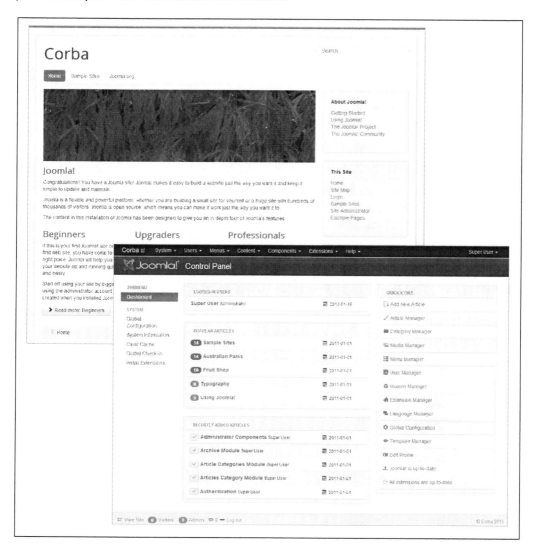

Your workspace – the backend

Joomla is a web application. It's a software tool that's installed on a web server and that's accessed through a browser. Creating and managing a site with Joomla is an online activity. Wherever you are, if you have Internet access you can log in to the Joomla administration interface to manage your site.

This means every Joomla site has a "staff entrance" that your site visitors will never get to see. It's the administration interface or backend of your site, accessed through a login page that's displayed when you add /administrator to the URL of the site. By default, only the site administrator has permission to log in to the backend; later on, the administrator can give other contributors access. Although there's also such a thing as frontend editing, generally you will administer your site using the backend. The backend is the interface for all site management tasks, such as adding content, changing menus, or customizing the layout.

And what's the frontend?

The public face of your Joomla site is called—you might have guessed it—the **frontend**. That's just another word for "your website as the visitor sees it".

In the rest of this chapter, you'll learn more about these two basic notions in Joomla. First, we'll take a closer look at the frontend (the final output of whatever you do in Joomla) by exploring the contents of the Joomla example website. After that, we'll examine how the backend works and get our hands dirty with some real-life content management activities.

Exploring the frontend – the website as the user sees it

Let's first take a closer look at the elements of the default Joomla example site home page. This will give you a good overview of the different modules that Joomla features out of the box.

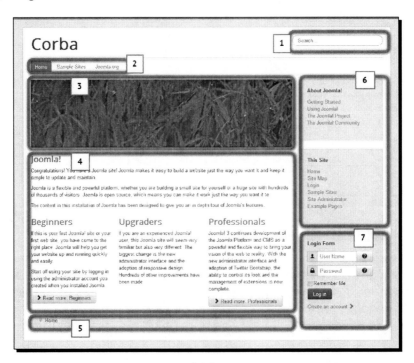

In the preceding screenshot, you see what the home page looks like after you've installed Joomla with the **Learn Joomla** sample data. As you can see, the example is focused on presenting quite a lot of information, the home page pulling the reader towards the content through intro texts and several menus. There's one main image, the header image that stays unchanged on all pages.

The previous screenshot of the home page shows the following elements:

- **(1) Search box**: The search results are shown in the main content area
- **(2) Top menu**: A menu at the top of the page
- **(3) Header image**: Displays a selected image on one or more pages
- **(4) Mainbody of the home page**: Contains introductory texts of selected articles
- **(5) Breadcrumbs**: Shows the pathway to the current page
- **(6) Two different menus**: **About Joomla** and **This Site**
- **(7) Login form**: For registered users

This site with example content perfectly demonstrates what Joomla is capable of. The fact that it's already packed with articles, menus, and extras gives you a great opportunity to try out Joomla's capabilities and decide for yourself which features fit your site's needs.

You're certainly not limited to building the kind of information-rich sites the example site demonstrates. In *Chapter 1, Introduction: A New and Easy Way to Build Your Website*, you've seen a few other examples of Joomla sites ranging from small personal blogs to huge corporate and e-commerce sites. Joomla 3 even comes with sample data showcasing other types of sites, such as blogs. However, you can only select the sample data type when installing Joomla; unfortunately, it isn't possible to see the effects of other sample data unless you re-install the CMS. But don't worry, the **Learn Joomla** sample data we're using in this book is the most comprehensive set of sample data—so that's your best choice if you want to get a good grasp of all that Joomla has to offer. Later on, you'll learn how to customize the **Learn Joomla** sample site to create a much cleaner look that may fit your needs better.

Time for action – tour the example site

Let's take a closer look at the demo site and see some real-life examples of page layouts. You'll see how the content in the mainbody and the modules in the surrounding content area change depending on the menu hyperlink you click:

1. Enter the URL of your site (for example, `http://www.mysite.com`) in your web browser. If, in *Chapter 2, Installation: Getting Joomla Up and Running*, you have installed Joomla into another folder, the URL would be `http://www.mysite.com/otherfoldername`. You'll recognize the home page, as displayed in the following screenshot. The mainbody (the visible part of it outlined in the screenshot) consists of four article intro texts.

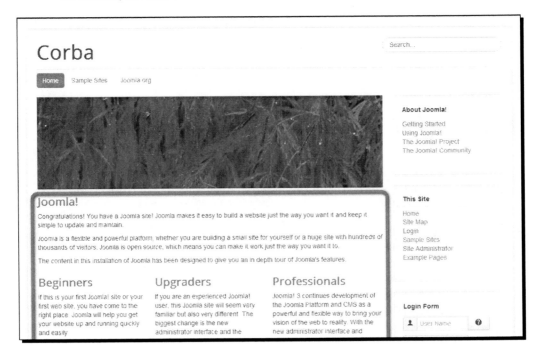

2. Let's explore how the layout changes on a different page. In the **About Joomla** menu, click on **Getting Started**. You'll notice that the mainbody displays just one article, which is the most common type of page content. The login form isn't displayed on this page. Again, the mainbody is outlined in the following screenshot:

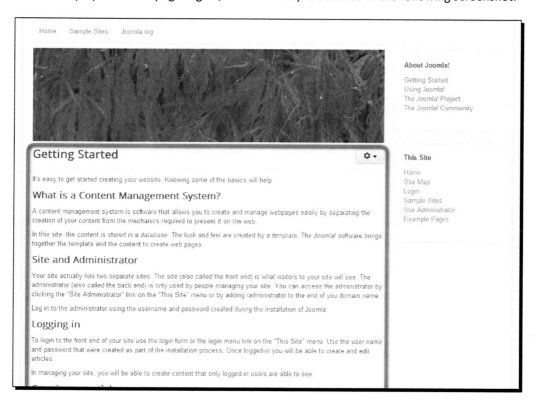

3. Let's have a look at another type of page layout. In the **About Joomla** menu, click on **Using Joomla** and on **Using Extensions**. This link takes you to a page in which the mainbody starts with a a short introductory text describing the main category, **Extensions**. Below this is a list of links to (and descriptions of) subcategories of the **Extensions** category, such as **Components**, **Modules**, and **Templates**:

What just happened?

At first sight, the Joomla example site may seem overwhelming. There are many bits of content, many menus, and different types of web page layouts. But, in fact, many pages on Joomla sites are built around the three-page layouts you've just discovered: the home page (showing featured articles), content pages (with one main article in the mainbody), and "pages in between". These "pages in between" function as overview pages linking to one or more content categories. Overview pages can contain either short descriptions of content categories or introductory texts to the articles themselves (just like the ones you've seen on the home page). These overview pages help users discover the site contents by offering them an overview of articles on related topics.

You've also discovered how the mainbody can be combined with different modules. In the example site, the home page contains a login form in the left-hand column. On other pages, this block isn't displayed.

Exploring the example content

Take some time to browse the rest of the Joomla example site. You'll notice that there is more to explore than just pages with "classic content" (articles, text, and images) that we've seen so far. Although classic content pages may be at the core of many websites, in a dynamic site all kinds of dynamic content can be displayed in the mainbody. Try out the **Login** link in the **This Site** menu on the home page, or try out the **Search** box. You'll see that the mainbody will show a login form page and search results.

For now, we won't go any deeper into these different types of dynamic content—though it's important to realize that they exist and that they take Joomla's capabilities much further than just plain old "presentation of text and images". We'll cover this subject in more detail in the next few chapters.

Have a go hero – get familiar with the other example sites

Are you ready to explore a link to quite a different site layout? In the horizontal top menu, click on the **Sample Sites** link. You'll see a new menu appearing in the right column, featuring links to **Australian Parks** and **Fruit Shop**. In the **Fruit Shop** menu, click on the **Welcome** link. You're in for a bit of a shock—you're taken to a completely different website!

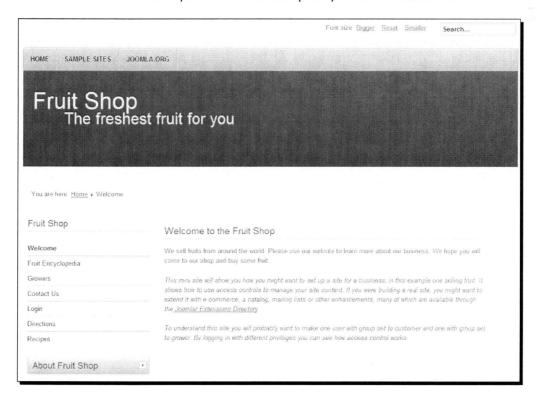

The **Fruit Shop** sample site appears to be a separate website—not only the content, but also the site design is quite different. Don't let this confuse you. It's all part of one big Joomla example site, the one where you've installed Joomla with the **Learn Joomla** sample data. The trick is that the menu links pointing to the Fruit Shop "site" have specific templates assigned to them. As a template in Joomla controls the overall look and feel of the site, the Fruit shop menu links appear to open a totally different site. However, when you click the **Home** link, you'll notice you'll be taken to the default sample site home page again.

Applying templates to specific menu links within the site can give visitors the impression of exploring a separate set of websites. Usually, you'll probably use just one template in your website. However, you can use different templates to give different parts of the site—for example, site sections focused on particular product groups or services—a distinct look and feel. You'll learn more about assigning templates to specific site parts in *Chapter 11, Creating an Attractive Design: Working with Templates*.

Taking control – administering your site in the backend

The backend is the cockpit of your Joomla jet. It's the administration interface that allows you to manage your site. It's organized neatly, so you should learn to find your way around it pretty fast. We'll have a closer look at the backend interface right now.

Time for action – logging in to the backend

To enable us to get a closer look at the administrative interface of Joomla, let's see how you can access the backend of the site and enter the **Joomla Control Panel**.

1. In the address bar of the browser, enter the address of your website and add /administrator to it. If your site is http://www.mysite.com, type http://www.mysite.com/administrator in the address bar.

2. You've already had a short look at it after you installed Joomla in the previous chapter—the secret entrance to your site. You'll see a login prompt:

3. Enter your username and the password you've created when installing Joomla (see also *Chapter 2, Installation: Getting Joomla Up and Running*). Click on the **Log in** button.

4. After you've successfully entered your credentials, you'll enter the actual administration interface: the backend home page (the Control Panel). This interface provides access to all of the functions that you need as a site administrator, (such as adding content, changing menus, customizing the layout, and so on):

What just happened?

You've logged in to the backend of your site, and—lo and behold!—you've entered the Control Panel, only accessible to users with special access rights. You'll be coming back there for every site management activity. As the site administrator, you'll probably want to add a bookmark in your browser of the /administrator URL.

Taking a closer look at the Control Panel

Let's look at the **Control Panel** in more detail. In the following screenshot, the four main screen areas of the Control Panel are outlined:

In the preceding screenshot, I've added numbers to clarify the five sections of the Control Panel. Let's have a closer look at each of them:

Top menu (1)

The horizontal top menu is an essential feature of the Control Panel. This is really where all of the action is. Each main menu item gives access to a drop-down list featuring all of Joomla's content management tools and functions. These are the main menu items:

- **System**: Set global configuration options, perform system maintenance
- **Users**: Manage users, manage users access rights, send mail to users
- **Menus**: Add and manage menus and menu links
- **Content**: Add or change articles, change site structure, manage media (images)
- **Components**: Manage special features, such as banners and contacts
- **Extensions**: Manage extensions, templates, and languages to extend the functionality and capabilities of your website
- **Help**: Joomla's online help function and support pages

This top menu is the one you'll use over and over again when working on your site. For now, we'll first have a look at the other panels and controls; after that we will start exploring the wide range of capabilities hidden behind all of the top menu items.

The Submenu and System menus (2)

The **Submenu** and **System** menus in the left column gives you quick access to the subcomponents of the current page. The menus and menu options that appear in this column are context sensitive, offering options related to the choices you make in the horizontal top menu bar.

Information panels (3)

These three information display lists containing the **Last Logged-in Users**, **Popular Articles**, and **Recently Added Articles**. The purpose of these panels is to give you a quick overview of up-to-date information on your site's users and content. Click on any of the items in the list to edit it. For example, clicking the title of a popular article will take you to the page where you can edit the article.

Shortcut list (4)

Named as the **Quick Icons** section, this displays a series of icons/hyperlinks that offer quick access to frequently used functions such as adding a new article or changing site settings. You can also access all these functions through the top menu.

Preview and Info Bar (5)

At the bottom of the administrator screen there's a horizontal bar that always remains visible. In this part of the Control Panel you'll find the following functions:

- **View Site**: Open the website's home page in a new browser tab or window.
- **Visitors**: Information on the number of visitors that are currently logged in on the frontend of the site.
- **Admins**: The number of users that have logged in in the backend of the site. Currently that's just one person—you.
- **Messages** (a little envelope icon): Indicates the number of unread private messages. These are messages sent to you by other site users.
- **Logout**: Logout from the backend.

In the far left at the top of the menu bar, you'll notice that your site name is displayed. This is the site name you entered previously, when installing Joomla. If you followed along in the *Chapter 2, Installation: Getting Joomla Up and Running*, you'll see the name of the example we'll be building in this book, **Corba**. You'll probably often use the shortcut this site name offers: clicking this name allows you to quickly go to the front of the website in a new browser tab. Another useful shortcut: If you click on the Joomla logo that's shown on all backend screens in the blue top bar, you're taken back to the **Control Panel**, the start screen of the backend.

Understanding backend tools and controls

The Control Panel is the home page of the backend. Whatever action you want to perform, the dozens of links on the Control Panel page lead you to the appropriate tools or **Managers**, as Joomla calls them. Examples are the **Article Manager**, the **Menu Manager**, and the **User Manager**. That's where the real action takes place.

Although there are many different Managers and other types of administration tools, it's quite easy to grasp the way they work. All of the interface pages share the same base layout and show a toolbar in the upper-right position of the screen. In the following screenshot, you can see the control buttons of Joomla's **Article Manager** toolbar:

Many Manager pages share commonly used features, such as **New**, **Edit**, **Publish**, and **Trash**. Let's take the Article Manager as an example and look at the functions of the toolbar buttons in more detail:

- **New**: Create a new article
- **Edit**: Edit an article
- **Publish**: Make an article visible to your visitors
- **Unpublish**: Make an article invisible to your visitors (without throwing it away)
- **Featured**: Assign a special status to the article, to display it in an overview of selected (featured) articles on the front page or on another page showcasing featured articles
- **Archive**: Archive articles and make these accessible only through a special menu link to archived content
- **Check In**: Unlock articles that are currently marked as checked out (this option can be useful if articles are locked because another content editor didn't properly save the article and finish the editing session. Using the **Check In** option, the article is unlocked and users will be able to edit it again.)
- **Trash**: Send an article to the Trash (to delete it)
- **Batch**: Select any number of articles and click on **Batch** to move or copy all selected articles at once, or change article access levels
- **Options**: Change general article settings
- **Help**: Browse to Joomla's online help

The toolbar is context sensitive. It will display the buttons relevant to the current activity. When you select an article and click on the **Edit** button in the **Article Manager** you'll be taken to the article editor screen.

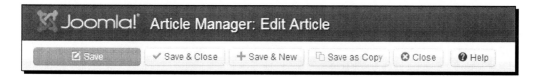

In this screen, you'll see the following set of toolbar buttons:

- **Save**: Save changes, without closing the current window
- **Save & Close**: Save changes and closing the current window (return to the Article Manager)
- **Save & New**: Save changes and open a new empty article editing screen. This allows you to quickly create a series of articles without having to close the **New Article** screen
- **Save as Copy**: Save the current article and leave the current screen and its contents open for you to edit a copy of the article you have just saved
- **Close**: Cancel without saving any changes
- **Help**: Access Joomla's online help

As you can see, most toolbar buttons are self-explanatory. Note, however, the difference between the **Save** and **Save & Close** buttons. Click on **Save** to save changes without leaving the current page. You'll find that when editing the text of an article, it's easiest to click on **Save** now and then to store changes without leaving the current screen. When you're satisfied with the results, click on **Save & Close** to close the editing screen. The same applies to any occurrence of **Save** and **Save & Close** on other Joomla interface screens.

Clicking on the **Save** button every now and then, when writing a long article, will ensure your article contents are saved. You can lose all of the unsaved changes when you leave the article editor open (without action) for more than 15 minutes. Later in this chapter (see *Time for action – setting Joomla preferences*) you'll learn how to change this 15-minute setting to allow you to take some more time for your well-deserved coffee breaks.

Getting your feet wet – start administering your site

We have had a first look at the **Control Panel** screen layout and the main backend toolbars. You're probably curious to try out how the thing actually works! I'll test your patience just a little more. First, we'll make some more sense of the Control Panel and find out what you really need to know to get started on this impressive toolbox. After all, its main menu bar consists of seven menu options with more than 40 submenu items. That's a wealth of CMS power—but it's also quite daunting.

We won't go into all of the menu items and their capabilities here; rather, you'll learn how to use the important menu options as you go along building your site in the following chapters. For now, let's go ahead and see what the primary functions are.

Three types of backend tasks

Roughly, the seven options in the **Control Panel** menu bar consist of three clusters. Some you'll use on a daily basis, some you'll only have to deploy every now and then. In the following diagram, you can see what these three groups are. In the rest of this chapter, we'll have a closer look at them not in the order they appear on the menu bar, but in order of their relevance in your day-to-day content management activities.

Let's try out an example of each of these three types of content and site management actions:

- **Content management example**: Creating and publishing content
- **Extension management example**: Adding a module
- **Site management example**: Changing site settings

Content management example – let's create some content!

It's fine to have an example site filled with some dummy content about Joomla, but you probably want to make your mark by adding your own content. Publish something, anything, to your own Joomla website.

Time for action – publishing your first article

Let's look at the steps required to publish your first article:

1. Navigate to **Content | Article Manager** (alternatively you can use the **Article Manager** quick icon in the **Control Panel**).

2. In the toolbar, click on the **New** button (the green one with the plus sign).

3. Alternatively, you can use the fly-out menu **Content | Article Manager | Add New article**. This will take you to the **Article Manager: Add New Article** screen even faster.

4. In the **Article Manager: Add New Article** screen, fill out the **Title** field as shown in the following screenshot. Enter a title (for example, **My first article**) and add some article text in the text editor box. Any text will do; for now we're just playing around in the example site.

5. Leave the **Category** drop-down box as it is: it's okay to have this article assigned to the **Sample Data-Articles** category. You'll learn how to create categories and organize content in the next two chapters.

6. Make sure **Status** (under **Details**) is set to **Published**. This is the default option.

7. Set **Featured** to **Yes** to make sure your article will be shown on the home page.

8. Click on the **Save** button in the toolbar in the top left-hand side of the page. Joomla will inform you that it has successfully saved changes to your article.

9. Click on **View Site** in the Preview and Info Bar section of the screen. This will take you to the home page of your site.

You're done! As you can see, your first article is now published on the front page.

What just happened?

In a few steps you have created and published brand new content. By choosing the **Featured** option, you've made sure the article text is shown on the home page. Don't worry, you'll learn how to create articles on other content pages and make them accessible through menu links in the next chapter.

Extension management example – adding a module

You've just added an article to your site. However, in Joomla you can also easily add other types of content. By using extensions you can add new functionality to the site. One example of an extension at work is the login form block on the home page.

Extensions are separate additions to Joomla. You can download them from the Web and add them to your Joomla installation in a few clicks. Because there are many extensions available, Joomla is nearly limitlessly extendable. By default, some (mostly quite simple) extensions are included in the default installation. In the next example, you'll activate one of these included extensions: the most read articles module. This adds a little block (module) to the site that automatically lists the most popular items.

Time for action – adding a module to the site

You are logged in to the backend of the site and want to add a block with links to the most read articles on the site. Let's add this block (or as Joomla calls it, a module).

1. Navigate to **Extensions | Module Manager**. Click **New**. A list of available module types is displayed:

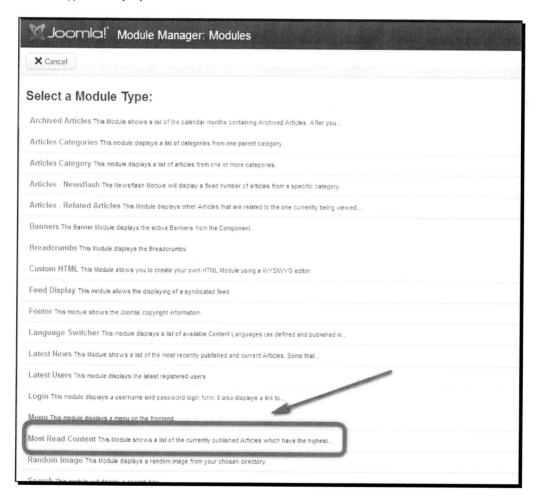

2. Click on the name of the module type you want to add, **Most Read Content**.

3. The **Module Manager: Module Most Read Content** screen opens. This is where you manage the settings of this module. Change the details as follows:

   - **Title**: Enter a title that will appear above the list of hyperlinks to appear, such as **Popular**.

   - **Position**: Select the location on the page where the module is displayed. Click **Type or Select a Position** to display a drop-down list containing all available positions. Scroll down until you see the positions for **Protostar**, the current site template. Now select **Right [position-7]**, which means that the module will appear in the right column.

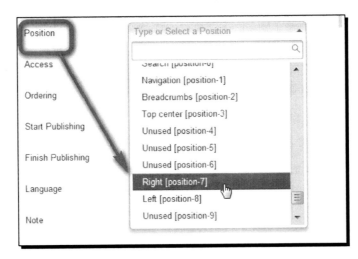

4. Click on the **Menu Assignment** tab heading to select the pages where you want the module to appear. Select **Module Assignment: Only on the pages selected**.

5. By default, all pages are selected, so to make your selection, first click **Select: None to deselect all pages**.

6. To find the **Main Menu** items we're looking for, click on the minus sign to the left-hand side of the **About Joomla** menu name; this will collapse this menu (hide all menu items). Also click on the minus sign to the left of **Australian Parks** and **Fruit Shop** too. Now the **Main Menu** menu items are easily visible.

7. Just below the **Main Menu** heading, select the **Home** link. This way the module will appear on the homepage only:

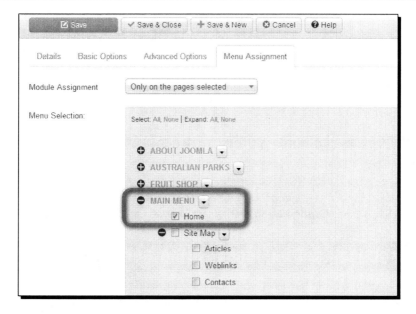

8. You can leave all other settings unchanged. Click **Save** and click **View Site** to see the results.

What just happened?

A new block is displayed on the home page. It's dynamically populated with hyperlinks pointing to the five most read articles. The beauty of a module like this one is that you can set it once and then forget about it. There's no need for manual maintenance—when other articles become more popular, Joomla will automatically update the list.

Extensions can be easily switched on and off. By switching an extension off, you don't delete anything. The extension and all of the settings you've chosen for it remains available in the backend, but it isn't visible any more to the site visitor. This way, you can still decide to use it again later. To make the module block containing most read articles invisible, go back to **Extensions | Module Manager**, click on the name of the newly created module (**Popular**) and change the **Published** setting back to **Unpublished**.

Site management example – configuring basic site settings

The **Site** menu and **Users** menu in the **Control Panel** menu bar offer you some more advanced functions, ranging from database maintenance to user management. In the course of this book you'll learn which functions are important for day to day site management. For now, we'll take a look at the **Site | Basic Configuration** settings where you can set Joomla preferences.

Time for action – setting Joomla preferences

When browsing the Joomla backend, you may have noticed that after a certain amount of idle time Joomla will ask you to log in again. By default, Joomla kicks you out when you've been logged in for 15 minutes without any activity. When developing a site it can be quite annoying to have to log in every time you return to your desk with a fresh cup of coffee. Let's change this with the **Session Lifetime** setting in the Joomla preferences.

1. From the **Control Panel**, navigate to **System | Global Configuration** (you can also click on the **Global Configuration** link in the **System** menu on the left-hand side; it's a shortcut).

2. **Global Configuration** is divided into **Site** settings, **System** settings, **Server** settings, **Permissions**, and **Text Filters**. Click on the **System** tab to show the appropriate settings panel:

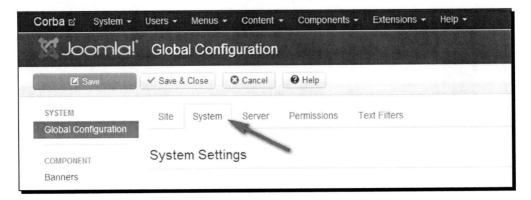

3. On the **System** page, scroll down until you see the **Session Settings** heading. Change **Session Lifetime** to **45** minutes.

4. Click on **Save** in the toolbar. From now on, you only have to log in again if you leave the Joomla backend untouched for more than 45 minutes.

What just happened?

You've just made your life as an administrator a little easier by changing one of the default system settings. You can now leave your computer idle—more specifically, don't perform any actions in the Joomla backend—for 45 minutes before Joomla prompts you to log in again.

Have a go hero – explore the configuration options

Check out the other **Global Configuration** options, but be careful. It's best to leave most of the settings unchanged. Don't touch the **Server Settings** and **Database Settings** options (on the **Server** page) unless you know what you're doing as these contain critical data that Joomla needs to function properly. However, you can easily change some harmless **Site** settings. Maybe you would like to change the site name (the name shown in the backend header bar) or replace the default Joomla text in the **Metadata Description** field with a few appropriate words to let search engines know what your site's about. If you're not yet familiar with these concepts, however, that's fine. You'll learn more about the options you need later on in the book.

Looking for all the answers?

In the course of this book, you'll learn much more about the Control Panel and the sort of functionality it has to offer. However, we won't cover every tiny little detail of the administration interface. Luckily, Joomla offers an exhaustive online reference to all backend menus, submenus, options, settings, and screens. In the backend, click on Help in the Global Configuration screen. There's a wealth of up-to-date information from the Joomla help site.

Pop quiz – test your knowledge of Joomla basics

Q1. What's makes a CMS-based website different from a traditional, "static" website?

a. A CMS consists of an unlimited database of web pages.

b. A CMS doesn't use traditional coding languages, such as HTML.

c. A CMS dynamically builds web pages by gathering content blocks from a database.

Q2. What's the backend of a Joomla-powered website?

    a.   It's the interface where administrators log in to change site configuration settings.

    b.   It's the interface where administrators log in to build and maintain the site.

    c.   It's the part of the site that's only accessible for registered users.

Q3. How can you rearrange the page layout of your site and move about content blocks?

    a.   By moving and deleting articles.

    b.   By using the **Module Manager** to change the position and visibility of modules.

    c.   By using the **Article Manager** to change the position and visibility of articles.

Summary

In this chapter you learned about what makes building websites with Joomla special, what the frontend of your site can look like, and how to use the backend Control Panel.

- You've seen what the differences are between static websites and websites built the Joomla way. A Joomla powered website is a collection of building blocks, dynamically constructed from the database.

- The frontend of the website—the site as your visitor experiences it—is constructed out of different building blocks. The central part of the page is called the mainbody; the surrounding blocks are called modules.

- Joomla offers a great number of options to present information in the central content area, the mainbody. Moreover, you can combine the mainbody with almost any combination and number of modules in the header, in the footer, in the left-hand side column, and the right-hand side column.

- Every Joomla site has a backend; a **Control Panel** to administer your site. When you log into the backend, you can manage content, add new features, change settings, and so on. You add an article through the **Article Manager**, rearrange elements on the page through the **Module Manager**, and change site settings in the **Global Configuration** panel.

In the next chapter, we'll get up to speed and take things much further. Now that you've experimented with Joomla a bit, you'll create a fully functional website that perfectly meets your first client's demands—and it will be finished in an hour!

4

Web Building Basics: Creating a Site in an Hour

In the previous chapter, you have acquainted yourself with the Joomla interface, explored the example site, and tried out Joomla's administration interface.

You know your way around, you've got a good grasp of how things work—so now it's high time to start building a website! In this chapter, you'll build a complete site in just one hour. Imagine, you've just got a call from your first client. They have founded a club that is about to get some media attention, but they still haven't got a website they can refer to. They need a website and they need it fast. Can you help them out?

That's a perfect opportunity to put your new web building toolkit to the test. And, well, being new to Joomla, maybe you'll need a little bit more than just one hour. However, if you start now, you're certain to meet tomorrow's deadline—and have time left to have dinner in time, take a hot bath, and grab a movie too.

In this chapter, you'll learn to:

- ◆ Remove Joomla's sample data to create a blank canvas for your site
- ◆ Customize the site's template
- ◆ Add content: create a framework, add articles, and add menu items

◆ Add new features: create a contact form and a special message block

◆ Finish your very first, fully functional Joomla-powered website.

What you will be making

In the following screenshot, you see what you will be building throughout this chapter. Although it still uses the basic layout of Joomla's sample site, it's perfectly tailored to the client's specifications:

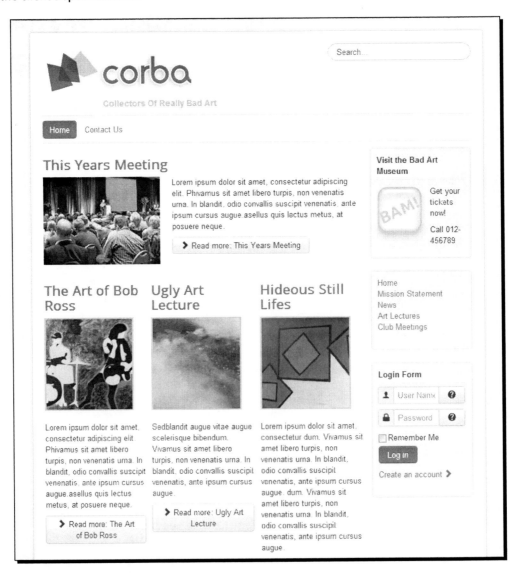

Meet your client

Allow me to introduce you to your first client! It's a club that proudly calls itself Collectors Of Really Bad Art (or CORBA). They just love horrible amateur paintings and other forms of ugly art that mostly end up dumped in the trash heap or turn up in charity shops. According to the CORBA philosophy, ugly art is worth collecting for its own ugly sake. Now that a big newspaper is about to write an article about CORBA, the collectors club needs a website to broadcast their message and tell the public what they're all about. You may not be into art, but you are into the art of building websites, so you're just the one, the CORBA people need.

CORBA's wish list is as follows:

- The look and feel of the site should fit with the logo and colors found on the club's stationery
- The site should present several content pages in a well organized way, providing a solid basis for further expansion
- The home page should show a selection of news items on bad art collecting
- Visitors should be invited to get in touch; there has to be a contact form

Logging in again

If you want to follow along with the exercises in this chapter, I'll assume you're logged in to the backend of your site. Remember, it takes just two steps:

- In your browser, log in to the backend, by adding administrator to the URL of your website: `www.mysite.com/administrator`.
- At the login prompt, enter your username and password and click on the **Login** button. Once you are logged in, you'll see the Control Panel. The Control Panel is the home page of the backend.

Cleaning up – removing the sample data

In *Chapter 2, Installation: Getting Joomla Up and Running*, you installed Joomla with the example site data. You'll only do that once, when you're new to Joomla and want to have a first look at its possibilities. In the previous chapters, you've explored the sample content. Now that you are starting to build your own site, you don't need all that content anymore. Unfortunately, there is no "Uninstall Sample Data" button. You can install Joomla again without sample data, but in this case we'll just clean up the sample site.

Admittedly, cleaning up Joomla may seem about as exciting as wiping clean a wall-to-wall classroom blackboard before the lesson starts. However, it's a good way of preparing yourself for your very first Joomla site. You'll find that stripping Joomla's example site will give you some useful insight into the way it's constructed. Bit by bit, it will reveal the different types of content that have been used to fill the empty CMS framework.

If you have installed Joomla with no sample data you can skip the next two steps.

Step 1: Removing sample content

Let's first remove the sample content now. It consists of three groups:

◆ Actual content: Articles and the containers Joomla uses to organize articles; these are called **categories**. We'll learn more about them in the rest of this chapter.

◆ Menu links to these articles or to categories.

◆ Modules: Little prefab function blocks, such as the login form.

Time for action – deleting articles and categories

To remove content, you always start with the actual articles. That's because you cannot remove containers (categories) as long as they're not empty.

1. Navigate to **Content | Article Manager**.

2. Above the article listing, on the right-hand side, you'll notice three drop-down boxes: **Title**, **Ascending**, and **20**. The number 20 indicates the amount of articles shown in this article listing screen. Click on the **20** button and change the value to **All**.

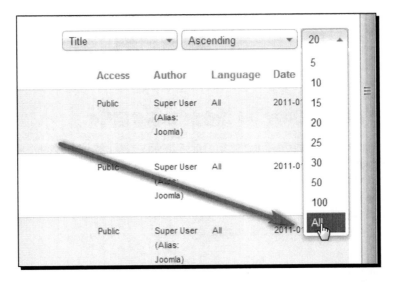

3. Now the full list of example articles is displayed on the page.

4. Select the checkbox at the top of the list (just to the left-hand side of the **Title** heading). This way all of the items in the column are selected:

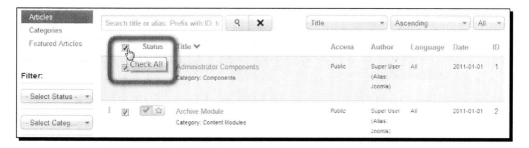

5. Click on the **Trash** button in the toolbar. Joomla shows a message confirming that the articles have been trashed.

6. When articles are in the trash, they're still in Joomla's database should you wish to restore them. However, you won't be needing these articles again. To permanently delete them, in the **Select Status** drop down, on the left-hand side of the screen, select **Trashed**.

7. All trashed articles are displayed on the page. Again, select all the articles and now click **Empty Trash**. All the articles are deleted.

Now remove the sample categories. These are containers for articles that no longer exist.

8. Navigate to **Content | Category Manager**. Make sure all categories are displayed. In the drop-down box indicating the number of displayed articles, select **All**.

9. Tick the top row checkbox to select all of the categories. Deselect just one category: **Uncategorised**. We want to keep this one, as it is used for articles that do not fit a regular category.

10. Click on **Trash**. You'll see a message confirming that the categories have been successfully trashed.

11. To permanently delete the categories, in the **Select Status** drop-down select **Trashed**. Select all categories and click **Empty trash**. All categories are permanently deleted.

Have a look at the frontend of the site. You'll notice all of the content has been removed from the example site except for the menus and the **Login** and **Search** module:

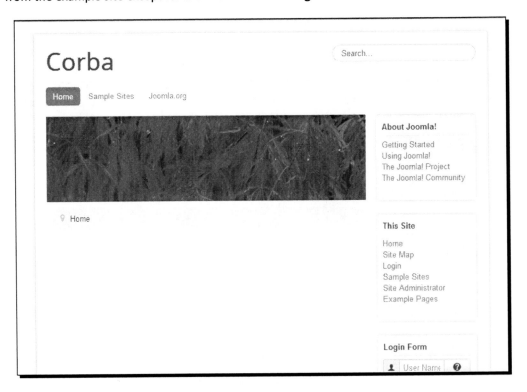

In this example, the site header shows the current site name. If you've followed along in *Chapter 2, Installation: Getting Joomla Up and Running*, this will be Corba, the name of the example client we'll use in the rest of this book. If you want to change the site name displayed in the header, you can do this by navigating to **System | Global Configuration | Site Settings | Site Name** and changing the current value.

Step 2: Deleting menus and other modules

Apart from articles and categories, the example site contains menus and modules. (Actually, menus themselves are modules too—you'll learn more about this in *Chapter 8, Helping Your Visitors Find What They Want: Managing Menus*, about creating navigation on your site.)

Time for action – deleting menus

Because much of the example menus are redundant for our goal, we'll delete them. Not to worry—you can always create new menus. We'll just delete the specific instances of the menus that were used in the example site.

1. Go to **Menus | Menu Manager**. Select three example menus you won't be needing any more, namely **About Joomla**, **Australian Parks**, and **Fruit Shop**. Do not select **Main Menu**, **Top**, and **User Menu**. We'll keep these three more generic menus because we can re-use them in our new site.

2. Click on the **Delete** button. A warning message appears; click **OK** to confirm you want to delete the menus and their contents and associated menu modules. You'll see a confirmation message and have just three menus left in the **Menu Manager** screen:

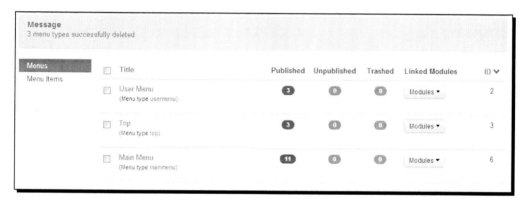

Although we'll keep the Main Menu, we don't need the redundant links it contains (to content that has just been deleted). The only link we need to keep is the **Home** link, as it's necessary for any Joomla site to function properly. You'll know the drill of deleting items by now, as the steps involved are comparable to those needed to remove articles or categories.

3. Navigate to **Menus | Main Menu**. Alternatively, you can just click on the **Main Menu** title if you've still got the **Menu Manager | Menus** screen open. Select all menu items, except for **Home**. Click on **Trash** to delete the selected menu items.

4. As you won't be needing these menu links any more, you might as well permanently remove them from the trash. In the **Select Status** drop-down list, select **Trashed**. Select all of the items, click on **Empty Trash**, and confirm.

What just happened?

To be able to put together your first Joomla site, you've deleted of a lot of sample content: articles, categories, and menus. The site is almost empty now.

Have a go hero – cleaning out the list of modules

The example site contains many examples of modules that are redundant for our own site. You probably haven't even seen them all in action, as most of them are only shown on their specific demonstration page in the example site. However, you can safely delete these module examples. Don't worry—you can always re-create any of these modules again. (As an example, we'll create a new module in the course of this chapter, and we'll find out more about modules in the coming chapters on extending Joomla). By deleting modules, you just throw away the specific instances of these modules that were used in the example site, not the module functionality.

The module deletion drill will seem familiar by now. In short: in the **Extensions** drop-down menu, click on **Module Manager**. The Module Manager displays a list of modules that are in use. Make sure all are displayed. In the select box indicating the number of displayed items, select **All**. Click the select box to the left of the **Status** heading. Now de-select generic modules that you will be using in your own site: make sure to keep **This Site**, **Top**, **User Menu**, **Search**, **Login Form**, and **Breadcrumbs**. (Be careful, as there are similarly-named modules that you *can* delete, such as **Breadcrumbs** in position **None**, and the module named **Login**.)

After you've deleted all modules you don't need (using the **Trash** button), have a look at the site. The results are impressive: articles, categories, menus, and redundant modules have disappeared. We're left with a blank canvas perfectly suitable for the new site.

Remember, installing Joomla with sample data is only recommended when you're new to Joomla and want to get familiar with the system by exploring its page layouts, menus, modules, and so on. When you already know Joomla, it's both easier and faster to start building your site without first installing sample data.

Building your new site in three steps

You've now got a blank canvas. The site is empty, there's no content, and there are just a few basic layout elements. It's high time to start building something new, cool, and attractive! In the rest of this chapter, you'll add new content to replace the content that we've just deleted when deconstructing the example site.

We'll do this in three steps:

1. **Customize the layout**: Tweak the basic layout to fit your needs.

2. **Add content**: Design a structure for your content (using categories) and add articles that fit the content framework.

3. **Add extras**: Add further functionality to your site, such as a contact form or a little content block drawing attention to a specific topic.

Step 1: Customizing the layout

In *Chapter 3, First Steps: Getting to Know Joomla*, you've seen that the overall site layout (columns, colors, typography, and so on) is set in the site's template files. Joomla allows you to edit the current template using the **Template Manager**. In this case, we'll replace the Joomla logo by your client's logo image and tweak the header text a little.

Time for action – creating a copy of the current template

First, let's make a copy of the current template. This is the best approach if you want to modify the current template. You avoid the risk that any code changes will be overwritten if the original template should ever be updated. Joomla allows you to easily create a copy of all of the template's files in a new folder.

1. To create a copy, go to **Extensions | Template Manager**. Click **Templates** in the submenu on the left-hand side.

2. In the **Template Manager | Templates** screen, click the link **Protostar Details and Files**. You're taken to the **Template Manager | Customise Template** screen. Click on the **Copy** button. Enter a name for the template copy (for example, `Protostar_copy`). You can use only letters, numbers, dashes, and underscores. Click **Copy template** in the pop-up screen. The pop-up closes. Now click **Close** to return to the **Templates** screen.

3. Finally, switch to the **Template Manager | Styles** screen by clicking the **Styles** link in the menu on the left-hand side. Here you can set the new template to be the default one. Click the white star next to **protostar_copy - Default** to make this your new default template. The star turns orange.

What just happened?

You've used Joomla's built-in template copying machine to create an exact copy of the template you want to use and change. You now can leave the original template untouched, which can come in handy should you wish to return to its default settings. Moreover, you can now safely change the settings and code of the copied template without worrying that your changes will be overwritten by an update of the original template files.

Now that you've created a copy of the Protostar template, it's time to customize this copy a little. After all, we don't want our design to look like any default Joomla site. We'll make our mark by creating a new logo image and add it to the template.

Time for action – preparing a new logo image

Let's first create a new logo image.

1. Open up your image editing tool. In this example, we'll use Adobe Photoshop, but any image editor will do.

2. A logo image of about 270 pixels wide and 90 pixels high will fit nicely in the existing template header space (in *Chapter 11*, *Creating an Attractive Design: Working with Templates*, you'll learn how to take a look at the HTML and CSS to find out the dimensions used in different parts of the page design). Click on **New**. In the **Width** and **Height** boxes, fill in `270` and `90` pixels respectively. Choose **Background Contents: Transparent**.

3. In Photoshop, the PNG file shows a grey and white "checkerboard" background. This indicates that the background is transparent, which means the colors of the header background will shine through. This way, the logo image you create blends in nicely with the overall design.

4. Now you can create any logo you like. Let's skip the details, as these depend on the specific needs of your site and the tool you are using. For this example, I've created a contemporary logo using a free font: **Quadranta**, from `www.dafont.com` (see `www.dafont.com/faq.php` for installation instructions). Apart from this, I have applied an outline, a drop shadow effect and I've added a few shapes (colored distorted rectangles) to make my design look like a contemporary logo.

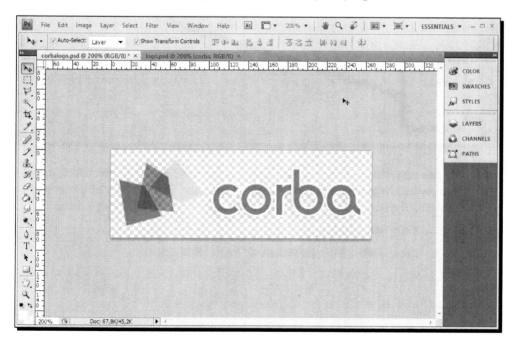

5. Save the image as a PNG file. In Photoshop, click on **Save for Web and Devices**, choose the PNG-24 file format, and save the image as `corbalogo.png`. Make sure to check the **Transparency** checkbox to preserve the transparent background. Click on **Save**.

6. In the next screen, choose a location on your computer and click on **Save** again. Your logo image is ready!

7. In the backend of the Joomla site, you can now upload and "activate" the new logo image file.

8. Go to **Extensions | Template Manager**. The current (default) template is called **Protostar_copy**. Click on the **protostar_copy – Default** link. Click the **Options** tab. You'll see a **Logo** option that allows you to select a logo image file. Click **Select**. A pop-up window opens.

9. In the pop-up window, click **Browse...** (you may have to scroll within the pop-up to see it) and browse to the **corba_logo.png** file on your computer. Click **Start upload**.

10. The **Upload Complete** message is displayed. Now click on the thumbnail of the new logo image (the filename will automatically appear in the **Image URL** field) and click **Insert**.

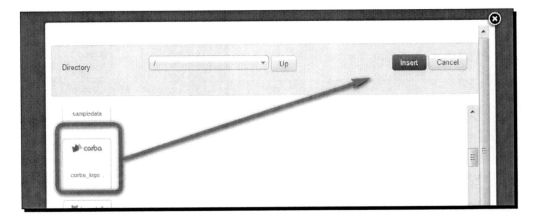

11. The pop-up window closes and you return to the **Template Manager: Edit Style** screen. The new logo image has been set. However, we'll also change a few other settings to customize the template. In the **Options** section, change the following values:

  ❑ **Title**: Enter **CORBA**.

  ❑ **Description**: Enter **Collectors Of Really Bad Art**.

12. Click **Save & Close** and click **View site** to see the output:

As you can see, the new logo and the new tag line now both appear, just as we had expected.

Living without Photoshop—free alternatives

Photoshop may be a fine graphic editing tool, but it's not exactly cheap. The standard Windows graphics editor Paint can do the job—but its capabilities are very, very basic. Fortunately, there are many excellent and free Photoshop alternatives. You can even have essential Photoshopping capabilities on your computer without installing a thing. Just browse to `www.pixlr.com`, click **Open Photo editor** and start creating and editing!

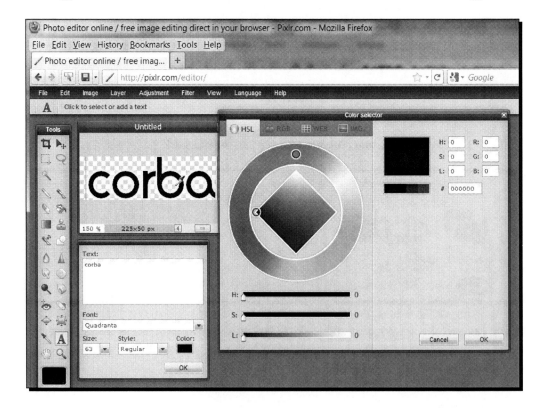

If you're looking for free graphic editing software programs, do a web search for **Paint.NET** or **GIMP**. Both are very capable programs; Paint. NET is beginner-friendly and at the same time quite powerful. The **GIMP**, an acronym for **GNU Image Manipulation Program**, is arguably the most popular free Photoshop contender. It's an open source program that's available for all platforms (Windows, Apple OS, and Linux) and features a truckload of photo retouching and image editing tools.

Time for action – tweaking the design details

Maybe you're happy with the template as it is, now that you've personalized the logo and tagline text. But in many cases you may want to customize the design even more. To do this, you have to edit the CSS files of the template. CSS (Cascading Style Sheets) define the design of the site—the HTML code provides the basic structure of the page—CSS is used to customize the layout, color, and typography. We'll come back to the principles of CSS in a minute, but the best way to find out how it works is to play around with it a little. As an example, we'll change the style of the tagline text. Right now it's pretty small and inconspicuous, so let's make it bigger and bolder.

1. Go to **Extensions | Template Manager** and click the **Templates** menu link on the left-hand side. Click **Protostar_copy Details and Files** to edit the copied template. This will take you to the screen showing the (editable) files of the current template. Click **Edit css/template.css**. This is the CSS file that the `Protostar_copy` template currently uses.

2. The **Template Manager** editor screen opens. Here you can edit or add the CSS code to the `template.css` code file. The file doesn't contain any particular style for the site description at this moment; the look of the tagline is determined by the general CSS markup for all paragraph text. Luckily, the tagline text does already have a specific "CSS name" (or a class, in CSS terms) applied to it. If you were to look in the page's HTML code, you'd see this line of text has `the.site-description` class applied to it. All you have to do to change the styling of the tagline text is to add CSS code that adds some meaning to the currently "empty" `.site-description` class. This will tell the browser how to render the tagline text. To do this, add the following code at the beginning of the code screen:

    ```
    .site-description {
        color: silver;
        font-size: 14px;
        font-weight: bold;
        padding-left: 104px;
    }
    ```

3. To clarify, the code `color: silver` indicates the text should have a gray color, `font-size: 14px` indicates the font should be a bit bigger than the original value, `font-weight:bold` indicates the tagline should be rendered as bold text and `padding-left:104px` indicates the tagline should be placed 104 pixels to the right from its current position, aligning it with the logo text.

4. Click on the **Save & Close** button.

5. Click on **View Site** to see the results on the frontend. If you still see the old design, force your browser to refresh (reload the page) by typing *F5* (or, *Ctrl + R* or *Cmd + R*).

You'll notice the tagline looks much better and stands out a little more.

What just happened?

The new look for your site is beginning to take shape. You've replaced the original logo image, but you've also added a few lines in the CSS stylesheet of the current Joomla template.

CSS stylesheets? Come again?

You've just changed the code in one of the Joomla template files. Specifically, you've edited a CSS file. Now wait a minute... wasn't Joomla supposed to take the code editing effort out of managing websites? It certainly is—and it does—but if you want to really customize the appearance of your site, editing the CSS files is the way to go. Don't worry, you don't have to be a code wizard to be able to change the template CSS to suit your needs.

Now what exactly is CSS? We'll get into the subject of templates in more detail in *Chapter 11, Creating an Attractive Design: Working with Templates*, but here's a short introduction into what stylesheets are and what they do:

- ◆ You probably know web pages are documents containing HTML code. HTML tells the web browser what content it should display and roughly where this content is placed on the web page.

- ◆ These HTML documents can be linked to **Cascading Style Sheets** (**CSS**) files. These CSS files tell the web browser how the data in the HTML file should be displayed. CSS is a relatively simple set of rules that define the web pages' colors, fonts, page layout, and more.

As CSS instructions are stored in a separate file, these layout instructions can be linked to (and used by) any number of HTML documents. In other words—changing one line in a CSS file can change the appearance of a number of web pages using that CSS file. You've just seen an example of this when you made all pages on the site display a bigger tagline by editing the `template.css` file.

Joomla's built-in CSS editor screen makes it easy to quickly tweak the current template's layout details; however, you do need to have some knowledge of CSS for this. If you're new to CSS, you can find a wealth of information on the Web. Just Google the phrase "introduction to CSS" or "CSS tutorial" and you'll be presented with some great resources. To get a quick introduction, have a look at `www.yourhtmlsource.com/stylesheets/introduction.html`.

We'll be exploring CSS in more detail in *Chapter 11, Creating an Attractive Design: Working with Templates*.

Have a go hero – explore layout settings

As you've seen, there are different ways to influence the look and feel of your current template. The first way is by using the options that are built into the template that allow you to select different settings and values (via **Template Manager | Styles**); the second way is by editing the template stylesheet (the actual template code, via **Template Manager | Templates**).

Have a go and experiment a little with the built-in template options. Get a feel for the effects that the different options have by trying out some width settings and color combinations. Pick your flavor, click on **Save**, and click on **View site** to see the output on the frontend.

You'll notice that template options only allow you to change a limited set of options. It's far more powerful to take a look under the hood and edit the template CSS file or files in the Joomla editor. That way, your layout options are only limited by your CSS skills. It's a good idea to take another look into the `template.css` file in the template editor CSS files to get a feel for what coding in CSS is like—you'll notice that CSS rules are, for the most part, written in plain English and don't look at all difficult to understand.

Step 2: Adding content

The customized template looks good, but the site's still empty. It's high time to actually populate it with some articles! In the previous chapter, you already created one simple article in the Joomla example site. However, when you create your own site you'll want to choose a more structured approach.

Creating a foundation first: Making categories

If you have experience in designing static websites, you've probably added new pages to the site in two steps. You start making a new HTML document—the page—and then added a link to that page, making sure your new content can be found.

In Joomla, you have to take a little preparatory action. Before you make new pages, it's common practice to first create containers for your content. These containers are called categories. You can create as many categories as you want. Categories hold articles. We won't go into the specifics just now, as we'll be exploring the ins and outs of of organizing content in the next chapter. For now, let's experiment a little and see how using categories in Joomla works.

As you've got a tight deadline to meet, we'll follow the three steps of content creation the quick and dirty way. For this basic site, one category split up into two subcategories will do for us to be able to classify all content.

Time for action – creating a News category

Your client, CORBA, wants to publish a range of articles on the current club activities on their site; that's what they're all about. How can we categorize these articles the Joomla way? Let's first add a category as a container for these news articles.

1. Navigate to **Content | Category Manager**. Click on the **New** button. (Alternatively, you can click on the **Content | Category Manager | Add New Category** fly-out menu item).

2. The **Category Manager: Add A New Articles Category** screen opens. In the **Title** field, type **News**. Don't worry about the other fields; you can leave them empty for now.

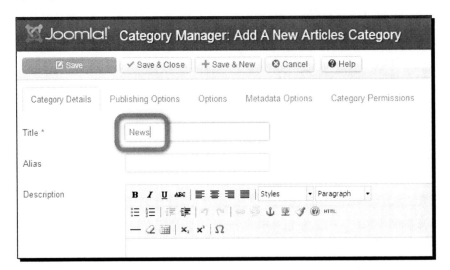

3. Click on **Save & Close**. A message is displayed (**Category successfully saved**) and you're taken to the **Category Manager** screen. You'll see the results—apart from **Uncategorised**, there's one other category now, **News**.

What just happened?

In Joomla, you create content groups (categories) before you can actually start adding articles and menu links. However, when you add categories in the backend, you'll notice nothing changes on the frontend. To get them to display, we'll add content to the category and create a menu link pointing to category content later.

Creating articles and using the Images and Links fields

Now we come to the core of content management. Let's actually start creating content! We'll make some articles, apply the appropriate formatting, and add images.

Time for action – creating an article

First, let's create an article in the **News** category:

1. Navigate to **Content | Article Manager | Add New Article**. The **Article Manager: Add New Article** screen opens.

2. In the **Title** box, type the title of the article (in this example, **Bad Photography Exhibition**).

3. In the **Category** drop-down box, select **News**. Now you see why you needed to create a category before. Without these you cannot assign any new article to the appropriate "containers" within your overall site structure.

4. In the editor screen, write the article. In this example, we'll just use dummy text. It's easy to copy and paste any amount of fake paragraph text from www.lipsum.com.

5. To divide the article text into an intro text and the main article text, position the cursor at the beginning of the first line below the first paragraph. Click on the **Read more** button at the bottom of the editor screen. A red dotted line appears indicating the separation between intro text and main article text.

6. Finally, we'll add an image to the article. Below the article editor screen, you'll notice there's an **Images and links** section. This feature allows you to add an image, which Joomla will show at the beginning of the article text and/or the article intro text. In this case, we'll add images to the intro of the article. To do this, click **Select** in the **Intro Image** field. A pop-up screen with thumbnails of the available images in Joomla's default image folder appears. Click the icon of the `sampledata` folder. Navigate to `sampledata/parks/landscape` and select one of the available images by clicking on its thumbnail.

7. In the **Image float** drop-down box, click on **Left**. This will make the image appear to the left-hand side of the text. Click on **Insert**. The pop-up window closes:

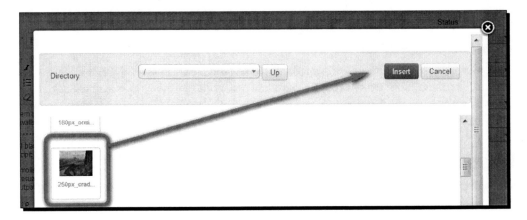

Although the image will be shown on the frontend, it isn't visible in the backend article text. To check whether you've chosen the desired image, point your cursor to the eye symbol in the **Intro Image** field. This will display a small thumbnail of the selected image:

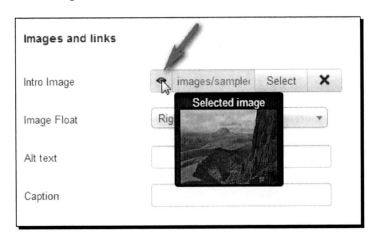

8. Repeat the previous two steps to add a **Full article image**. Again, select an image (in this case, preferably a bigger size image) and make the **Image float** to the **Left**.

This is what the **Article Manager: Add New Article** screen looks like once you've completed inserting all of the article data:

9. Click on **Save & Close** to save changes you've made. You're taken to the **Article Manager: Articles** screen. The details of the article are displayed in the articles list:

10. The new article is ready, but if you now click the **View site** link, you might be disappointed. There is no sign of your new article on the website! That's because you have to take one last step and add a menu link.

What just happened?

You've created a full-blown article, consisting of text and images. To add images, you've used Joomla's **Images and links**, a nifty new feature. After all, it's a common scenario for web content that images are placed at the very beginning of an article. Joomla's **Images and links** fields make it more convenient to create a set of articles using fixed layouts. They allow for a fool-proof way of inserting different images placed exactly at the beginning of the article intro and of the full article text.

To enable Joomla to separately display the intro text, (with a **Read more** link to the full article) you used the **Read more** button in the article editor. This divides the article text into an intro text and the main article text. In the editor, the separation is indicated by a red dotted line.

You'll probably remember seeing this division at work on the sample site home page that contains several short intro texts. Only when visitors click on the accompanying **Read more** link are they taken to a page with the full article text.

Have a go hero – add more images to articles

When you want to add images to articles, you're certainly not limited to the **Images and links** feature you've used in the previous examples. It's possible to place images anywhere on an article. Just position the cursor at the beginning of any paragraph and click the **Image** button at the bottom of the editor screen. We'll use this way of adding images later in this book. Here's a quick walkthrough of the steps involved:

To the article you just created, you added an image from Joomla's default image set. For testing purposes that's okay, but in real life you'll want to add your own images. To do this, place the cursor at the beginning of any article paragraph and click on the **Image** button at the bottom of the article editor screen. In the pop-up screen, you'll see an **Upload files** box. Click on **Browse files** to find an image file on your hard drive. Select the image file and click on **Start Upload**. A thumbnail of the uploaded image will appear among the other thumbnails (you may have to scroll down if there are a lot of images). Click on the desired thumbnail. Choose the appropriate **Align** setting and click on **Insert**. The pop-up window closes; your picture is inserted.

Making content visible on the site: Creating a menu link

The article you've just created is ready and it's stored in Joomla's database—but it's still invisible on the frontend of the site. That's because there's no link pointing to it. The **Main Menu** (titled **This Site**) is empty, except for the **Home** link.

Time for action – adding a menu link

Let's finish the three steps of content creation and add a link to your article:

1. Navigate to **Menus | Main Menu | Add New Menu Item**. The **Menu Manager: New Menu Item** screen opens.

2. Next to the **Menu Item Type** box, click on the **Select** button and select **Articles | Category Blog**. This menu link type tells Joomla to display a page containing intro texts and **Read more** hyperlinks to all content from a specific category. You'll see what that looks like in a minute.

3. In the **Choose a category** drop-down box, select **News**.

4. In the **Menu Title** field, type **News**. Click on **Save**.

What just happened?

Creating just one link to the **News** category changes a lot on the frontend. The site now looks as follows:

◆ The home page is still empty, but the menu does contain a new link, **News**.

◆ When the visitor clicks on the **News** link, they are shown a **Category Blog** page. This is an overview page of all contents of the **News** category. The overview consists of intro texts and **Read more** links to the full articles. For now, there's just one article intro text. When you add new articles to the category, they will automatically be added to this overview page:

♦ When the visitor clicks on the **Read more** link, he is taken to the full article. The breadcrumb trail just below the article reflects the category structure: **Home | News | Bad Photography Exhibition**:

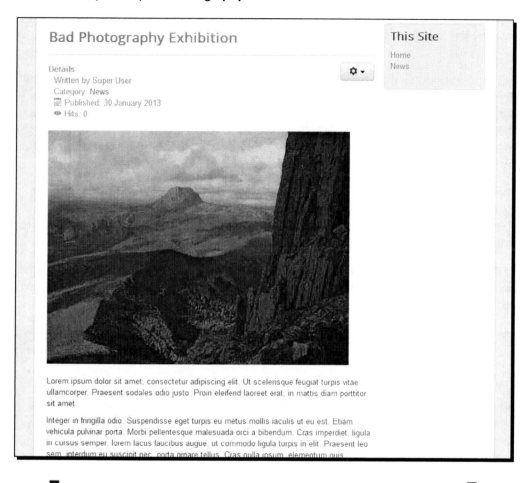

In the previous screenshot of the **Category Blog** page, you see the **Intro Image** is displayed aligned to the left of the intro text, just as it should. However, at the time of writing, the **Image Float** settings of images added though **Images and links** fields have no effect. This appears to be due to a bug in the Protostar template. When you read this, the issue has probably been solved. However, if you experience problems aligning images you inserted using **Images and links**, check the website accompanying this book (www. joomm.net) for a simple solution.

Now that's the all-important power of menus

The previous example illustrates the power of Joomla menu links. Just by adding a menu link you make content accessible in several ways. Whatever you add to the category you've set up, no new menu links are needed. Any new content will show up through the **News** category link that you have already created.

It's important to notice that Joomla menu links are very special. They don't just point to existing pages; rather, they determine what page will be displayed. The **Category Blog** Menu Item Type you've just deployed, contains dozens of options and settings (which we will try out later). Choosing a particular menu item type and tweaking its settings tells Joomla exactly what to fetch from the database and how to display it. That's why you see such an impressive list of Menu Item Types when you add a new link to a menu. In fact, these Menu Item Types represent different preset ways to display all kinds of content.

The **Category Blog** layout makes Joomla display bits of articles in a "blog style"; that is, as a series of short intro texts on one page. If you would have created a direct menu link to the new article using an **Article Layout**, the menu link would have pointed to the same content in a different presentation—the full article page.

In *Chapter 8, Helping Your Visitors Find What They Want: Managing Menus*, we'll dive deeper into the art of creating menu items and the effects that different Menu Item Types and their settings have on the final results, a broad range of web page types.

Have a go hero – create more categories and articles

For the example site you'll need a few more categories and articles. Your client wants to publish content on two specific subjects: Club Meetings and Art Lectures. This calls for two new categories. You can add these using the same steps you took to create the **News** category. First, add one more category called **Club Meetings** and click **Save & New**—this will save the first category and open a blank new screen to immediately create a second one. Create a second category called **Art Lectures** and click **Save & Close**. The Category Manager should show the results; in all you've added three categories.

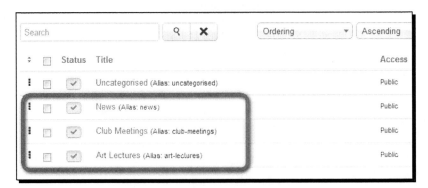

Add a few dummy articles to the categories. To do this repeat the steps you just took in *Time for action – create an article*.

A quick way to add new (dummy) articles is using the **Save as Copy** button in the **Article Manager: Edit Article** screen. Open any article you want to use as a base for a new article and change the article **Title**. Make the **Alias** field (found under **Publishing Options**) empty and click on **Save as Copy**. That's all, you've created a new article. To create more articles, repeat these steps: change the title, clear the alias, click **Save as Copy**. Of course, you can change more details of the article if you like—change some article text, add another image, or assign the article to a different category. In any case, saving the article as a copy is a lot quicker than just creating a series of separate new articles and filling out all the details.

To follow along with the examples used in this book, create articles using the titles displayed in the following screenshot. In this example, three articles have been added to each of the two new categories:

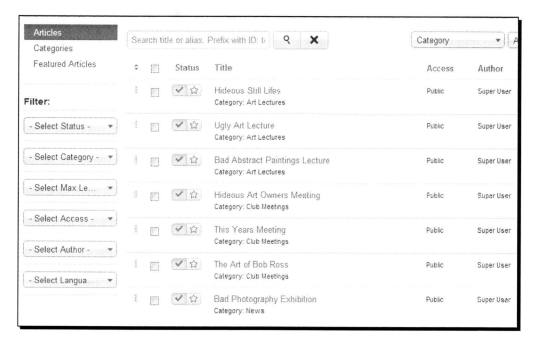

As you can see, the **Article Manager** displays an overview of the entire site contents. In the **Title** column all of the articles are shown; below each title you can see the **Category** to which the article is assigned.

In your case the order of the articles in the listing may be different from the order shown in the previous screenshot. By default the articles are ordered by **Title**, but in the previous screenshot you've seen them ordered by **Category**. To change the way the articles are sorted, click on the drop-down box above the article listing (on the right-hand side).

By defining a couple of categories you've now got a foundation to add any amount of content on the main subjects. In later chapters, we'll expand this structure.

Creating menu links to the new content

Now that you've added some more categories and articles, the next step is to make that content accessible through the menu. You've already seen how this works: go to **Menus | Main Menu | Add New Menu Item**.

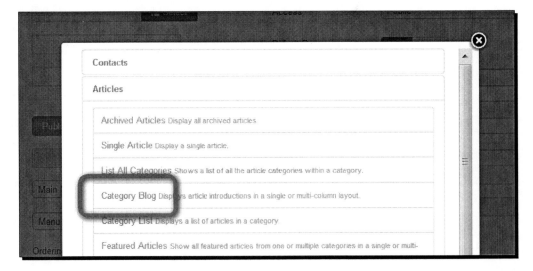

First, add a new menu item of the **Articles | Category Blog** type. Call this menu link **Art Lectures** and make it point to the **Art Lectures** category.

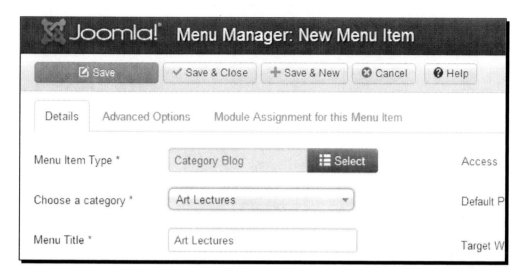

After you've saved this menu link, create the same type of menu link for the **Club Meetings** category. (Remember, in cases like these the **Save & New** button is your best friend!)

The Main Menu should now contain a total of four menu items: **Home**, **News**, **Art Lectures**, and **Club Meetings**. Click **View Site** to have a look at the frontend. You'll notice the site is beginning to take shape. If you click a link pointing to any of the categories, Joomla displays the intro texts of the articles in that particular category. If you've added a picture to the intro texts, the result should look something like the following screenshot—an overview page containing intros of all category content. Don't worry if the actual order of articles is different in your setup; by default articles are arranged with the newest ones on top.

You'll learn how to change this in *Chapter 7, Welcoming your Visitors – Creating Attractive Home Pages and Overview Pages,* on creating category overview pages.

In this example, all articles contain an (right aligned) image in the intro text. You'll agree that this makes the category blog overview page look quite attractive, even if we haven't changed any of the default settings.

Adding individual content pages: uncategorized articles

For now, your client would like to have just one different type of content page on their first website. Let's say they'd like a page on their mission statement. As there's no need for more content like this, it would be overkill to create a category to accommodate this article. Luckily, Joomla allows you to add uncategorized articles. You've probably noticed there's a default category called **Uncategorised** (which is, admittedly, a strange name for a category!) just for this purpose. Uncategorized articles are ordinary articles except for one thing; when adding them, you assign them to the "Uncategorized category".

Time for action – adding uncategorized articles

Let's create a Mission Statement page by adding an uncategorized article.

1. Navigate to **Content | Article Manager**. Click on **New**.

2. In the **Title** box, enter **Mission Statement**. In the **Category** drop-down box, make sure **Uncategorised** is selected.

3. In the text editor area, add the Mission Statement text and add an image, if you like. For this example, we've entered the following text:

   We all know the works of great art throughout the centuries. But what about bad art? Much of the creative output of really lousy artists has been discarded, thrown away because of its lack of artistic value. Let's not let that happen any more!

The beauty in ugliness

Collectors Of Really Bad Art is a club for bad art lovers. We seek to find and promote the beauty that's hidden behind superficial ugliness. Tour our website to discover that beauty too!

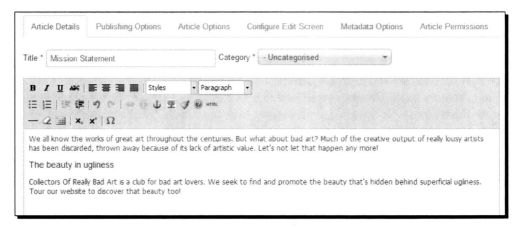

4. Click on **Save & Close**.

   The uncategorized article is finished—we just need a menu link to make it visible.

5. Navigate to **Menus | Main Menu | Add New Menu Item**.

6. In the **Menu Manager: New Menu Item** screen, we'll create a link to a single article. Let's select the appropriate **Menu Item Type**; click on **Articles | Single Article**. The pop-up screen closes.

7. Click the **Select** button next to the **Select an Article** box to choose the article this menu link will link to. In the pop-up box, select the **Mission Statement** article. The pop-up window closes.

8. In the **Menu Title** box, enter **Mission Statement**.

9. Click on **Save & Close**. Click on **View Site** to admire the results. The menu now displays a new link to the **Mission Statement** article.

Your first uncategorized article is ready.

What just happened?

Uncategorized articles are a perfect solution to place content on your site that doesn't fit the categories structure. For now, you've added one uncategorized article and a menu link pointing to that specific article. On the frontend of your website, the output is as follows:

◆ A new menu link is displayed as the last item in the Main Menu:

◆ Clicking on the **Mission Statement** link reveals a single article page:

Have a go hero –rearrange the Main Menu using drag-and-drop

You'll have noticed that Main Menu items are shown in the order that you've created them. The last two menu items you've just added are displayed at the bottom of the menu. You can change the order of items in the main menu by navigating to **Menus** | **Main Menu** and clicking on the three vertical dots to the left-hand site of any of the article titles. You can now drag-and-drop the article to the desired position. Try this out now. For example, try to move the **Mission Statement** article link to the second position:

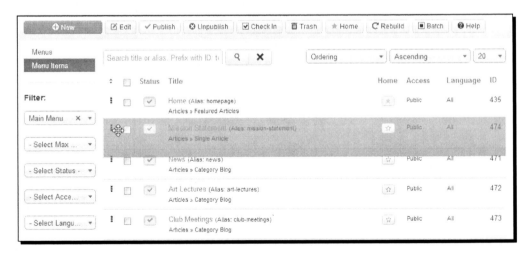

No need to save this new setting; when you have a look at the frontend of the site, you'll immediately see the effects.

Hiding the menu title

The main menu as it's displayed on the front end has a title: **This Site**. You probably want to edit or delete that title; generic web site menus don't need a title. To change the title of the menu, you need to edit the menu module properties. To do this, go to **Extensions | Module Manager**. Click on the **This Site** title. The **Module Manager: Module Menu** screen menu opens. Select **Show Title: Hide** and save changes. From now on, the menu title is hidden.

Putting content on the home page—at last!

Now that you've stuffed your site with content, there's one essential page to take care of. As we haven't added anything to the home page yet, its main content area is still empty.

It may seem strange that you do not start with the home page when adding content; after all, it's the official entrance to the site. However, you do need to have the actual content— articles—before you can start publishing anything on your home page. After all, the home page is usually a selection of content items—teasers, images, or hyperlinks—drawn from the rest of the site.

Adding items to the home page

How do you control which pieces of content are shown on the home page? When you write a new article (**Content | Article Manager | New**), or edit an existing article in the Article Manager, you can choose whether you want the article to be displayed on the home page. In the **Article Manager: Edit Article** screen, set **Featured** to **Yes**.

Another way to quickly add items to the home page (or remove them) is to use the Article Manager overview screen (**Content | Article Manager**). A white star in the **Status** column indicates the article is not displayed on the home page. Clicking on the star changes its color to orange. This indicates the article will be displayed on the home page, as this is by default set up to show all featured articles. We'll try this out right now.

Time for action – assigning articles to the home page

Let's add a couple of articles to the home page through the Article Manager.

1. Navigate to **Content | Article Manager**.

2. In the **Status** column, click on the white star next to four articles: **Hideous Still Lifes**, **Ugly Art Lecture**, **The Art of Bob Ross**, and **This Years Meeting**. The white star turns orange. The results are shown in the following screenshot. Four articles are set to show on the home page:

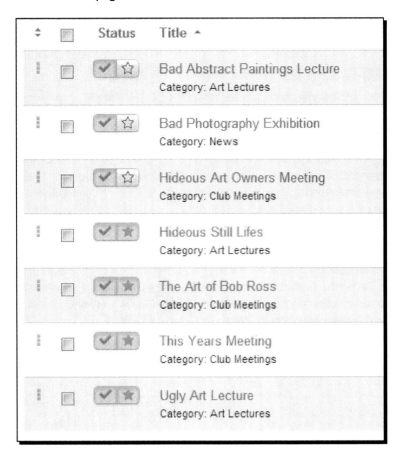

3. Click on **View Site**. You've got a home page filled with content! Four articles are displayed on the home page as intro texts with **Read more** links:

What just happened?

By clicking on the icon in the **Featured** column in the Article Manager, you have added four articles to the home page. On the frontend, these four articles are now shown in the default Joomla home page layout; the first intro text is displayed in the full mainbody width, the other intro texts below are presented in three columns. We'll leave this for now—but rest assured, you'll learn how to tweak these display options to your heart's content in later chapters.

There's more to the home page than just featured articles

How do you determine what's shown on the homepage? Partly you do so by indicating which articles should be featured. By default, featured articles appear on the home page. They are shown in the main content area or mainbody. That is the part of the page where the four intro texts are displayed in the preceding screenshot. But there's more to the home page—the entire page the user sees when they click on **Home**. That page also contains modules, such as menus and the search function. Whether a module is displayed on the home page, is something you control through the settings of the modules themselves. You can see an example of this later on in this chapter, when we add a module to the site.

Step 3: adding extras through extensions

You've just taken a few giant leaps! You have customized the layout of your new site, framed a structure, and have created and published the contents to match. If this were a static HTML site, this would be about it. This would be all there was to a website. In Joomla, however, the fun has just begun. You can now add functional or even just stylish extras. For this, you'll use Joomla's components and other extensions—that's where the Joomla's real magic power lies.

Components and Extensions, what's the difference?

To manage Joomla's extended functionality, you'll find yourself working with both the **Components** and the **Extensions** menu in the backend. In fact, components are extensions too—they also extend Joomla functionality. Components are found under the separate **Components** menu in the Joomla backend, as they are more powerful and more complex; they're applications within the Joomla application. Through the **Extensions** menu, you can find modules and plugins. These are smaller add-ons that can contain all sorts of dynamic information. Sometimes, components and modules are designed to work together.

In spite of the differences between the different types of extensions, behind the scenes they generally serve the same purpose. They all enhance your site's functionality.

For now, we'll be using components and other extensions that are included in the default Joomla setup. Later, you'll probably want to add other extensions. There are thousands of them available on the Web, providing whatever functionality you might want to add to your site. You'll learn more about adding extensions in *Chapter 10, Getting the Most out of Your Site: Extending Joomla*.

Add a contact form

Let's take care of one of the last items on your client's wish list and enable site visitors to get in touch through a contact form. Adding this form will take two steps. First, we'll create a contact; after that, we'll create a menu link that displays a contact form.

Time for action – creating a contact

Let's add a contact, that is, someone whose (mail) address and other contact details can be displayed on the form page and who will receive the form data in their mailbox.

1. Navigate to **Components | Contacts**. The **Contact Manager** opens. Click on **New**.

2. In the **Contact Manager: Contact** screen, enter the details for the contact. In the **Name** box, enter **CORBA Staff**:

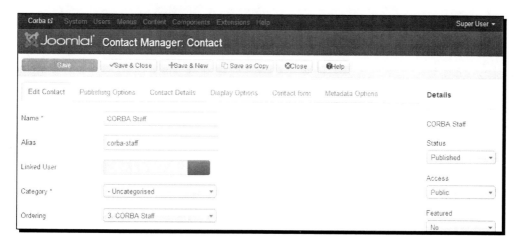

3. In the **Category** drop-down list, select **Uncategorised**. There's no need for different types of contact categories on our site.

4. Click the **Contact Details** tab to enter the contact information details you want to display. In this case, it's okay to just fill out the **Email** box and the **Telephone** box. It is important to specify a valid e-mail address, because this is where the form data will be sent to. In the **Position** field, enter something like **Staff Bureau** or **General Enquiries**—this is the text that will be displayed above the telephone number.

5. Click on the **Display Options** tab to specify whether you want to show or hide specific contact details on the contact form page. In this case, the default options are okay. You could, of course, display more contact details to offer visitors various ways to respond.

6. Click on **Save & Close**.

What just happened?

To be able to create a contact form, you have first created a contact. Using the Joomla Contact Component, you can build a comprehensive system of contacts organized by contact categories. For our goal, just one contact name and e-mail address will suffice.

Time for action – creating a Contact Form menu link

Now that a contact exists you can add a link to a contact form to the main menu:

1. Navigate to **Menus | Top**. We'll add the new link to the horizontal top menu.

2. Click on **New**.

3. In the **Menu Item Type** list, select **Contacts | Single Contact**.

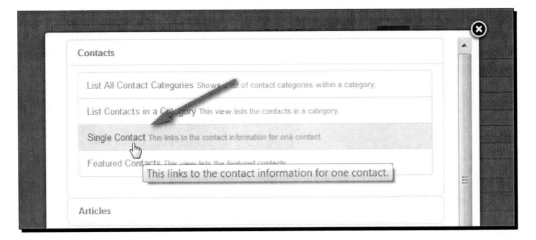

4. Click on the **Select** button next to the **Select a Contact** textbox to select the appropriate contact, **CORBA Staff**.

5. Enter a **Menu Title** for the menu item (for example, **Contact Us**). Make sure **Menu Location** is set to the **Top** menu.

6. Click the **Advanced Options** tab to access the **Contact Display Options** section. Choose **Display format: Plain**. Otherwise, the contact form will be displayed in separate (sliding or tabbed) panels—which is not what we want.

7. Click on **Save & Close**. The site now has a **Contact** menu link that displays a contact form:

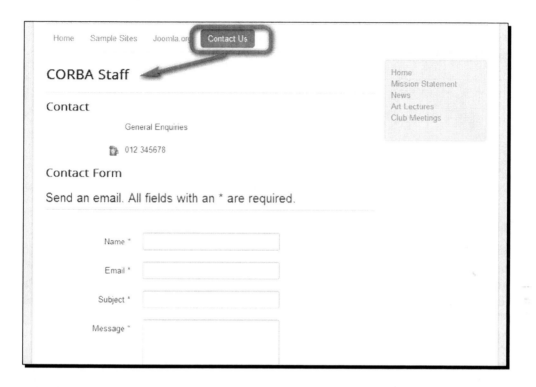

What just happened?

You have used the Contacts Component to create a contact and added a menu link to a contact form. Again you have experienced how powerful menu links are in Joomla. Just by selecting the **Menu Item Type: Single Contact** you have created a menu link that takes the visitor to a contact form page.

Have a go hero – clean up the Top Menu

If you're using the Top Menu that's left from the Joomla sample data, the menu still contains some redundant example links. You'll know how to remove them: go to **Menus | Top**, select the menu links you don't need and click **Trash**. You can keep the **Home** and **Contact Us** menu links:

Adding a special message block

The CORBA people are pleased with the current site, but they would like you to draw a little extra attention to their upcoming Ugly Art Exhibition in the Bad Art Museum. Could you maybe place some sort of message block on the home page, instead of just adding another article? In Joomla, you can. For this purpose, you use one of the modules that are available in Joomla, called **Custom HTML**. In this module block, you can add all desired content (text, images, hyperlinks, and more) and you can place the block in a specific position on specific pages.

Time for action – creating a message block

To add a message block about the Ugly Art Exhibition on the home page, we'll add a new module of the Custom HTML type.

1. Go to **Extensions | Module Manager** and click **New** to create a new module.

2. In the **Select a Module Type** screen, select **Custom HTML**.

3. Enter a **Title: Visit the Bad Art Museum**.

4. In the **Position** drop-down list, scroll to find a list of available positions for the current template, **Protostar**. Select **Right [position-7]**. This will add the block to the right column of the current template. (You'll learn more about finding out what positions are available in *Chapter 11, Creating an Attractive Design: Working with Templates*.)

5. Click on the **Custom Output** tab to enter any content the module block should contain. To insert an image, click on the **Image** button at the bottom of the editor. If you use the example files for this book, upload and insert the `bam_logo.png` image file.

6. Add some text. In this example we're entering a short text: **Get your tickets now!** and a phone number. The editor screen now looks like this:

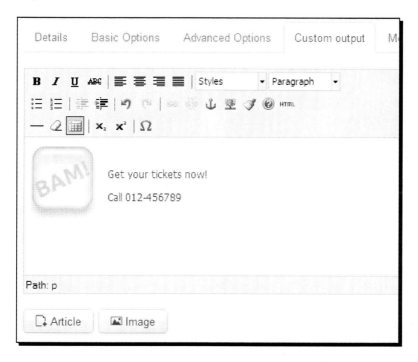

7. Finally, let's determine on which pages the module will appear. Click on the **Menu Assignment** tab to select **Module Assignment: Only on the selected pages**. Click **Select None** to deselect all pages. Now select only the **Home** page.

8. Click **Save & Close** and then click **View site**:

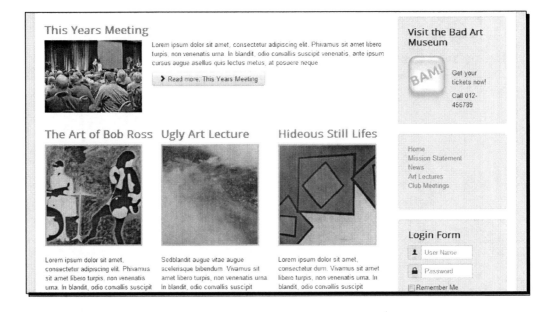

What just happened?

You've used a simple but very flexible little module in Joomla, called Custom HTML. Your site now shows a special info block in the right-hand side column of the home page.

Wrapping up: Changing site settings

The one-hour website is finished. However, there are a few adjustments to be made in the backend.

Time for action – changing the site configuration

The site configuration still shows some default values that don't match the new site contents. Let's enter the appropriate site name and add site metadata.

1. Navigate to **System | Global Configuration**.

2. In the **Site Settings** section, enter the **Site Name: CORBA - Collectors Of Really Bad Art**. In **SEO Settings** section, select **Include Site Name in Page Title: After**. This way the site information will be shown in the title bar or the current tab of the visitors' web browser:

3. In the **Metadata Settings** section (you may have to scroll down to see it), add some text. The meta description is used in search engines result pages. In the **Site Meta Description** box, enter: **CORBA is an international club of Collectors Of Really Bad Art**.

4. Joomla also offers you the possibility to add site meta keywords. Most search engines ignore meta keywords these days, but it won't hurt to enter a few keywords that characterize the site's contents: bad art, ugly paintings, bad painting, CORBA. Save your changes by clicking **Save & Close**.

What just happened?

By entering a few lines in the **Global Configuration** screen we've made sure the right site name shows up in the visitors' web browser and search engines pick up the right information about the site's contents.

Pop quiz – test your basic Joomla knowledge

Q1. What can you use the built-in Joomla CSS editor for?

    a.   To add some content containers

    b.   To change the appearance of your site

    c.   To change menu settings

Q2. In what order do you add articles and menu links?

    a.   Create menu links first, then add articles

    b.   Add articles first, then create menu links

    c.   You can choose whatever order you like

Q3. What methods does Joomla provide you with to insert images in articles?

    a.   You can add images in fixed positions through the **Images and links** fields found in the article editor screen

    b.   You can insert images anywhere you like in the article text by using the **Image** button below the article editor text field

    c.   You can use both methods mentioned above, whatever is more appropriate for your goals

Q4. What do you use components and extensions for?

    a.   Adding extras, such as newsletters or contact forms

    b.   Adding content that only registered users can see

    c.   To quickly add new content

Summary

You may not be aware of it, but you did actually do an incredible job. Your first Joomla website is up and running!

- You've built your site in three steps. First you customized the layout, then you added a framework for content, and then you added further functionality (such as a contact form) to your site.

- You have personalized the look of the site by editing the template files. You can edit the template CSS files directly in the **Template Manager** editor screen.

- Before you created content pages, you created the containers they belong in. These containers are called categories. You also added uncategorized articles: content pages that don't fit any category.

- You've seen that, to make content visible on your site, there has to be a menu link pointing to it.

- You've added items to the home page by changing their **Featured** setting.

- You added extra functionality to the site by using components and extensions. Using the Contacts component you added contact details and a contact form.

In this chapter, we followed the fast and simple approach and used only the basic capabilities of the system, leaving most settings at their default values. Building on this, it is possible to create much bigger, complex, sophisticated, and cool sites. The next chapters will cover the subjects we've touched upon in more detail.

In *Chapter 5, Small Sites, Big Sites: Organizing your Content Effectively*, we'll look specifically at the site's structure; how can you organize the content of your site, whether it's a ten page personal website or a big corporate site? You'll find out that Joomla's system of categorizing content makes it easy to create a site that's user-friendly, expandable, and easily manageable.

5
Small Sites, Big Sites: Organizing your Content Effectively

In the last chapter, you saw that creating a website in Joomla revolves around three major tasks: designing a layout, creating content, and adding extras. The central part is, of course, creating content. You can have a Joomla site using a simple default template, you can have a site without adding extra functionality, but you can't have a site without content. That's why, in the next few chapters, we'll concentrate on managing and creating content. In later chapters, you'll work on layout and adding extras.

In this chapter you'll learn how to:

◆ Translate a basic site map to a workable blueprint for a Joomla-based site

◆ Design a clear, scalable framework for your content, group your content using Joomla's system of categories and subcategories

◆ Use uncategorized pages to build sites that don't require a multi-level content

Building on the example site

The CORBA site you developed in *Chapter 4, Web Building Basics: Creating a Site in an Hour,* was a great little site, perfectly suited for your client's initial purposes for their first Web presence. Now it's time to make room for growth. Your client has a big pile of information on bad art that they want to present to the public. You are asked to design a site framework that makes it easy to add more content, while at the same time keep it easy for visitors to quickly find their way through the site.

Can you do that? You most certainly can! Joomla allows you to build sites of all sorts and sizes, whether they consist of just a few pages or thousands of them. If you plan ahead and start with a sound basic structure, you'll be rewarded with a site that's easy to maintain and extend. In this chapter, we'll review the site you've just built and look at the different ways the content can be structured—and rearranged, if need be.

Grouping content – a crash course in site organization

To lay the groundwork for your site, you won't use Joomla. The back of a napkin will do fine. Draw up a site map to lay out the primary content chunks and their relationships. View your site from a user's perspective. What do you think your visitors will primarily look for, and how can you help them find things fast and easily?

Designing a site map

To create a site map, first collect all information you plan on having on your website and organize it into a simple and logical format. Let's have a look again at the CORBA website you built in the last chapter. The following is the basic outline of the site you've created up to now:

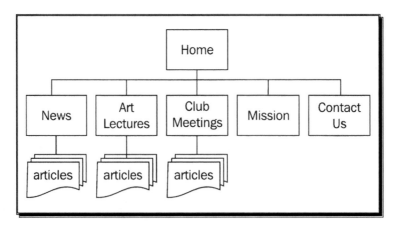

As site maps come, this is a very basic one. **News**, **Art Lectures**, and **Club Meetings** are categories that hold several articles on these three topics. **Mission** is a basic web page (an article). **Contact Us** is a contact form page. This structure was good enough to start with, but it won't do if CORBA wants to expand their site.

Time for action – create a future-proof site map

Let's make some room for growth. Imagine that your client's planning to expand the site and add new content. They have come up with the following list of subjects they want to add to their site:

◆ A few pages to introduce the founding members of CORBA

◆ Facts on bad art: history, little known facts, and so on

◆ Reviews of bad art, bad art galleries, and so on

◆ Club activities other than lectures and meetings, such as art exhibitions

What's the best way to organize things? Let's figure out which content fits which type of container.

1. The information on CORBA founders fits in a new category, **About CORBA**. This will be a category containing just a few articles: apart from an article on CORBA founders, the existing uncategorized Mission Statement article can be moved here too.

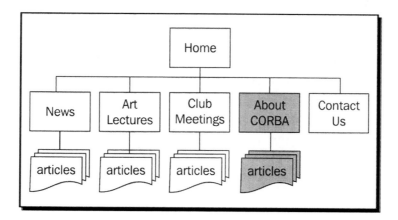

2. Up to now, we've created content groups that are just one level deep: categories holding articles. However, In Joomla, categories can hold as many other categories as you like. To organize all content on bad art, it would be good to have an extra level: a main category on **Bad Art** containing two subcategories: articles with **Reviews** and articles containing **Facts**.

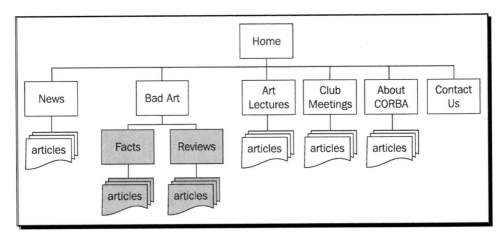

3. Now, how do we accommodate for the content on the "activities" the client wants to add? We've already got two categories that both contain information on things CORBA organizes: lectures and meetings. It makes sense to add a new top-level category **Activities**, as this is really the common denominator for both the **Art Lectures** and **Club Meetings** article groups.

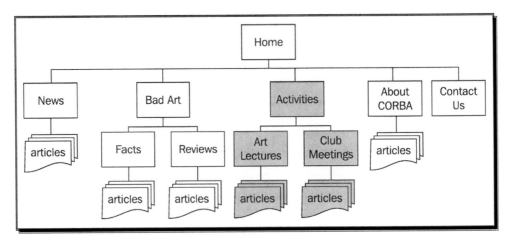

Of course, it's up to you to decide if you want to make two or more categories part of one main category (in this case **Activities**). You could also have three top-level categories on different types of activities. However, grouping content, as outlined previously, does have advantages when managing and presenting content. By putting all content in one main container, you can, for example, choose to create one menu link to display all content of **Activities** in one overview page, regardless of the category of activity they belong to. We'll see an example of this later in this chapter.

What just happened?

You've laid a foundation for your site—on paper! You've created a set of content groups (categories, in Joomla terms). Some of these categories contain subcategories.

Before you actually start using Joomla to create categories, it's a good idea to sketch a structure for the content that you have in mind. Basically, no matter how big or small your website is, you'll organize it just like the example you've just seen. You'll work from top to bottom, from the primary level to the lower levels, defining content groups and their relations. In Joomla, you can have as many subcategory levels as you like. However, try to keep your site map lean and clean. Choose an organization that makes sense to you and your visitors. A complex structure will make it harder to maintain the content, and eventually, when building menus, it will make it harder to design clear and simple navigation paths for your visitors.

Tips on choosing main categories

- It can be useful to choose categories based on the main intentions people have when they come to the site. What are they here for? Is it to *browse products* or to *join a workshop*?

- Common choices for main categories are: Products, Catalogue, Company, Portfolio, About Us, Jobs, News, and Downloads.

- Try not to have more than five to seven main categories. Once you have more than that, readers won't be able to hold them all in their heads at once when they have to choose which one to browse.

Transferring your site map to Joomla

Let's have a closer look at our new site map and identify the Joomla elements. This, and any, Joomla site is likely to consist of four types of content.

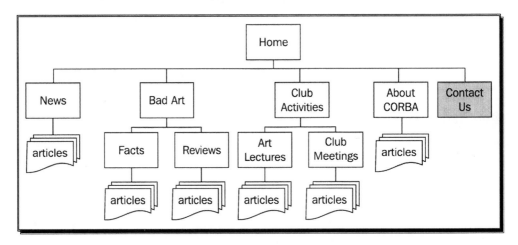

The following are the content types in our CORBA site map:

Content type	Description
Home	Obviously, the top- level item will be the home page.
Categories	The main content groups we can identify as categories. This small site has four main categories, two of which contain two categories. In Joomla, you can present articles in a given category on category overview pages.
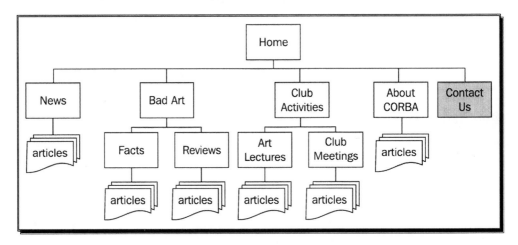 *(articles icon)*	Each of the categories hold actual content: this is what will end up in Joomla as articles.
Contact Us	The home page, categories, and articles are all about article content—that is, they're all "text and images". However, most sites are likely to also contain a different type of content: items containing special functionality. An example is the contact form in the site map shown previously. Other examples are guest books, order forms, photo galleries.

What's the purpose of uncategorized articles?

In this site map, we have placed all article content in categories. However, more often than not you'll find there are one or two articles that don't really belong in any category: a Disclaimer page or a simple About Us page. In Joomla, you can add these as uncategorized articles. You've seen an example of those when building your first site in the last chapter.

Moreover, uncategorized articles come in handy when building a very small site of just a few pages. Instead of creating categories that each hold just one article, you can leave all content uncategorized. You'll see some examples of this at the end of this chapter.

Another way to make use of uncategorized articles is as a placeholder for articles that have not yet been assigned to a category. Later, you can always group uncategorized articles by placing them in a (new) category.

Basically, the four groups outlined previously are all there is to a Joomla site. When you've got your site blueprint laid out, you won't meet any surprises when building it. You can transform any amount of content and functionality into a website.

How do you turn a site map into a website?

What's the best way to get from the site map on the back of your napkin to a real-life Joomla site? In this book, we'll work in this order:

1. **Organize**: Create content containers.

   You've seen that much of the site map we just created consists of content containers, categories. In this chapter, we'll create all necessary containers for our example site.

2. **Add content**: Fill the containers with articles.

   Next, we'll add articles to categories. Articles are the "classic content" that most web pages are made of. For our example site, we'll work on article contents in the next chapter.

3. **Put your contents on display**: Create the home page and content overview pages.

   Next, you'll want to guide and invite visitors. You can achieve this using two special types of pages in the site map, the home page and Joomla's category overview pages ("secondary home pages"). You'll focus on deploying these page types in *Chapter 7, Welcoming your Visitors: Creating Attractive Home Pages and Overview Pages*.

4. **Make everything findable**: Create menus.

The top-level items in your site map will probably end up as menu items on the site. To open up your site to the world you'll create and customize menus helping visitors to easily navigate your content. This is the subject of *Chapter 8, Helping Your Visitors Find What They Want: Managing Menus*.

And what about the special content stuff?

In the preceding list, we've only accounted for "classic content", such as articles, home pages, overview pages, and menus linking it all. We haven't yet mentioned one essential part of the site map, the special goodies. On a dynamic website you're likely to have much more than just plain old articles. You can add picture galleries, forms, product catalogues, site maps, and much, much more. It's important to identify those special pages from the beginning, but you'll add them later using Joomla's components and extensions. That's why we'll first concentrate on building a rock-solid foundation; later we'll add all of the desired extras.

Let's start with step one now, and get our site organized!

Creating categories and subcategories

Let's log in to Joomla again and turn to the first step in the task list outlined previously, creating content containers. In the previous chapter you've already had a foretaste of how you create categories in Joomla. It's pretty straightforward, and the same goes for creating categories within categories (called subcategories or nested categories). Let's find out how this works for our example site.

Time for action – create a category and subcategories

We've seen that the CORBA site could do with some extra content containers. We've already outlined on paper what categories are needed, so let's add the first new category, About CORBA:

1. Navigate to Content | Category Manager | Add New Category

2. In the **Category Manager: Add A New Articles Category** screen, fill out the **Title** field. In this example, type About CORBA:

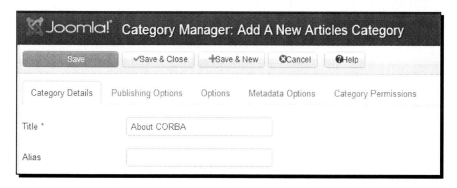

3. Leave the other values unchanged; click on **Save & Close**. You're taken to the **Category Manager** list. The **About CORBA** category is now shown in the **Category Manager** list.

4. According to our site map, the next few categories we need are nested: one main category (**Bad Art**) containing two subcategories (**Facts** and **Reviews**). To add them, in the **Category Manager** screen, click **New**.

5. In the **Category Manager: Add A New Articles Category** screen, type `Bad Art` in the **Title** field.

6. Click on **Save & New**. This button makes it easier to create a series of categories; in one go, the current category is saved and the **Add A New Articles Category** screen opens.

7. Enter the details for the next category you want to create. In the **Title** field, add **Facts**. In the **Details** section on the right-hand side of the screen, locate the **Parent** drop-down box and select **Bad Art** as shown in the following screenshot:

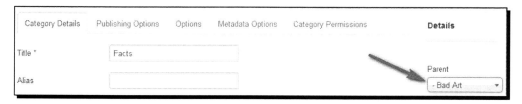

8. Click on **Save & New** again. In the next screen, enter the title of the next new category: **Reviews**. Make sure this category is also a subcategory of the **Bad Art** parent category. Click **Save & Close**. You're done!

What just happened?

You have added an **About CORBA** category and a category on **Bad Art** with two subcategories. **About CORBA** will contain just a few articles (such as the Mission Statement). As **Bad Art** is a much more important subject on our site, it contains a few subcategories that will allow you to classify lots of bad art content in a logical way.

In what case do you need more subcategory levels?

Since Joomla 1.6, there are no limits to the number of subcategories any category can hold. However, it's best to keep the number of category levels limited, as every new layer of content adds complexity to your site. In our example site, a single level of subcategories is all we need. On large sites, it can certainly make sense to use more levels of content organization. Imagine a site featuring product reviews. The following outline illustrates how such a site could use four levels of categories to organize a main category of "reviews" into subcategories of product types, brands, and models:

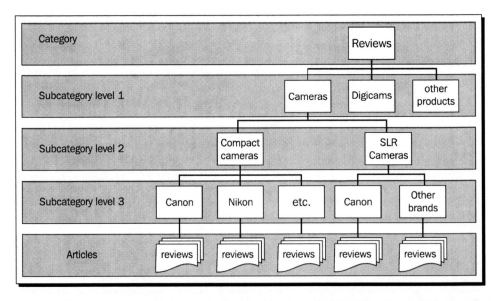

Have a go hero – rearrange existing categories

Let's return to the CORBA site map; the category tree of the example site is nearly finished. One thing left to do is to group the two separate categories we already created in the previous chapter, **Art Lectures** and **Club Meetings**. You need to make these into subcategories of a new main category: **Activities**. Luckily, in Joomla it's easy to rearrange categories and move them up or down in the "category tree".

To do this, first create a new category called **Activities** and click on **Save & Close**. Now open the existing **Art Lectures** category (in the **Category Manager** screen, click its title) and change the **Parent** to **Activities**. Do the same for the **Club Meetings** category. In the **Category Manager** screen, the results are displayed as follows:

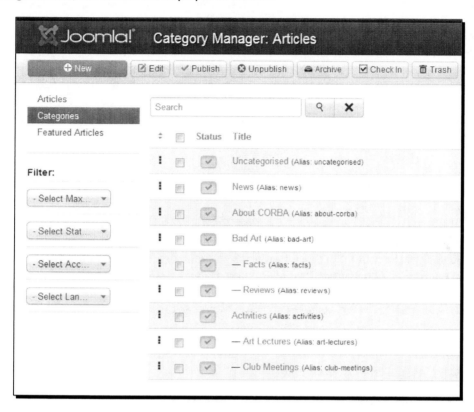

 You can easily recognize subcategories in the **Category Manager** screen, as they are always displayed indented. A first-level subcategory is displayed indented one position, a second-level will be displayed indented two positions, and so on.

You're done! The site map we've outlined on paper before is now turned into a Joomla category tree. It consists of four main categories, two of which contain subcategories. It's a clear and logical structure.

Adding content to new categories

By adding new categories, you've made room for growth. We'll leave these containers empty for now; in the next chapters, we'll add articles to them. However, if you do want to add some (dummy) content to any of the new categories, you can do this by repeating the steps you took in the last chapter (see the section *Step 2: Adding content* under *Building your new site in three steps* in *Chapter 4, Web Building Basics: Creating a Site in an Hour*). In short, navigate to **Content | Article Manager** and click on **New**. Add a title, and in the **Category** drop-down box select any of the new categories. Add some article text and add a `Read More` link after the first paragraph to enable Joomla to separately show the introductory text and the body text. Click on **Save & New** to quickly open a new, empty article editor screen, or click **Save as Copy** to save the current article and to leave the article editor and its contents open for you to create a copy, changing details as needed.

Displaying main categories and subcategories on your site

Categories are content containers; they tell Joomla how to group things in the backend. Now, how do you get the content in those containers to show up on your website? You've already seen in *Chapter 4, Web Building Basics: Creating a Site in an Hour*, that one way to do this is by adding a menu link of the category blog type. This way, you already have added menu links to the **Art Lectures** and **Club Meetings** categories.

Let's go into creating menu links that point to categories in some more detail. How do you go about creating a menu link to display the contents of the new **Activities** main category (top-level category) and its subcategories?

Time for action – create a link to point to a main category

Creating a menu link to point to a category requires the following steps:

1. Navigate to **Menus | Main Menu** and click on **New**.
2. The **Menu Manager: New Menu Item** screen opens. In the **Menu Item Type** section, select **Articles | Category Blog**.

3. In the **Choose a category** drop-down list, select **Activities**.

4. Enter a menu title (that is, `Activities`) and click on **Save & Close**.

As you can see in the following screenshot, **Activities** now shows up as the last menu item in the **Menu Item Manager**. The order in which the menu items are presented here is the same order they'll be in the **Main Menu** on the website. If you would like to move the **Activities** link up in the **Main Menu**, just click on the three little blocks in the **Ordering** column to drag and drop any menu item to the desired position. (The **Ordering** column is the one on the left-hand side with two little blue triangles pointing up and down in the top row.) In this example, we'll leave the order unchanged.

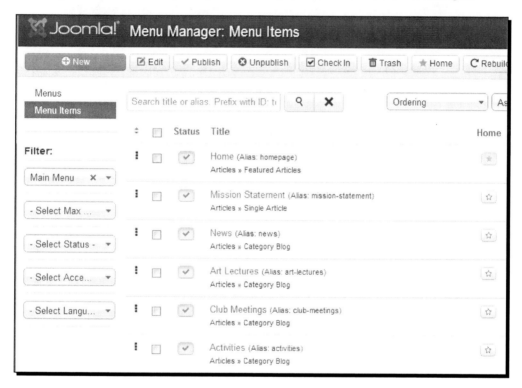

5. Click on **View Site** and click the new **Activities** link in the main menu to check out what's changed on the frontend:

Rather uninviting, isn't it? As you can see, a menu link to a top-level category (that holds other categories) displays differently from a direct link to a category, such as the direct menu links to **Art Lectures** and **Club Meetings** categories you created earlier. Because the top-level **Activities** category is empty, the **Activities** menu link points to a page that contains no more than just two links to the subcategories. However, if you were to add an article to the **Activities** category, the display would change as follows:

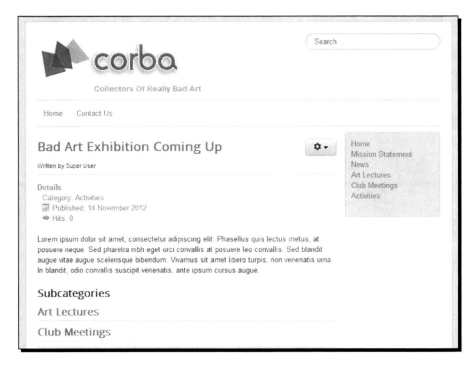

As you can see, the **Activities** link now points to a page containing intro texts from the main category (in this case there's just one article in it) and at the bottom of the page there are two links to subcategories. When the visitor clicks the **Art Lectures** or **Club Meetings** link, they will be taken to a page showing the contents of that specific subcategory.

Have a go hero – explore the possibilities of category pages

When categories contain subcategories, the default setup of category blog pages require visitors to click through on the links to subcategories at the bottom of the page to see what articles they contain. However, it's also possible to get the articles from all subcategories to show on the **Activities** page. Let's have a peek at the possibilities right now; in later chapters we'll explore overview pages like these more thoroughly.

To change the layout of the **Category Blog** page, go to the **Menu Manager** screen again and edit the **Activities** menu item by clicking the **Title** menu item. Click the **Advanced Options** tab to access the **Blog Layout Options** and set **Include Subcategories** to **All**. Save the changes.

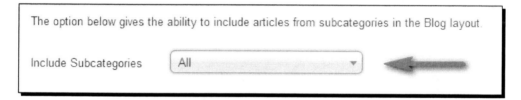

When the visitor clicks the **Activities** link on the frontend, a page will be displayed containing article intro texts from the main category **Activities** and both subcategories, **Art Lectures** and **Club Meetings**:

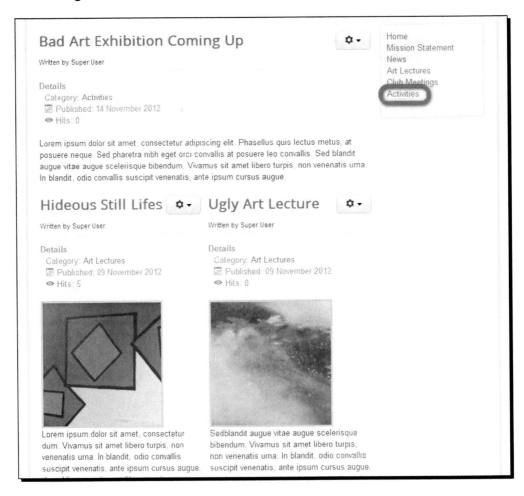

You'll note that changing one small setting makes quite a difference. Feel free to explore the other options of the **Category Blog** menu item type and get a taste for their effects on the page display. And that's just the beginning: there's much more to categories content presentation than just the **Blog Layout Options**. You can choose to display category contents in many other formats. For now, using the **Category Blog** format will do just fine; you'll learn about the other ways of displaying category contents in *Chapter 7, Welcoming your Visitors: Creating Attractive Home Pages and Overview Pages*.

If you've followed along with all the previous Time for Action sections, you've now got a rather messy menu containing separate links to both **Activities** and to its subcategories, **Club Meetings** and **Art Lectures**. That's okay for now; we'll clean up and rearrange our site menus in *Chapter 8, Helping Your Visitors Find What They Want: Managing Menus*.

Refining your site structure

It's a fact of life: you probably won't get your site structure right in one go unless you've got a really simple, really static site. Is that a bad thing? No, it isn't—because websites evolve and Joomla makes it easy to go ahead with a provisional structure and to change things when needed. Maybe because new content has become available that has to go into a new category. Or maybe because when you're actually adding content, you learn that your well-organized site isn't altogether logical after all. That's fine; keeping a close eye on the structure of your website is a continuous process. And luckily, categories, once defined, can be changed easily without any consequences for the articles they may contain. You've seen how easy it is to add new ones, and it's equally simple to move content from one category to another.

Time for action – move content from one category to another

The main **Activities** category contains a couple of articles that you may want to move to the **News** category. Let's clean up the **Activities - Meetings** category and move anything topical into the **News** category:

1. Navigate to **Content | Article Manager**. From the list, select the items you want to move from the **Meetings** category to the **News** category. In this example, we've selected one article:

2. Click the **Batch** button. A popup box called **Batch process the selected articles** appears. In the **Select category for Move/Copy** drop-down box, select the target category, **News**. Then click **Process**:

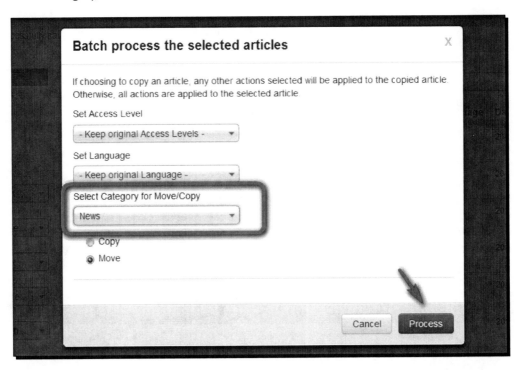

3. A message is displayed: **Batch process completed successfully**. In the **Article Manager** screen, the selected article is now part of the **News** category:

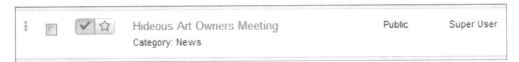

What just happened?

You've understood the real-life challenge of content management! Now you're not only able to create a sound content structure for your website, but you also know how to improve on it. You can move any amount of existing content to another category.

Have a go hero – moving entire categories

Sometimes you might want to move an entire (sub)category and all its contents to another main category. Try this out for yourself—it's not much different from moving articles, as you've just done. Imagine you'd like to move the **Reviews** subcategory from the **Bad Art** main category to another main category. In the **Category Manager** screen, select the category you want to move. Click the **Batch** button and in the **Batch process the selected categories** screen use the **Select category for Move/Copy** drop-down box to select the target category. Click **Process** to move the category to its new main category. It's just as straightforward to move the entire category—including all of its article contents—back again. This flexibility is great when you're setting up or restructuring your site.

Renaming categories

As we've just seen, Joomla allows you to easily rearrange your site structure and its contents. You can also *rename* categories that already contain articles; no content will be lost.

Time for action – rename a category

On your client's website there's an **Activities** category. Your client wants to make it clear that this site section is not about the activities organized by other art societies—it's only about CORBA. Could you please change the name of the section to **CORBA Activities**?

1. Navigate to **Content | Category Manager** and click on the title of the **Activities** section to open it for editing.

2. In the edit screen, change the title to CORBA Activities.

3. In the **Alias** field, remove the existing alias (remember, the alias is Joomla's internal name for the article used when creating user-friendly URLs). Leave this box blank; Joomla will fill it with CORBA-activities when you apply or save your changes. You can check that now by clicking on **Save**. You'll notice the **Alias** box is filled out automatically.

4. Click on **Close**. In the **Category Manager**, the new title and alias are displayed.

What just happened?

By changing a category name, all of Joomla's internal references to the name are updated automatically. All articles in the renamed category will reflect the changes you made. In the **Article Manager**, for example, all items that belonged to the **Activities** category are now updated to show they are in the **CORBA Activities** category. No manual labor here—and more importantly, nothing is lost!

Have a go hero – name and rename!

Using appropriate, short, and descriptive labels for categories (and for the menu links pointing to them) is essential. After all, these are the words that guide your visitors to the content you want them to discover. It's a good idea to tweak these labels until you're perfectly happy with them. When you change the names of categories, you might want to change menu link labels too, as these don't automatically change with the category name. Try to find short and appropriate menu link labels. To change menu link labels, navigate to the **Main Menu**, select any of the menu items and change what's in the **Title** field (such as **Activities**).

 When changing **Titles** (of categories or menu link items) make sure to clear the contents of the **Alias** box. Joomla will automatically create an **Alias** for the new title.

Changing category settings

You've already created a good deal of categories without altering any of the default settings. In some cases, however, you may want to have some more control over the category details. In the following table you can see the options that are available in the **Category Manager: Edit An Articles Category/Add A New Articles Category** screen.

The screen is organized in five main sections, accessible through tabs: **Category Details, Publishing Options, Options, Metadata Options,** and **Category Permissions**. These screens allow you to enter more details on the contents of the category (by adding a description), to determine whether a category is visible or not for specific user groups, and so on.

Let's have a look at the options that are available when creating or editing a category.

Adding or editing categories: an overview of the settings	
Title	The category title as it will be displayed. You can use lowercase, uppercase, and spaces.
Alias	Leave the **Alias** box blank. The **Alias** is the internal name of the item. When you save the category, Joomla will automatically fill in the category name in lowercase letters without spaces or special characters. If the **Title** is **About CORBA**, the alias will be about-corba. The **Alias** will be shown in the page URL (www.example.com/about-corba.html) when using Joomla's search engine-friendly URLs (see *Chapter 12, Attracting Search Engine Traffic: SEO Tips and Techniques*, on attracting search engine traffic).

Description	In the **Description** text editor area, you can enter and format a short descriptive text introducing the subject of the category.

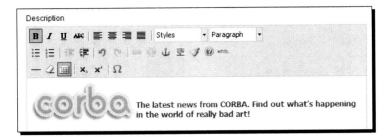

Category descriptions can be displayed at the top of pages displaying category contents (provided the **Category Description** is set to **Show** in the **Advanced options** of the menu link pointing to that category overview page).

For more on category descriptions, see *Chapter 7, Welcoming your Visitors: Creating Attractive Home Pages and Overview Pages*, on category overview pages.

Details

Parent	Select - **No parent** to create a top-level category or select any of the existing categories to add a subcategory.

Status	The status can can be **Published** (visible on the front of the site), **Unpublished** (not visible on the site, but still visible in the backend), **Archived** (moved to the archive; you can make archived articles/categories visible with a special menu link), or **Trashed** (moved to the trash). Unpublishing categories can be useful when your site is live and you're preparing a new category. Using this option, your site visitors won't know the category is there until you publish it.
Access	By choosing the appropriate **Access** setting, you control who have access to this category: all visitors (**Public**), registered users (**Registered**), or users with special rights (**Special**). The default value, **Public**, should be okay. When you start working with different user types on your site, you can change these settings (see *Chapter 9, Opening Up the Site: Enabling Users to Log In and Contribute*, on user access levels). You can also create special access levels.
Language	If you have a multilingual site, this drop-down list box allows you to select the language for this category.

The **Publishing Options** tab

Created by	Select the user who will be displayed as the author of this category

The **Options** tab

Alternative Layout	A powerful feature that lets you select a custom layout for the current category, provided the selected template (or component) allows for these additional layout options. A template may contain so-called template overrides, custom layouts that overrule Joomla's default layouts of categories. More information can be found on `http://tinyurl.com/jlayouts` (a shortcut URL pointing to `http://downloads.joomlacode.org/trackeritem/5/8/6/58619/introtoaltlayoutsinversion1-6v2.pdf`).
Image	This option affects how overview pages of category contents are displayed. At the top of these pages an image and a short description can be shown. Here you can select the image that will be displayed with that description. However, you can also choose to insert an image into the description itself, as shown on the previous page in the example given under **Description**.
Note	This little feature can prove to be really useful: in the **Note** field, you can add notes for yourself or for others who have access to the backend. For example, you can describe the purpose of the category ("New generic category on club activities").

The **Metadata Options** tab

Meta Description **Meta Keywords**	Metadata are added to the HTML document source code. It's the information that's not displayed on the web page, but search engine spiders do process it. Metadata for a category override global metadata or menu item metadata. You can add a short **Meta Description** and **Meta Keywords** for categories. Not all search engines use **Meta Keywords** to index content, but the **Meta Description** is certainly important. For example, Google uses it search results pages to describe the page contents.
Author	Add a **Meta Author** to make it possible for search engines to display the author of the document.
Robots	The **Robots** meta tag is used to indicate whether search engine spiders should index the contents of this category or not.

The **Category Permissions** tab

Public, Guest, and so on	The **Category Permissions** tab allows you to determine what different user groups are allowed to work with this category. An example is that you can determine which user groups can edit or create content in this category. You can read more about permissions in *Chapter 9, Opening Up the Site: Enabling Users to Log In and Contribute*.

Building a site without using categories

When organizing your site content you might end up with articles that do not belong in any category. These you can add as uncategorized articles. Usually, uncategorized articles contain static content, such as an About Us page or some legal information. However, you can also choose to build your site using uncategorized articles only.

Sometimes, Joomla's powerful multi-level site organization capabilities are just too much. Very small sites—"brochure sites" of some five to ten pages—without secondary page levels, can consist of uncategorized articles only.

Let's say your local yoga teacher asks you to develop a website. She probably wouldn't need much more content than shown in the following diagram:

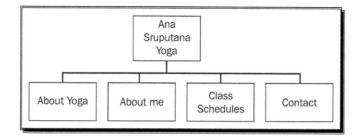

In this case, there are no layers of content below the menu link level. There will probably be five menu links: **Home**, **About Yoga**, **About me**, **Class Schedules**, and **Contact**. Three of these will each point to an article (**About Yoga**, **About Me**, and **Class Schedules**). The **Contact** page could also be a plain article, but let's assume this is—just like we've seen before—a contact form generated by Joomla's **Contacts** component. This is how we could translate the preceding site map in Joomla terms:

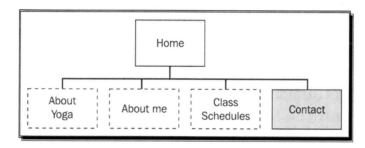

The boxes with grey dotted outlines represent uncategorized articles; the box with a grey background represents a special functionality page (in this case a **Contact** form).

This same simple one-level structure would be appropriate for all kinds of small sites with a dedicated subject matter, that is, a portfolio site for a one-man company or an event site. A copy writing company would have a Joomla site structure similar to the following:

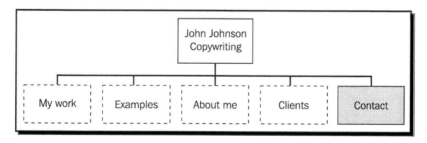

For an event site—such as a site for a congress or seminar—a structure like the one shown in the following diagram would be fine:

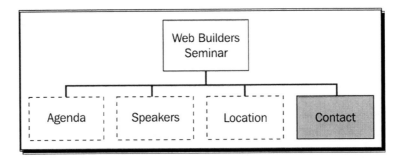

Although you'll leave much of the built-in functionality for managing big, content-rich sites untouched, it's still worthwhile to use Joomla for sites like these. All the other advantages of Joomla still hold, such as the ability to add any extra functionality you like. If your client wants a registration form for his seminar site, or a photo gallery for his portfolio site, you can add these using Joomla extensions. And, of course, your client will be able to manage and update content easily.

How do you go about building a small site?

Creating a small site like the examples previously shown simply means you'll skip a few steps, as there's no need to create any categories. These are the actions it takes:

1. Create the uncategorized content pages (articles) you need.
2. Add menu links to the **Main Menu**. In this case, you'll link directly to articles instead of categories.

An example is as follows, a three-page site based on a "clean" Joomla installation (without sample data). Creating the basic setup of a tiny site like this takes just a few minutes.

In this example, in our new and empty Joomla site we've created four uncategorized articles. We've set them all to display on the homepage (as **Featured Articles**).

For each of these articles, we've added a menu link in the **Main Menu** (via **Menus | Main Menu | Add New Menu Item**).

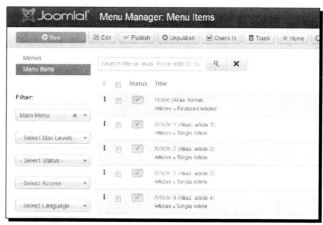

This is what the visitor sees. The **Main Menu** contains four links to articles; the **Front Page** shows intro texts of the articles with **Read more** links.

When the visitor clicks on a link, the full article is shown.

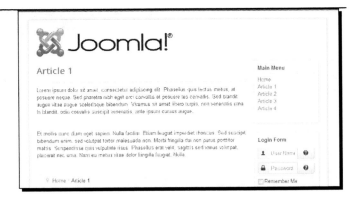

That's all there is to setting up a tiny one-level website in Joomla. Write a few articles and create links pointing to them. After that, you can focus on the extras you might want to add (see *Chapter 10, Getting the Most out of Your Site: Extending Joomla*, on extending Joomla) and the design (see *Chapter 11, Creating an Attractive Design: Working with Templates*).

Downsize the home page too

For a very small site, you can still build the home page using Joomla's default **Featured Articles** system. Select a few articles to display (fully, or only as intro texts) on the home page. However, you may want something more simple for this type of site. It's possible to show just one particular article as your own, customized home page content. You'll read more about this approach in *Chapter 6, Creating Killer Content: Adding and Editing Articles*, on home page display options.

Have a go hero – organize a site!

Imagine you've been asked to build an informative website for a small company. How would you go about this? Think of what you want to achieve, create an outline of the main and secondary categories, and translate this outline to Joomla. What would be your main categories and subcategories, where would you put uncategorized articles?

And how about creating a small website about yourself? Using the site-structuring skills you've acquired in this chapter, go ahead and create a great structure that would be both realizable in Joomla and appealing to your visitors.

Pop quiz – test your site organization knowledge

Q1. What's the best order in which to build Joomla-based sites?

    a.   Start with extensions, add content, add menu links, add content containers.

    b.   Start with menu links, add content containers, add content, add extensions.

    c.   Start with content containers, add content, add menu links, add extensions.

Q2. What can you use uncategorized articles for?

    a.   To display articles that have not yet been authorized.

    b.   To display articles that do not belong to categories.

    c.   To display articles that are displayed on the homepage.

Q3. How can you get categories to display in the frontend?

    a.   Categories are backend stuff; they're only displayed in the **Category Manager**.

    b.   A category can be displayed by adding a specific menu link that points to a category overview page.

    c.   Categories are automatically displayed on overview pages when added to the **Category Manager**.

Summary

In *Chapter 3, First Steps: Getting to Know Joomla*, you've learned that Joomla retrieves content from a database, block by block. Together these blocks form a web page. That's why you begin building a site by creating categories; you start with the core of the site, a well-organized content database. In this chapter, we've learned what it takes to create content categories and to build a future-proof framework for site content.

Specifically, you've learned the following:

   ◆   Every website, big or small, requires planning. It all starts with creating a logical site map reflecting the structure of the content you have in mind. Keep it lean and clean. Bear in mind that visitors will want to get to the content they're looking for as fast as possible.

   ◆   To transfer your hand-drawn site map to a working Joomla site, first identify the different Joomla content elements in it. This will help you build the site step by step.

- The main content containers are categories and subcategories. You'll create these first, before adding content. To show category contents on the site, you add menu links pointing to categories. At any time, you can rearrange and rename categories or move their contents.
- Small sites, with just a few content pages, can consist of uncategorized articles only.

In the next chapter, we'll jump from organization to creating content. We'll fill the containers we've made with different types of articles.

6

Creating Killer Content: Adding and Editing Articles

Once you have created a framework of categories and subcategories, things can move pretty fast. There's nothing to stop you from creating a content-rich site—whether you want to add a dozen, hundreds, or even thousands of pages. In this chapter we'll focus on adding and editing articles, the type of content that's essential to most sites. Later, you might want to add other types of content (such as image galleries or forums); we'll deal with those in Chapter 10, Getting the Most out of Your Site: Extending Joomla.

When creating the example site in Chapter 4, Web Building Basics: Creating a Site in an Hour, you've already seen how you can create a new article using the default settings. You've left all of the extra function buttons and parameters alone. But in real life, you'll probably want more control. You want to make your content look great, add pictures, and specify exactly how to display things and what details to display. Joomla allows you to edit articles and tweak article settings to fit your needs exactly.

In this chapter you'll learn:

- ◆ Creating, editing, and formatting articles
- ◆ Split an article into intro text and body text
- ◆ Dealing with long articles: splitting them into a series of pages
- ◆ Adjusting general article settings

So let's get it started!

Articles and content pages, what's the difference?

You might be tempted to think an *article* is the same as a *page*. Strictly, it isn't. You've read before that Joomla doesn't think in terms of pages. Joomla figures any web page is constructed of a whole lot of database-driven bits and pieces—and almost any combination of those bits and pieces can turn up on the visitor's browser as a web page.

Although in Joomla, an article will certainly be at the center of a content page, there's bound to be much more to that page. Around the article there will be all kinds of other dynamic content—yes, those bits and pieces again. Be that as it may, for the sake of simplicity we'll just use the word page (or content page) for articles now and then.
As long as we're aware that content pages may contain more than articles, that's OK, isn't it? Don't tell Joomla; it will be our secret.

Creating and editing articles: beyond the basics

Over the last few chapters, you practiced adding and editing articles. Let's recap the steps involved:

- To create a new article, navigate to **Content | Article Manager** and click on **New**. Alternatively, use the shortcut menu option **Content | Article Manager | Add New Article**.

- Any of these two methods will open the **Article Manager | Add New Article** screen.

- To edit an existing article, navigate to **Content | Article Manager**. Select the article (select the checkbox on the left-hand side of the article title) and click on the **Edit** button in the toolbar. There's also a shortcut available—just click on the title of the article to open it in the **Article Manager: Edit Article** screen.

Apart from the screen titles, the **Add New Article** and **Edit Article** screens are identical. You're already familiar with some of the most important functions; in this chapter, we'll boldly go to sections we haven't explored yet.

The Article Editor is shown in the following screenshot:

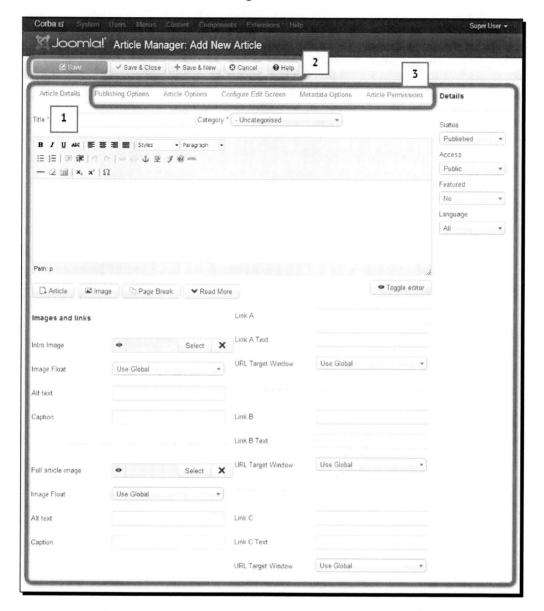

The article editing screen consists of four sections. The actual text editing area offers you a simple word processor-like interface for entering and formatting text. Above the article text you add the **Title**, select the appropriate **Category**, and so on. On the right-hand side you can set the article **Details**—for example, whether it should be published, or whether it should be a featured article. Below the editor screen the **Images and links** fields allow you to add images that will be displayed at the start of the article and a set of links (URLs) that can be displayed above or below the article.

The article editing screen consists of the following sections:

◆ The toolbar buttons mainly allow you to save the article (or cancel changes).

◆ The upper part of the screen contains five tabs. Clicking any of these tabs reveals a screen where you can set specific options.

◆ **Publishing Options**, **Article Options**, and **Metadata Options** allow you to set up the article to display and behave just as you need it to. You'll learn more about them in the *Adjusting article settings* section later in this chapter.

◆ **Configure Edit Screen** is an advanced feature allowing you to customize the appearance of the article edit screen for users that have permissions to edit this article. You can specify which article options should be available in the edit screen.

◆ Through the **Article Permissions** tab, you can set permissions for user groups at the level of this specific article. Using permission settings you can control whether specific user groups can or cannot see this article, or if they are allowed to edit it. You'll learn more about permissions in *Chapter 9, Opening Up the Site: Enabling Users to Log In and Contribute*.

Let's now explore the power of the Joomla article editor. We'll find out how we can tweak articles to get them to display exactly as we want them to.

 In the **Add New Article** screen, you'll usually have to select the **Category** the article belongs to. When adding a number of articles to the same category, you can set one specific category to be already selected when you open the **Add New Article** screen. To do this, in the **Article Manager: Articles** screen, select the desired **Category** in the **Filter:** list. Now this category will be the default one when you click **New** to create a new article.

Making your words look good: formatting article text

Your client, CORBA, wants to add some new content to their site explaining the characteristic qualities of bad art. You've been sent a text file and have been asked to turn the contents into a new page. Can you please create a new article and make it look good?

Time for action – add styling to article text

Let's create a new article and see how we can format it adequately.

1. Navigate to **Content | Article Manager** and click on **New**.

2. In the **Title** box, enter **Just What is Ugly Art?** This is the type of factual content that fits the **Facts** category, so let's select the **Bad Art** main category and the **Facts** subcategory:

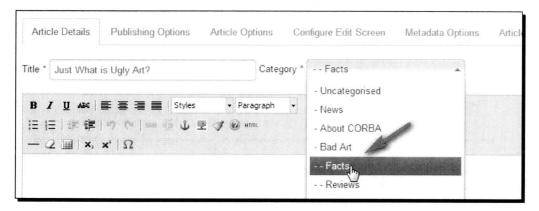

3. By default, **Status** (found under **Details**) is set to **Published**. Let's set it to **Unpublished**. This way, the article will remain invisible to your site visitors until you're finished with it (and publish it).

4. We don't want this article to show up on our home page, so leave **Featured** set to **No**.

5. In the text editor screen, add some article text. If you want to copy text from a word processor document, first strip out all of the formatting. That way you avoid invisible word processor tags messing up your article text. To do this, open the Notepad application on your PC (or TextEdit on a Mac) and paste the text from the word processor into the Notepad or TextEdit document. This will give you a clean text-only file that you can copy and paste into the Joomla editor window. Right-click and select **Paste** from the pop-up menu.

6. In this example we've added five paragraphs—a short introductory text and four separate paragraphs. Type a subheading above each of the four paragraphs. In the example we've used the subheadings **Abstract Chaos**, **Poor Anatomy**, **Too much detail**, and **Hideous Colors**.

7. Let's use the text editor tools to change the basic formatting of the text. Put the cursor anywhere in the line containing the subheading **Abstract Chaos**. Click on the **Format** drop-down box (it shows the **Paragraph** format by default) and select the predefined **Heading 3** format as shown in the following screenshot:

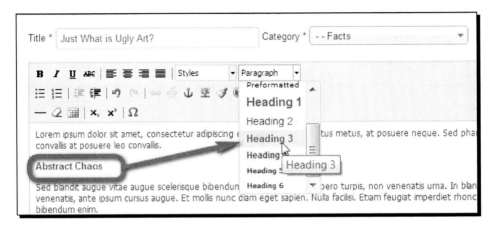

In the previous screenshot, the **Heading 3** format is being applied to an article subheading. As the main article titles in Joomla usually have a **Heading 2** format, the **Heading 3** format is suited for the next level (the subheadings within an article).

Want more formatting control?

The font style of the heading is now set to the **Heading 3** format. What this actually looks like depends on the CSS stylesheet of the template you're using. In the default Joomla template we're using, the **Heading 3** style is preformatted as a blue Open Sans font. When you install a different template, your headings and all other CSS-defined layout will probably look completely different. And if you really want to get creative and create a mouthwatering article layout, you'll want to change the template CSS styles yourself and adapt them to your needs. Don't worry, we'll get to the ins and outs of templates and styling in *Chapter 11, Creating an Attractive Design: Working with Templates.*

8. Select the other three subheadings and apply the **Heading 3** style to these too. When you're done formatting the text, click on **Save & Close**.

This article editor screen gives you a rough impression of what the article will look like, but it isn't a reliable preview of the article: on the frontend, the fonts used and the overall layout can be quite different due to specific template CSS styles. This means you'll probably always want to check what the article looks like by navigating the frontend of the site as soon as the article has been published. To have this preview available while editing an article, it's a good idea to open the frontend article in a new browser tab, and switch between the two-tabbed browser windows using the *Ctrl + Tab* key combination. You can see how this works later in this chapter after we've added a menu link for the current article and set the article status to **Published**.

What just happened?

You've created a new article in the **Facts** category and formatted some text using the word processor-like interface of the text editor. While preparing your text, you can set it to be invisible (unpublished); later on, you'll publish the finished text in one click.

Have a go hero – change the formatting

Feel free to open the article you've just created and play around to explore the different text formatting options. Check out how to apply indenting, bulleted lists, and so on. You may want to select the first paragraph and apply bold styling to really make it stand out as the leading paragraph. Applying styles to the selected text works just like you'd expect it to in word processing software. Use the *Enter* key to start a new paragraph; use *Shift + Enter* to start a new line (but not a new paragraph).

Make sure to check out the **Toggle Editor** button. Clicking on it changes the editor to a plain text editor showing the HTML code of the article text:

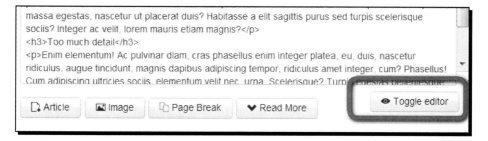

This can be particularly useful if you know your way around HTML; sometimes you may want to directly edit the HTML code or check it for unwanted tags. You can go back to the **What You See Is What You Get (WYSIWYG)** view by clicking on the **Toggle editor** button again.

Extending the text editor

Joomla ships with the text editor you've just used. It's actually an extension called **Tiny MCE**. If you would like to have some advanced text editing controls, you can set Tiny MCE to its **Extended** view. Just navigate to **Extensions | Plug-in Manager** and click on **Editor - TinyMCE** to edit the settings.

In the **Basic Options** section, select **Functionality: Extended**. This will add some useful buttons to the editor screen, such as a **Paste as plain text** button and a **Paste from Word** button that lets you copy text from a Word document while automatically stripping all Word formatting that's not needed on a web page. The extended text editor toolbar looks similar to the following screenshot:

If you still find Tiny MCE's capabilities too limited, you can easily replace it by another (free) text editor. A very popular one is the Joomla Content Editor (JCE). You'll read more about replacing the default text editor in *Chapter 10, Getting the Most out of Your Site: Extending Joomla*.

Adding images to articles

You've just created an all-text page on art. That's not really what makes your visually-oriented visitors tick. Let's show them what it's all about and add some images!

Imagine you've been sent some image files by mail and you've copied them to your hard drive.

Before uploading images, make sure they are resized to the proper dimensions for use on your web page. It's not a good idea to upload a big image and resize it in the editor screen, as loading the image file will considerably slow down the web page's display in the browser. Moreover, Joomla doesn't contain image-editing capabilities, so you cannot change image dimensions or crop images once they're uploaded. To resize images, use either an image editing software (such as Photoshop or GIMP) or pick a simple online resizing tool such as http://www.picresize.com. Search for **web image formats** to find more information and tutorials on the best image formats and image sizes for use on the Web.

Time for action – uploading images

To add images to an article, you'll first use Joomla's **Media Manager** to upload the image files to the web server:

1. Navigate to **Content | Media Manager**. The **Media Manager** displays the files available in the default image folder.

2. We'll create a specific folder for the files we want to add. Click on the **Create Folder** button. A text field appears where you can type the name of the new subfolder. In this example, we've entered **paintings**. Now click the second **Create Folder** button:

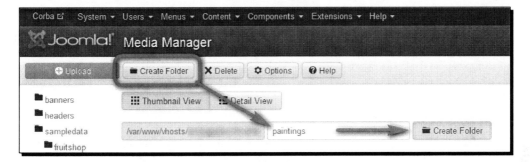

3. Click on the icon of the new paintings folder:

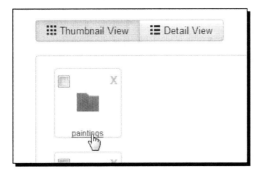

4. You'll be shown an empty folder. Add a new image by clicking on the **Upload** button in the toolbar.

5. Click on the **Browse** button at the right hand side of the **Upload file** textbox, select about five images from your computer's hard drive, click on **Open**, and then click on **Start Upload**.

6. A message appears, indicating the upload is complete. The **Files** section of the **Media Manager** shows thumbnails of the uploaded pictures:

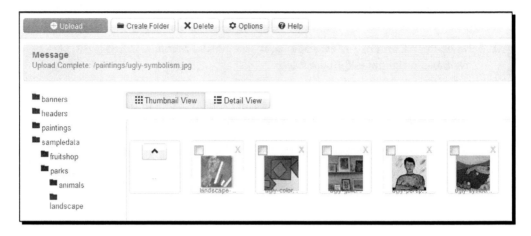

What just happened?

You've uploaded a set of pictures ready to be inserted into any article. By default, Joomla's Media Manager will look for images that are present in the `images` directory of the web server folder in which Joomla has been installed. Joomla doesn't, however, display the name `images` when you browse the Media Manager; it just shows the images and a list of subfolders. When you create new subfolders in the Media Manager, you actually add subfolders to the `images` root folder.

It's a good idea to create subfolders if you want to keep different groups of images organized (for example, `paintings`, `sculpture`, `staff`, and `meetings`). This way, you won't end up with all image files piled up in one big default image folder.

 If you'd like to use another folder as the default base directory, navigate to **Content| Media Manager** and click **Options**. In the **Component** section, change the **Path to Image Folder**. For example, entering `/images/paintings` as the default path would make Joomla look in this folder when you insert article images.

Time for action – inserting and aligning images

Now, let's insert the images you've just uploaded into the article text:

1. Navigate to **Content | Article Manager** and open the article, **Just What is Ugly Art?** to edit it (by clicking on the article title).

2. Let's place an image in each of the article paragraphs. Place the cursor at the beginning of the first paragraph below the introduction text, just after the first subheading:

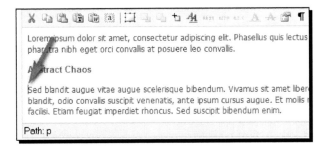

3. Click on the **Image** button at the bottom of the text editor screen:

4. A pop-up screen opens displaying the contents of the `images` root directory. Select the appropriate subfolder by clicking on the paintings folder icon.

5. Select the image you want to insert. Joomla automatically adds the path to the image in the **Image URL** field:

6. Scroll down in the pop-up window to add the other relevant details as follows:

- ❑ In the **Image Description** box, type a description. This text isn't displayed, but it informs search engines what the picture is about. It will also show up when the visitor uses a non-visual web browser.

- ❑ In the **Image Title** box, enter a title. This is shown only when the web visitor hovers the mouse pointer on the image. Select **Yes** in the **Caption** drop-down box only if you want to have Joomla display the title text as a caption just below the image.

- ❑ In the **Align** drop-down box, you can choose how the image will be aligned—to the left, to the right, or centered. Let's select **Left** for the first image. In the next screenshot, you can see the effects of right and left alignment of pictures.

7. When done, click **Insert** in the upper-right corner of the pop-up screen to close it and add the image to the article.

8. Place the cursor in the next paragraph and repeat steps 4 to 6. Do this until every paragraph of the article body text contains a picture.

9. The **Article Text** editor screen roughly shows what the article text will look like; this is okay to get a first impression of the output. In the following example, some are aligned right relative to the text, some are aligned left:

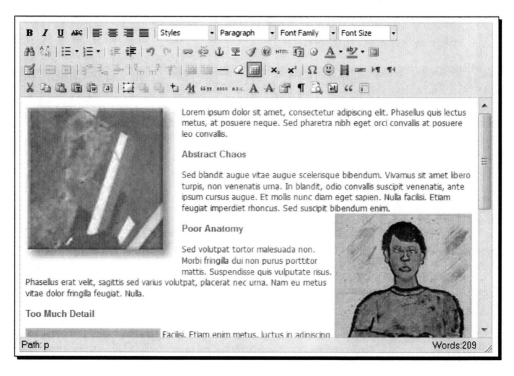

10. As the article is ready for display, let's get it to show on the frontend of the site. First, make sure the **Status** of the article is set to **Published**. Now, add a menu link to the **Facts** category to make its contents (even if that's just this one article) visible. You'll know the drill from previous chapters—go to **Menus | Main Menu | Add New Menu Item**, select **Category Blog** as the **Menu Item Type**, select the **Facts** category, add a **Menu Title** (that is, **Facts on Bad Art**) and save the menu link. That's it; you can now see the article output on the frontend by clicking on the **Facts on Bad Art** menu link.

Just What is Ugly Art?

⚙▾

Written by Super User

Details
  Category: Facts
  📅 Published: 19 November 2012
  👁 Hits: 0

Lorem ipsum dolor sit amet, consectetur adipiscing elit. Phasellus quis lectus metus, at posuere neque. Sed pharetra nibh eget orci convallis at posuere leo convallis.

Abstract Chaos

Sed blandit augue vitae augue scelerisque bibendum. Vivamus sit amet libero turpis, non venenatis urna. In blandit, odio convallis suscipit venenatis, ante ipsum cursus augue. Et mollis nunc diam eget sapien. Nulla facilisi. Etiam feugiat imperdiet rhoncus. Sed suscipit bibendum enim.

Poor Anatomy

Sed volutpat tortor malesuada non. Morbi fringilla dui non purus porttitor mattis. Suspendisse quis vulputate risus. Phasellus erat velit, sagittis sed varius volutpat, placerat nec urna. Nam eu metus vitae dolor fringilla feugiat. Nulla.

Too Much Detail

Facilisi. Etiam enim metus, luctus in adipiscing at, consectetur quis sapien. Duis imperdiet egestas ligula, quis hendrerit ipsum ullamcorper et.

Phasellus id tristique orci. Proin consequat mi at felis scelerisque ullamcorper. Etiam tempus, felis vel eleifend porta, velit nunc mattis urna, at ullamcorper erat diam dignissim ante. Pellentesque justo risus.

Hideous Colors

Rutrum ac semper a, faucibus nec lorem. Nullam eget quam tellus, eget sagittis justo Class aptent taciti sociosqu ad litora torquent per conubia nostra, per inceptos himenaeos. Proin ante enim, tincidunt ut interdum in, adipiscing quis tortor. Nulla turpis lacus, rutrum in adipiscing ut, porttitor ac ante. Sed euismod, mauris a

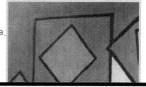

What just happened?

Adding pictures to articles is a pretty straightforward process. You upload the desired image files and use the **Image** button to tell Joomla where you want them displayed.

Have a go hero – adjusting the image settings

After you've inserted an image, you may want to adjust the display settings. To create some gutter space between the images and the surrounding text, click on the **Insert/edit image** icon (a picture of a tree) in the text editor toolbar.

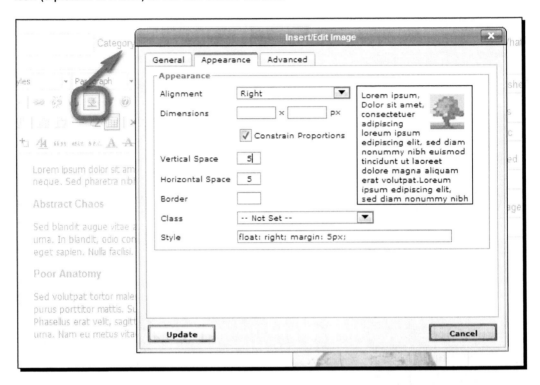

Click on the **Appearance** tab. Now you can set a value for **Vertical Space** or **Horizontal Space** (in pixels). This will create a little whitespace around the image, making it stand apart from the article text. Click on **Update** to apply the changes (yes, you're right; they'd better label this button as **Apply**).

The **Insert/edit image** button in the default editor (called TinyMCE) isn't really suited for inserting images. After clicking on this button, you can't browse to the image file, but have to know its exact location (URL). That's why there's a separate **Image** button below the text editor screen that's better equipped for inserting images.

When you want to upload images and create new folders, the **Media Manager** does the job. However, it does have a few limitations. Although you can add and delete files, you can't move them from one folder to another. Because of this, many Joomla users prefer to use an FTP program to upload files and manage the media folders on the web server. There are also many extensions available that enhance Joomla's image management capabilities. The Joomla Content Editor (see *Chapter 10, Getting the Most out of Your Site: Extending Joomla*) is a powerful replacement for the default text editor, which also makes uploading and inserting images much easier.

Changing the way the article displays

The article editor screen gives you much more power than just formatting text and adding pictures. You can also control how the article should be displayed: as one individual article, split into two parts, or even split in as many parts (subpages), as you like. Let's find out how we can enhance articles with these options.

One lump or two? Split the article into an intro text and main text

So far, we haven't added any instructions in our article to change the way it displays. Let's have a look at the frontend to see how it's displayed by default. To see again how our new article looks at the frontend, on the frontend **Main Menu**, click on the **Facts on Bad Art** link.

Earlier in this chapter, you created a link to the **Facts** category. As you've noticed (click on the **Facts on Bad Art** link to check this again if you want), the full five paragraph article shows up on the **Facts** category overview page. This is not how we want our article to be displayed. If we were to add more articles to this same category, they would all be fully displayed on a huge **Category Blog** overview page. To get Joomla to show just a short teaser text here, we'll now split the article, separating the intro text and the full article body text.

Time for action – creating an intro text

In the articles you created in earlier chapters, you've already seen it's good to add a separate intro text to an article. Now you know why—if you don't, the article can only be displayed fully on overview pages such as the category overview you just saw. Let's fix things by adding an intro text to our new article:

1. Navigate to **Content | Article Manager** and open the article that you just created (**Just What is Ugly Art?**) to edit it.

2. In the text editor screen, add a new first line. In this example, we've entered **The Characteristics of Truly Bad Art**.

3. Place the cursor just after this first line to indicate that you want Joomla to split the article here, and create a **Read more** link to point to the full article, click on the **Read more** button at the bottom of the editor screen. A red dotted line appears:

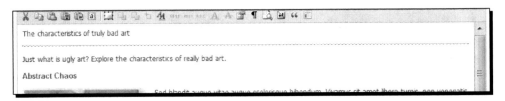

4. In the **Article Options** panel, set **Show Intro Text** to **Hide**. This means the intro text (the short teaser text we just created) will be hidden when the full article is shown. It will only be displayed on overview pages.

5. Click on **Save** and then click on **View site** to see the output on the frontend. You'll be taken to the home page. In the **Main Menu**, click on the **Facts on Bad Art** link.

Mission accomplished! Now, only the intro text and **Read more** link of the new article appear on the category overview page:

More teaser texts will be added to the overview when you add more articles to the category.

The full five paragraph article is shown (without the teaser text) when the visitor clicks on the **Read more** link:

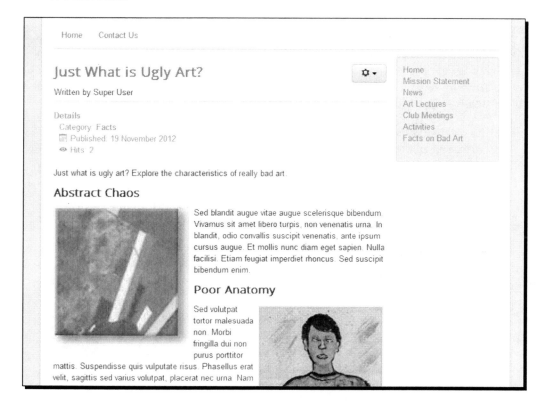

What just happened?

In principle, any article in Joomla can consist of one continuous text. Especially when writing short articles (think of blog posts), it's okay to create those kind of texts. But in many cases you'll want to split articles into an introductory text (a teaser text, in newspaper terms) and the actual article body text, allowing Joomla to publish the two parts on separate pages. By setting the intro text to hide, you can create a teaser text that's different from the intro text that's displayed as a part of the full article page.

Creating multipage articles

Suppose you have a long article with several sections, each covering a subtopic. Sometimes, you may find that such an article is too long to be fully displayed on a single page. It doesn't fit the content screen, you don't want the visitor to have to scroll all that much.

There's a tedious solution to this. It involves manually splitting the article by creating several individual short articles. But luckily, there's also a quick way out. By adding page breaks in a single article, Joomla will display this single article in the frontend as a series of separate pages, automatically adding navigation links and a table of contents.

Time for action – using page breaks to split up an article

Let's assume your client doesn't like the one-page article on ugly paintings. Instead of having one article with several subheadings, they'd rather see a couple of short pages that explain things step-by-step. To do this, we'll edit the existing article:

1. Navigate to **Content | Article Manager** and open the **Just What is Ugly Art?** article to edit it.

2. Select the page break locations. This is where Joomla will split the article into separate pages. In this example, we'll replace every subheading by a page break. Select the first subheading (**Abstract Chaos**) and delete it. Now click on the **Page Break** button at the bottom of the editor screen. A pop-up screen shows:

3. In the pop-up screen, enter the **Page Title** and **Table of Contents Alias**:

    □   **Page Title**: Enter a title for the new page. In this case, the text of the former subheading, **Abstract Chaos**. It will be displayed next to the article title, separated by a dash—**Just What is Ugly Art? – Abstract Chaos**.

    □   **Table of Contents Alias**: This is the link text that will appear in the **Table of Contents** of the multipage article. The **Alias** and the **Page Title** can be the same; however, it's best to keep the **Alias** text as short as possible.

4. Click on **Insert Page Break**. The pop-up screen closes and a grey dotted line is inserted to indicate the location of the page break.

5. Repeat steps 2 to 4 for each page break required and save the article. Click on **View site** to have a look at the frontend results. In the frontend **Main Menu**, click on **Ugly Paintings** and locate the intro text of the **Just what is Ugly Art?** article. Click on the **Read more** link.

Now, instead of one article Joomla has created a series of interlinked article pages. The first page the visitor sees is the first subpage. Pages include **<< Prev** and **Next >>** links to the previous and next page; the Table of Content's Aliases you've entered when creating page breaks now show up as hyperlinks in a table of contents featured on the right-hand side of every sub page:

What just happened?

Joomla lets you add page breaks to spread the content of a single article over multiple pages. To allow the visitor to move back and forth, a table of contents and Previous and Next navigation is automatically added to multipage articles.

Working with page breaks gives you an extra level of content below the article level. However, in general it's safe to assume that visitors don't like clicking multiple links to read one article. It's best to reserve multipage navigation for articles that easily break into logical chunks, such as step-by-step tutorials or portfolio pages showing different clients and projects.

Have a go hero: use sliders and tabs

The current release of Joomla offers some new and creative ways to put a lot of content on a single page, without displaying it all simultaneously. You don't have to use the default technique (as displayed in the previous section), where a long page is divided into several separate pages using a table of contents for navigation. Instead, you can now choose to divide the page contents using either sliders or tabs.

The following is an example—the page we've created before, is now divided into four panels. Panels slide out and slide in on a mouse-click. When the visitor clicks the title of any of the sections, the content of only that section is displayed.

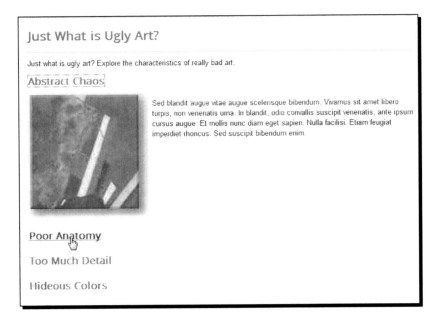

This technique is sometimes also called an **accordion**. To change the display of articles using pagebreaks, go to **Extensions | Plug-in Manager** and click the title of the **Content : Pagebreak** plug-in. Under **Basic Options**, select **Presentation Style: Sliders**:

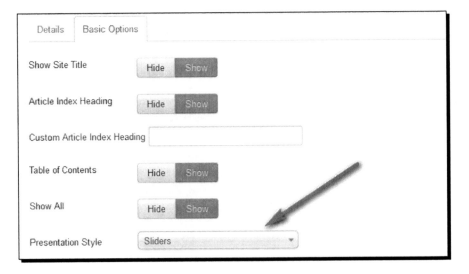

Save your changes and check the output of the article with page breaks you've created before.

 You can only choose one presentation style for all page breaks on the site. This means you can't have tabs on one article and sliders on another one. If you want to use more advanced tabbed pages and sliders (accordions), however, there are many Joomla extensions available. In *Chapter 10, Getting the Most out of Your Site: Extending Joomla*, you'll learn how to install and apply them.

Displaying images and links with articles

When editing or creating an article in Joomla, you'll notice that there's an **Images and links** section below the main editor screen. Joomla offers these fields for images and links to make it easier to create a series of articles sharing the same standardized layout—displaying an image at the top of the article and/or displaying a series of hyperlinks above (or below) the article. Although you're free to add images and hyperlinks to the article text itself, the **Images and links** fields allow for a foolproof way of inserting images and links displayed in a fixed position.

The advantage is that you (or other content contributors) don't have to repeatedly make sure that they insert images in the appropriate article location, which can easily lead to mistakes. By adding an Intro Image and setting its alignment, all article intro texts will share the same layout. The same holds for the three hyperlinks you can add through **Images and links**; if you want articles to start with one or more hyperlinks, you can enter these here. They will appear as a list of hyperlinks at the top or bottom of the article.

You've already seen a first example of using the **Images and links** fields in *Chapter 4, Web Building Basics: Creating a Site in an Hour*. Now let's take a closer look at how this feature works.

Time for action – adding images and links to an article

Let's create a new article in the **Facts** category to try out the possibilities of the **Images and links** feature:

1. In the backend, go to **Content | Article Manager | Add New Article**.

2. In the **Title** field, enter `An Overview of Bad Art Museums`. In the **Category** drop-down list, select **Facts**.

3. Enter a few paragraphs of dummy text. Insert a Read more-division after the first paragraph by placing the cursor at the start of the second paragraph and clicking on the **Read more** button.

4. The basic article is ready. Now let's use the **Images and links** feature. First, we'll add the Intro Image. In the **Images and links** section, click on the **Select** button for the Intro Image. A pop-up screen appears, allowing you to select (or in our case, upload and select) images.

5. As we haven't yet uploaded the appropriate images, let's do that now. In the **Upload file** section of the pop-up window, click **Choose files**. Select two images from your computer. If you are using the example images given in this book, upload `museum_small.jpg` and `museum_large.jpg`. Click **Open** and then click **Start Upload**. Both the images are now uploaded and their thumbnails appear.

6. Click on the `museum_small.jpg` thumbnail to select it and click **Insert**. You can click the little eye icon to check a preview of the selected image:

7. It's okay to leave the **Image Float** setting unchanged (**Use Global**). This way, the global setting (set through global article options) will be used. The image will be aligned to the left of the paragraph text.

8. Next, add a **Full article image**. Click **Select** to open a pop-up window. Click on `museum_large.jpg` to select it and click **Insert**.

9. The **Link** fields allow you to add a maximum of three hyperlinks that will be placed above or below the article text. In the textboxes for **Link A**, **Link B**, and **Link C**, enter the URLs that these hyperlinks should point to. For testing purposes, you can enter any URL here (for example, `www.google.com`).

10. Finally, add the link texts that will be displayed on the web page: **Link A Text**, **Link B Text**, and **Link C Text**. In this example, I've entered **Bad Art Museum Ohio**, **Museum of Bad Art (MOBA)**, and **Virtual Museum of Ugly Art**. Save the article.

You're done! Time to find out what the output looks like. On the frontend, click on the **Facts on Bad Art** link in the main menu. This will take you to the **Overview** page of the **Facts** category, proudly displaying your brand new article.

What just happened?

You've just created an article using the standardized layout Joomla offers through the **Images and links** fields. You'll notice that the **Facts** overview page displays the intro text and the small Intro Image you've added to the article. Clicking on the **Read more** button reveals the full story, including the full-size image and a set of links, displayed above the article text:

Have a go hero – tweak the article layout

Although the new article looks okay, the default settings may not be appropriate for your purposes. For example, it may seem strange to start an article with a row of hyperlinks that only make sense after the visitor has read the accompanying article text. Don't worry, it's easy to change the layout of the article through the article options. To find out how this works, open the article to edit it and click on the **Article options** tab. To change the position of the three hyperlinks, select: **Positioning of the Links: Below**. You may also want to hide a few article details that are displayed by default: set **Show Category, Show Author, Show Publish Date, Show Hits, Show Print**, and **Show E-mail** to **Hide**. As a result, the article output is clear and uncluttered—the focus is now on the main article text and the set of hyperlinks is shown after the main text. I'm sure you'll agree the Article options are a powerful way to customize the default display of articles and article details. We'll find out more about the options available in the next section.

An Overview of Bad Art Museums

Lorem ipsum dolor sit amet, consectetur adipiscing elit. Phasellus quis lectus metus, at posuere neque. Sed pharetra nibh eget orci convallis at posuere leo convallis. Sed blandit augue vitae augue scelerisque bibendum. Vivamus sit amet libero turpis, non venenatis urna. In blandit, odio convallis suscipit venenatis, ante ipsum cursus augue.

Phasellus lectus sem, fringilla eget consectetur in, ornare vitae odio. Praesent nec est et nisl adipiscing convallis. Phasellus consequat, urna nec viverra fermentum, erat augue bibendum felis, ut mattis magna neque et eros. Fusce lorem ligula, elementum non suscipit sed, ullamcorper eget massa. Vestibulum blandit, sem sed auctor luctus, nisl metus ultricies ante, et bibendum eros eros quis nisi. Nam sit amet quam eu ante venenatis lacinia sit amet ac nunc. Nulla ante erat, sagittis eu sodales sed, vestibulum vel enim. Vestibulum porta posuere mollis. Sed placerat adipiscing nisi in accumsan. Donec quis urna magna, et porttitor libero. Donec vel sem eu diam vulputate fringilla. Nunc cursus ligula nunc, ac dignissim turpis.

Nam eleifend ullamcorper nunc, a tristique tellus ornare nec. Vivamus semper nisl tempor diam blandit semper. Quisque non lacus orci, tempus feugiat urna. In auctor est a nulla pretium vitae vulputate leo consectetur. Class aptent taciti sociosqu ad litora torquent per conubia nostra, per inceptos himenaeos. Quisque luctus, ante quis placerat vehicula, arcu mauris mattis lectus, at viverra libero erat vitae augue. Morbi interdum vestibulum mi at suscipit. Etiam cursus mauris mattis nisl dignissim cursus. Vivamus luctus interdum metus, quis dignissim arcu imperdiet quis. Ut sed ipsum lectus. Nulla pellentesque quam quis neque tempus eget vestibulum metus blandit.

Bad Art Museum Ohio

Museum of Bad Art (MOBA)

Virtual Museum of Ugly Art

Tweaking the details: changing article settings

When editing an article, you can set a wide array of options. These allow you to control exactly which article details are shown, when the article will be published, and so on. It's a good idea to explore the options to make sure what combination of setting fits your needs best.

The following is an overview of the settings you can choose per article:

The Publishing Options tab

Alias	You don't have to enter anything here; Joomla will automatically fill out the **Alias** field based upon the article title. It's an internal reference that Joomla uses for the article URL.
Created by, Created by alias	By default, Joomla will display the name of the article's author. You can overrule this setting under **Article Options | Show Author** (see the following table). The author name is the name of the logged-in user who created the article. As long as you haven't created other user accounts, the Author name displayed will be **Super User**.
	If you want another name to appear with the article, you can enter an author alias here. When you have created accounts for other users, you can also select another user here by clicking the **Select User** button after the author name textbox.
	You can read more on creating user accounts in *Chapter 9, Opening Up the Site: Enabling Users to Log In and Contribute*.
Created Date	Change this value to manipulate the **Created Date** that Joomla can display with any article. By changing the date, you can bring an existing article to the attention of the visitor because it will reappear in lists or pages with new items.
Start Publishing, Finish Publishing	Sometimes, you'll have prepared content that should only be published for a given period of time; think of a temporary promotion, or a special New Years message. Use **Start Publishing** to enter the date when the new page should appear on the site; set a date in the **Finish Publishing** box to automatically unpublish content after a certain period.

The Article Options tab

Show Title, Show Intro Text, Position of Article Info, Show Category, Show Parent, Show Author, Show Create Date, Show Modify Date, Show Publish Date, Show Navigation, Show Icons, Show Print Icon, Show Email Icon, Show Voting, Show Hits, Show Unauthorised Links

These options control which details should be displayed with the article (in full article view). By default, these details are displayed at the top of the article.

In the following example, many of the article details are set to show. This is the default setup and it may result in a lot of "article clutter". It can be hard to find the actual article content in this detail overkill.

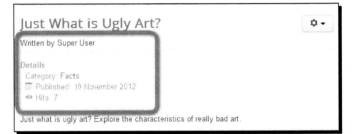

By using the **Position of Article Info** option, you can also set this information to display in a humbler position, at the bottom of the article:

However, whatever position you choose for the article details, it's best to only display useful information. Often, you can even leave out all extras, to save valuable screen real estate for the article text itself:

Selecting **Show Voting** will display a five-point scale below the article title when the full article is shown; visitors can rate the article:

Linked Titles, Link Category, Link Parent, Link Author	When set to **Show**, an article **Title**, **Category**, parent **Category**, or **Author** name are hyperlinks. This can be a very useful option, as it gives the visitor an alternative way to find content, apart from the menu system. By clicking on the hyperlink shown above or below the article, visitors navigate directly to the article/category/parent category or all articles by the same author.
Positioning of the Links	If you use the **Articles and Links** feature (covered later in this chapter), you can decide to display a set of hyperlinks in a fixed position—either above or below the article.
Read More Text	Entering a Read more text will replace the default Read more link text. If you were to enter the text **Full Story:** here, this would be displayed on the frontend as follows:

> › Full Story: Bad Abstract Paintings Lecture

Adding a specific text here can be better for usability, as it allows you to better guide your visitors towards the article content.

Alternative Layout	You can select a custom layout for the current article, provided the selected template (or component) allows for these additional layout options. A template may contain so-called template overrides, custom layouts that overrule Joomla's default layouts of categories. More information can be found on `http://docs.joomla.org/Layout_Overrides_in_Joomla_2.5`. The information here also applies to Joomla 3.x.

The Configure Edit screen tab

Show Publishing Options, Show Article Options, Administrator Images and Links, Frontend Images and Links	Here you can set whether you, as an administrator, want to hide the two previous options panels (**Publishing Options** and **Article Options**) for other users on this article edit screen. You can also set if you want to hide the next panel (**Images and Links**, see below) for users that have an Administrator account and/or for users that have frontend editing permissions. You'll read more on restricting access and permissions for user groups in *Chapter 9, Opening Up the Site: Enabling Users to Log In and Contribute*.

The Metadata Options tab

Meta Description, Meta Keywords, Robots, Author, Content Rights, External Reference	Metadata information is used by search engines. You can add an article description, meta keywords, and enter instructions for Robots (web search engine spiders). You'll read more on this in *Chapter 12, AAttracting Search Engine Traffic: SEO Tips and Techniques*.

The Article Permissions tab

In the **Article Permissions** section, you can set permissions for user groups at the level of this specific article. These permission settings allow specific user groups to see the article (or not see it), or allow them to edit it. You'll learn more about permissions in *Chapter 9, Opening Up the Site: Enabling Users to Log In and Contribute*.

Setting general preferences for all articles

The tabbed options panels in the article editor screen allow you to set preferences for specific articles. However, you'll probably want to select default preferences for all your articles—whether you want the author name displayed, whether the title should be a hyperlink, and so on. To enter these site-wide article preferences, navigate to **Content | Article Manager** and click on the **Options** button in the toolbar. These settings will apply to all articles. Of course, you can override these general settings by setting specific options when editing individual articles.

Let's have a look at the available general settings now. Go to **Content | Article Manager** and click on the **Options** button. You'll see a screen featuring nine tabs (**Articles, Editing Layout, Category**, and so on):

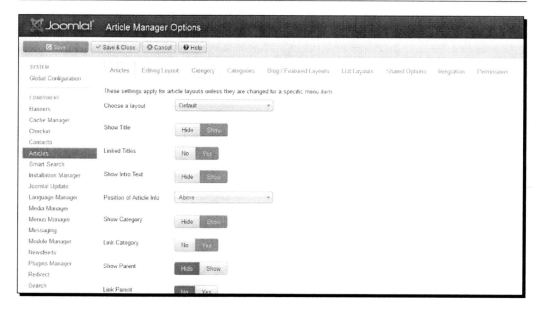

The Articles tab

The options under the **Articles** tab define the article properties (most of these settings you've already seen in the options panels of individual articles). The choices you make here apply to all articles. However, you can also set article options through menu items: when you create a link to an article or category, you'll also find the same set of **Article** options. The settings you choose for a specific menu item overrule the general settings.

An option that you'll only find in the **Article Manager Options** screen, is **Read More Limit**. The number you enter here, determines the maximum number of characters for the article title in a **Read more** button. This way, you can avoid the **Read more** button getting too big because of the length of the article title.

The Editing Layout tab

These options control what options are available on the article edit screen for other users than you (the almighty Super User). You can set whether you want to hide specific options panels (**Publishing Options** and **Article Options**) for users who have access to article edit screens. You can also hide the **Images and links** panel (allowing users to specify an image for the intro text and for the full article) for users that have an Administrator account and/or for users that have frontend editing permissions. You'll read more on restricting access and permissions for user groups in *Chapter 9, Opening Up the Site: Enabling Users to Log In and Contribute.*

The Category tab

Although this tab is displayed among the **Article Manager** options, the **Category** options don't apply to articles—they determine the way categories are displayed on category pages. The same set of options is available when you create a menu link to display categories (such as the **Category Blog** menu item type you've already used). Again, the general settings chosen here apply only when you don't make other choices for specific menu items.

One option that you will only find on the **Category** tab, is **Choose a layout**. Here you can determine how category overviews are displayed by default—either in a blog view or a list view. You'll learn more on the available category views in *Chapter 7, Welcoming Your Visitors – Creating Attractive Home Pages and Overview Pages*.

The Categories, Blog / Featured Layouts, List Layouts, and Shared Options tabs

Again, these options don't relate to individual articles. Rather, they affect the way overview pages, displaying articles or article teasers, are displayed. You'll learn more about these types of overview pages in *Chapter 7, Welcoming Your Visitors – Creating Attractive Home Pages and Overview Pages*. Here's a short introduction:

- The **Category** options affect pages that display multiple categories. You'll also find these options when you create a menu item type of a specific type, called **List of All Categories**.

- The **Blog / Featured Layouts** options affect article overview pages that use Joomla's Blog layout or Featured layout. This layout is used when you create pages through the **Category Blog** menu item type or the **Featured Articles** menu item type.

- The **List Layouts** options apply to overview pages that use a list view of items. You create list views (and find the same set of display options) by adding a Menu Item Type of the Category List or List of all categories type.

- The **Shared Options** apply to List, Blog, and Featured layouts.

The Integration tab

The Integration options are only relevant when you use news feeds (RSS feeds) on your website. The **Show Feed Link** option allows you to show or hide an RSS feed link. This will display a feed icon in the address bar of the web browser. The **For each feed item show** option allows you to control what to show in the news feed; the intro text of each article, or the full article. The choices made here can be overruled by the **Integration Options** settings of specific menu item types (such as a link of the Category Blog type).

The Permissions tab

Here you can set the default permissions for all article content. You can, for example, allow specific groups of users to edit or delete articles. You can read more about user permissions in *Chapter 9, Opening Up the Site: Enabling Users to Log In and Contribute*.

Archiving articles

As your site grows, you may want to clean up the site contents. You probably don't want to display outdated articles—such as last year's news—among your current content. In Joomla, there are different ways to achieve this. One option is to unpublish old articles. That way, the articles are still available in the backend, but the site visitor cannot see them anymore. Another option is to create an archive. Archived articles are still available, but they're no longer part of the "ordinary" site contents. You can make them visible through a menu link of the **Archived Articles** menu item type.

Archiving is something you do by hand. To archive an article (or multiple articles at once), select the desired article(s) in the **Article Manager** and hit the **Archive** toolbar button.

 If you want to automatically archive articles that are older than a given period of time, consider using Joomla extensions such as Auto-Archive. You can find it on the Joomla extension site (`http://extensions.joomla.org/extensions/news-production/timed-content`). Find more information on installing and using extensions in *Chapter 11, Creating an Attractive Design: Working with Templates*.

You can also change the article state to **Archived** when you've opened it in the article editor screen:

To see which articles have been archived, go to the **Article Manager** and select **Archived** in the **Status** select box:

You can still edit an archived article, which is quite useful. After all, although articles are archived, you might still want to correct a typo or delete some outdated information. To edit an archived article, just click on the article **Title** in the **Article Manager** to open the **Article Manager: Edit Article** screen.

To de-archive an article, select the article and change the **State** from **Archived** to **Published** (or **Unpublished**, if you don't want to display the article). Click on **Save** to commit the state change.

Time for action – creating a news archive

Let's create an archive for some old news pages on the CORBA site:

1. Navigate to **Content | Article Manager**. In the **Select Category** filter box, select **News** to see only the articles in that category.

2. Select the articles to be archived. In the following example, we've selected **Bad Photography Exhibition**.

3. Click on the **Archive** button in the toolbar.

4. A message appears to confirm the article has been archived. The article disappears from the article list. To see archived contents, select **Archived** in the **Select Status** drop-down list.

You've created a (tiny) news archive now, but there's no way for the visitor to see its contents. Let's create a link:

5. Navigate to **Menus| Main Menu| Add New Menu Item**. As the **Menu Item Type** for this link, select **Articles |Archived Articles**.

6. Enter a **Title** for the hyperlink: **News Archive**. Adjust any other settings you want and click on **Save**.

On the frontend, a link to the Archive is shown. Right now, there's just one article; however, if the site contains a substantial archive, the visitor can filter (search) archived articles by keyword or publication date.

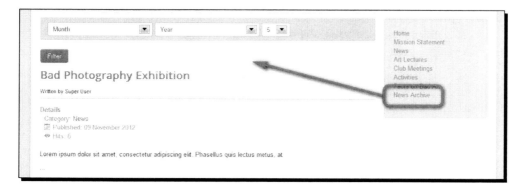

What just happened?

You've created an archive for outdated articles. Visitors can view an overview of the archive contents by clicking on the **News Archive** link in the **Main Menu**.

Pop quiz – test your article expertise

Q1. The article editor screen in Joomla allows you to do which of these three things?

    a.   Formatting article text.

    b.   Inserting images.

    c.   Controlling the start and end date of publishing.

Q2. What's the use of the Joomla Media Manager?

    a.   It allows you to manage all sorts of media (images, movie files, and MP3 files).

    b.   It allows you to upload images and insert them into an article.

    c.   It allows you to insert images that come with the default Joomla installation.

Q3. You open an existing article in the Joomla article editor and see a red-dotted line. What does that mean?

    a.   Text below the line will not be displayed.

    b.   The article text has exceeded the maximum number of characters allowed.

    c.   If needed, Joomla can separately display the intro text and the full article text.

Q4. How can you break a long article into a series of short ones?

    a.   By manually creating several individual articles.

    b.   By entering page breaks in an article.

    c.   By entering Read more links in an article.

Q5. What's the function of archiving articles?

    a.   Archived articles cannot be edited any more.

    b.   Archived articles aren't displayed in the frontend.

    c.   Archived articles are displayed in a special Archive part of the frontend.

Summary

In this chapter, you've mastered creating article content. This is what we covered:

- To create new articles or to edit existing ones, the **Article Manager** is your starting point. From there, click on **New** or select an article and click on **Edit**.

- The article editing screen allows you to style your contents and add images. If you want more text editing control, you can set the text editor to show an extra ("Extended") set of buttons.

- The **Media Manager** allows you to create new image folders. This way, you can keep the image files on the web server organized.

- There are several ways to display article content. It can be one continuous text page, but you can also split the article into an introductory text and the actual article body text.

- To break a long article into several interlinked subpages, you add page breaks to the article text. In the backend you've still got one article, in the frontend it will display as a series of pages.

You've now mastered the recipe that enables you to create as much killer content as you like. But all that beautiful content is useless if your site visitors fail to notice it's there. So, it's time to focus on your site's "shop windows"—the home page and other pages that draw your visitors' attention to the content.

In the next chapter, you'll learn how to create an inviting home page and alluring overview pages, giving visitors an irresistible preview of what your site has to offer.

7
Welcoming your Visitors: Creating Attractive Home Pages and Overview Pages

In the previous chapters, you've laid the groundwork for your site. First, you created content containers (categories and subcategories), then you created the actual content (articles). You've now got a bunch of neatly organized, attractive articles ready to be explored by a World Wide Web surfing audience. But how can you entice those casual web surfers to actually read all that valuable content? Why would they bother to drill down to the content of your site?

That's where the home page and overview pages come in. The home page lures your visitors in. Joomla's overview pages—"second-level home pages" that provide a quick overview of category contents—direct people to the articles they could be interested in.

In this chapter we will:

- Customize the home page settings
- Create a different kind of home page
- Create and tweak category overview pages
- Create different layouts for different types of overview pages

So, let's start tweaking the CORBA home page!

Up to now, you've set up the home page and category overview pages using the default options. But you may have noticed that Joomla offers dozens of options for these page types. Changing these options can completely alter the way content is presented. In fact, different settings can create very different looking pages.

To effectively welcome your visitors and entice them to read your valuable content, we'll create a better home page and effective category pages. In the following screenshots, you'll see the page types we're talking about. The basic layout of both home pages and overview pages is similar. On the left-hand side is the example home page in the default Joomla installation, on the right-hand side is an example category overview page found via the **About Joomla** menu (**Using Joomla | Using Extensions | Components | Content Component | Article Category Blog**):

Why do you need overview pages, anyway?

Typically, Joomla will lead your site visitor to a category content in three steps. Between the **Main Menu** and the actual content, there's a secondary page to show category contents. You can see how this works in the following set of screenshots:

A visitor clicks on a menu link.

They are taken to an overview page with article previews inviting them to click **Read more** links.

They click to read the full article.

As you can see, what's on the home page and the overview pages (and how it's presented) is vitally important to your site. It's the teaser texts, images, and hyperlinks on these pages that offer your visitors a first glimpse of the actual content. Of course, people don't always arrive at your site via the home page. Search engine results might take them directly to any page—including overview pages. One more reason to make those pages as enticing as you can!

> **Overview page, landing page, secondary home page?**
>
> Joomla doesn't have a name for overview pages. Among web builders they're also known as start pages, category pages, department pages, or landing pages. Whatever you like to call it, it's the same thing: a navigational page that provides an overview of site categories. In this book we'll call them category overview pages.

Creating the perfect home – mastering home page layout

By default, the homepage of any Joomla site is set up to display the following items:

- One introductory article text over the full width of the mainbody
- Three intro texts in three columns

As we haven't changed any of the homepage layout settings up to now, the example site homepage has the same layout.

This default setup is suited for many types of content-rich sites. But you're certainly not limited to displaying this one particular combination of intro texts and links in the central part of the home page (the "mainbody", as it is called in Joomla). There's a vast amount of choices on how to display content on the home page, and what to display.

Changing the way the home page is arranged

It's your client on the phone, telling you that—happy as they are with their new site—some CORBA staff members find the home page layout too distracting. They don't like the newspaper look that displays the content columns in different widths. Would you be so kind as to tone things down a little? If you could quickly show them an alternative layout, that would be fine. You hang up and dive into the homepage settings.

Time for action – rearranging the layout of articles on the home page

You decide to rearrange the items on the home page. Let's say you want a maximum of two intro texts, both in just one column. Apart from this, you would like to show a few hyperlinks to other articles that could be of interest to visitors browsing the home page. You may wonder where Joomla stores the home page settings. As we've seen in previous chapters, menu link settings often determine Joomla's page output—and this also holds for the **Home** link in the main menu. This menu link is of a specific Menu Item Type, **Featured Articles**. To change the appearance of the home page, we'll customize the **Home** menu link settings.

1. Navigate to **Menus | Main Menu**. In the **Menu Manager**, click on **Home** to enter the screen where you can edit the menu link settings.

2. Click the **Advanced Options** tab. In the **Layout Options** section, the current settings are shown as follows:

These are the "magic numbers" that determine the page lay-out. There's **1** leading article (which means it's displayed in full width), intro articles are shown in **3** columns, and there are **0** links to articles.

3. Change the values as follows: set **# Leading Articles** to **0**, **# Intro Articles** to **2**, **# Columns** to **1**, and **# Links** to **4**. This way just two articles will be shown in a single column and the rest of the featured articles is displayed as a set of hyperlinks.

4. Save your changes and click on **View site** to see the changes on the frontend. There are now two full-width intro texts. Although you have set **# Links** to **4**, beneath the intro texts only two article links are displayed. This is because up to now only four articles have been assigned to the home page. If you'll assign more articles to the home page, this list will grow to a maximum of four hyperlinks.

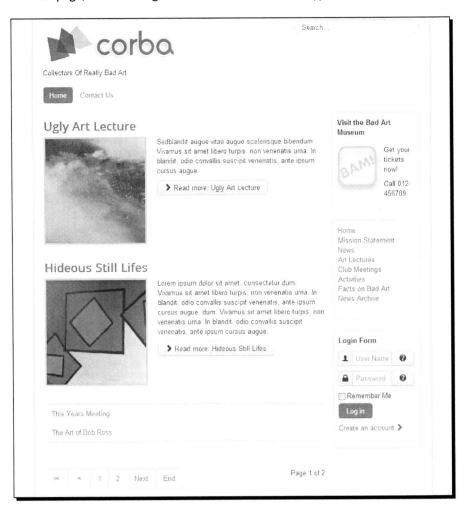

What just happened?

The settings of any menu item allow you to influence the look of the hyperlink's destination page. By default, the Joomla **Home** link of the main menu is of the **Featured Articles** Menu Item Type. In this case, you've tweaked the layout options of the **Featured** Articles menu link to change the home page mainbody. The magic numbers of the **Layout Options** section are really powerful as different values can completely change the way the page content is displayed.

Have a go hero – tweak home page layout options

Joomla offers you dozens of settings to customize the home page layout. Navigate to **Menus | Main Menu | Home** and click the **Advanced Options** tab to have a look at the different option panels, such as **Layout Options**. First, you will probably want to set **Pagination** to **Hide**. That way, you'll hide the pagination links (**< Start Prev Next Last >**) that Joomla displays when there are more articles available than can be shown on the home page as intro texts. In our example, the pagination links allow the visitor to navigate to a "second home page", displaying the intro texts of the two hyperlinks in the **More articles ...** list. Showing pagination links on a home page seems suited for weblog home pages, where visitors expect to be able to browse through possibly long lists of blog entries. On most other types of sites, web users aren't likely to expect multi-page home pages.

The options for the **Home** link (or any other **Featured Articles** Menu Item Type) allow you to also control exactly what details are shown for every article on the home page. Through the menu link settings you determine whether or not you want to show the author name, publication date, the category name, and much more. These article display settings in the menu link overrule the general settings found through **Content | Article Manager | Options**. For a full overview of all options available for the **Featured Articles** Menu Item Type, see the *The Featured Articles Menu Item Type – an overview of all options* later in this chapter.

Adding items to the home page

In the **More Articles ...** hyperlink list at the bottom of your home page, two hyperlinks are shown. That's because only four articles are set to display on the home page. To add a couple of articles, navigate to **Content | Article Manager**. Add any article by clicking on the white star in the **Status** column to the left-hand side of the article title. The grey star changes to an orange star.

In the following example, we've selected a **News** item (**CORBA Magazine Looking for Authors**) to be **Featured** on the homepage:

Want to see what this looks like up front? Just click on **View Site**. The new home page item is shown at the top. All other featured items are now positioned one position lower than before. You'll notice that the **Hideous Still Lifes** intro text has disappeared as this featured item has now slid down one position, to the list with article hyperlinks. This list now contains three articles instead of two.

Another way to add articles to the home page

Adding items to the home page takes just a few clicks in the **Article Manager Status** column. You can also add an individual article to the home page through a setting in the **Edit Article** screen: under **Details**, select **Featured: Yes**.

Controlling the order of home page items manually

Now that you've reorganized your home page layout, you'll probably want some control over the order of the home page items. To manually set the order, first edit the **Home** menu link. Click **Advanced Options** and under **Layout Options**, make sure **Category Order** is set to **No order**:

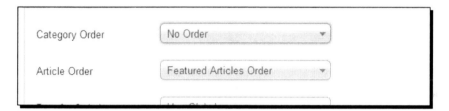

Click **Save & Close** and go to **Content | Featured Articles** and set the order as desired. First, set the value of the **Sort Order By** select box (by default it shows **Title**) to **Ordering**. Now you can change the articles order by clicking the three vertical squares to the left-hand side of any article title and dragging the article to another position. The intro texts and links on the home page will now be displayed in the order they have in the **Featured Articles** screen:

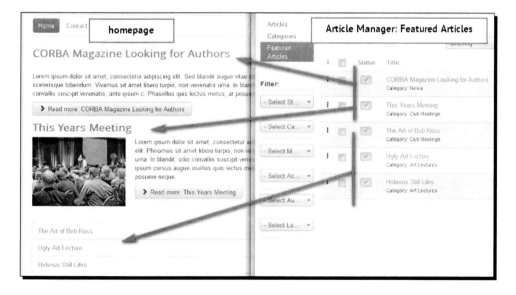

What's the use of the Featured Articles screen?

In the **Featured Articles** screen, you can't—as you might have expected—assign items to the **Featured** status. As you've seen, you can assign articles to the **Featured** status in the **Article Manager** (or in the article editing screen). You'll probably use the **Featured Articles** screen if you want to manually control the order of home page items, or if you want a quick overview of all featured articles. Apart from this, the **Featured Articles** screen allows you to publish, delete, or archive featured articles—but you can just as easily use the **Article Manager** for that too.

Setting a criteria to automatically order home page items

Having full manual control over the order of home page items can be convenient when you have a fixed set of content items that you want to show up on the home page, for example, when you have a corporate site and want to always show your company profile, an introduction to your products, and a link to a page with your address and contact details.

However, when your site is frequently updated with new content, you'll probably want Joomla to automatically arrange the home page items to a certain ordering criteria. Again, you can customize this behavior by editing the **Home** link in the main menu. Its **Layout Options** allow you to choose from a wide range of ordering methods.

Time for action – show the most recent items first

The visitors of the CORBA site will probably expect to see the most recently added items on the top of the page. Let's set the **Layout Options** to organize things accordingly.

1. Navigate to **Menus | Main Menu** and click the **Home** link to edit its settings.

2. Under the **Advanced Options** tab, you'll find the **Layout Options** offering several ordering options for featured articles. Make sure **Category Order** is set to **No order**, to avoid that specific category order settings overruling the article settings you choose. In the **Article Order** drop-down list, choose **Most recent first**.

3. As the **Date for ordering**, select **Create Date**. When ordering your articles by date, you'll probably want to display the creation date for every article. Navigate to the **Article Options** panel of the menu link and make sure **Show Create Date** is set to **Show**.

4. Click on **Save** and click on **View Site**. Now the most recent items are shown first on the home page:

What just happened?

You've told Joomla to put the most recently added items first on the home page. If you want, you can check this by opening a featured article, changing its created date to **Today**, and saving your changes; this article will immediately be displayed at the top in the home page layout. If you prefer to order home page items in another way (for example, alphabetically by title), you can do this by selecting the appropriate **Article Order** settings of the home page menu item (the **Home** link in the **Main Menu**).

The Featured Articles Menu Item Type – an overview of all options

You've seen that the **Home** menu is a link of the **Featured Articles** Menu Item Type. When adding or editing a **Featured Articles** menu link, you'll see there are are six expandable options panels available under the **Advanced Options** tab, offering a huge number of customization settings. Below you'll find a complete reference of all available options.

Dozens of dazzling options – isn't that a bit too much?

You've seen them before (when setting article preferences in *Chapter 6, Creating Killer Content: Adding and Editing Articles*), and now they turn up again, those seemingly endless lists of options. Maybe you find this abundance discouraging. Is it really necessary to check thirty or forty options to create just one menu link? Luckily, that's not how it works. You get fine results when you stick to the default settings. But if you want to tweak the way pages are displayed, it is worthwhile to experiment with the different options. See which settings fit your site best; in your day-to-day web building routine you'll probably stick to those.

Layout Options

Under **Layout Options** of the **Featured Articles** Menu Item Type, you find the main settings affecting the layout and arrangement of home page items.

Select Categories	By default, the home page displays **Featured Articles** from all article categories. You can, however, control exactly from which categories featured articles should be shown. For example, you might want to display only featured articles from the **News** category on the home page, and featured articles from another category on another **Featured Articles** page, introducing another category. You'll see an example of this in the section *Creating more than one page containing featured articles* later in this chapter.
# Leading Articles	Enter the number of leading articles you want to display, that is, intro texts displayed across the entire width of the mainbody.
# Intro Articles	The number of article intro texts that you want to show in two or more columns.
# Columns	Specify the number of columns; over how many columns should the **# Intro Articles** be distributed?
# Links	The number of hyperlinks to other articles (shown below **Leading** or **Intro Articles**)
Multi Column Order	Should intro texts in multiple columns be sorted from left to right (across) or from top to bottom (down)?

Category Order	Do you want to organize the items on the page by category title? You might want to do this when you have many items on your home page and you want your visitor to understand the category structure behind this. If you want to order by category, set **Show Category** (see **Article Options** explained in the next table) to **show**; that way, the visitor can see that the articles are grouped by category.
	The following **Category Order** options are available:
	◆ **No Order**: If you select this option, the items are displayed in the order you set in the **Article Order** field (the next option under **Layout Options**).
	◆ **Title Alphabetical**: Organizes categories alphabetically by title.
	◆ **Title Reverse Alphabetical**: Organizes categories reverse-alphabetically by title.
	◆ **Category Manager Order**: Organizes categories according to the order in the **Category Manager** and orders the category contents according to the **Article Order** (which you can specify below).
Article Order	You can order the items within the featured articles page by date, alphabetically by **Author name** or **Title**, **Most hits**, and so on. If you choose **Featured Articles Order**, then the items appear in the order they have on the **Content | Featured Articles** screen. This last option gives you full manual control over the order of items on the page. Note: the **Article Order** is applied only after the **Category Order**. **Article Order** only has effect if you choose **No Order** in the **Category Order** box.
Date for Ordering	If you've set the **Article Order** to **Most Recent First** or **Oldest First**, select the date for ordering: **Created**, **Modified**, or **Published**.
Pagination	**Auto**: When there are more items available than it can fit the first page, Joomla automatically adds pagination links (**<<Start <Previous 1 2 3 Next> End>>**). On the home page, in many cases, you'll probably want to set **Pagination** to **Hide**.
Pagination Results	If pagination links are shown, Joomla can also display the **Pagination Results**, the total number of pages (as in Page 1 of 3).

Article Options

The **Article Options** influence how articles are displayed on the **Featured Articles** page. For many extras you can select **Show**, **Hide**, **Use Global** (which means: use the settings chosen under **Article Manager | Options**), or **Use Article Settings** (use the settings chosen in the option panels of the individual articles).

The **Article Options** are similar to the options you can set in the general preferences for articles (**Article Manager | Options**, see the *Tweaking the details: changing article settings* section in *Chapter 6, Creating Killer Content: Adding and Editing Articles*). Here, you can depart from the general settings for the articles and make different choices for this particular menu item.

Show Title	Display article titles or not? It's hard to find a reason to select **Hide**.
Linked Titles	Should the title of the article be a hyperlink to the full article? By default this option is set to **Yes**. This is better for usability reasons, because your visitor can just click on the article title to read a full article (instead of just on a **Read more** link). It is also better because search engines love links that clearly define the destination (which article titles should do).
Show Intro Text	After the visitor has clicked on a **Read more** link, do you want them to see a page with just the rest of the article text (select **No**) or the full article including the intro text (select **Yes**)?
Position of Article Info	The **Article Info** consists of the article details, such as the publication date, author name, and so on. If these details are set to be displayed, do you want to display them above the article, below the article, or split (partly above the article and partly below it)?
Show Category	Select **Show** if you want to show the category name below the article title. Joomla will display the category (as shown in the following screenshot: **Category: Club Meetings**).

Link Category	If the **Category** title is shown, should it be a hyperlink to the category? In most cases it's a good idea to select **Yes** here: this provides visitors with a link to category contents with every article.

Show Parent	Select **Show** if you want to show the name of the main category (the parent category of the current article category) below the article title. This will look as follows:

> This Years Meeting
>
> Details
>   Parent Category: CORBA Activities ◄━━━
>   Category: Club Meetings
>   🖿 Last Updated: 30 November 2012
>   🖿 Created: 30 November 2012

Link Parent	Just like the **Category** title, the title of the parent category can be made a link to an overview page of the main category contents.
Show Author, **Link Author**, **Show Create Date**, **Show Modify Date**, **Show Publish Date**	Do you want to show the author name (and make it a link to a page with other articles by the same author), the creation date, the date the article was last updated, and/or the date on which the article was first published? By default, many of these options are set to **Show**. You may want to choose **Hide** if you've got a small site or a site that isn't regularly updated. In that case you probably don't want to broadcast when your articles were written or who wrote them.
Show Navigation	Select **Show** if want to display navigation links between articles.
Show Voting	Should readers be able to rate articles (assign one to five stars to an article)?
Show "Read more"	Do you want a **Read more** link to appear below an article intro text? You'll probably want to leave this set to **Yes**, but if the title of the article is a hyperlink, a **Read more** link can be omitted. Although Joomla displays the **Read more** link by default, many web builders just make the article title clickable and omit a separate **Read more** link.
Show Title with Read More	It's a good idea to display the article title as part of the **Read more** text, as this will make the link text more meaningful for both search engines and ordinary visitors.
Show Icons	Joomla can show a set of special function icons with any article. These allow the visitor to print the article, or to e-mail it. Do you want to display these options as icons or text links?
Show Print Icon, **Show Email Icon**	Show or hide the special function icons? It's often better to altogether hide these extras. Your visitors may want to use the print function, but any modern browser offers a print function with better page formatting options.

Show Hits	Should the number of hits per article (the number of times it's been displayed) be shown?
Show Unauthorized Links	Do you want to show hyperlinks to articles that are only accessible to registered users, or hide these articles completely?

The **Article Options** listed previously allow you to show or hide all kinds of details, such as **Author**, **Create Date**, and **Modify Date**. In the following image, you can see the result when most options are set to **Show**. Obviously, this results in too much "detail clutter".

On a website that's maintained by just one or a few authors, or a website that isn't updated regularly, you might want to hide author and date details. On a home page you'll probably also want to hide all of the special function icons (set **Icons**, **Print Icon**, and **Email Icon** to **Hide**). It's unlikely that visitors want to print or e-mail parts of your home page content. In the following image, all extras are hidden, which leaves much more room for actual content in the same space.

Hideous Still Lifes

Lorem ipsum dolor sit amet, consectetur dum. Vivamus sit amet libero turpis, non venenatis urna. In blandit, odio convallis suscipit venenatis, ante ipsum cursus augue. dum. Vivamus sit amet libero turpis, non venenatis urna. In blandit, odio convallis suscipit venenatis, ante ipsum cursus augue.

Sed pharetra nibh eget orci convallis at posuere leo convallis. Sed blandit augue vitae augue scelerisque bibendum. Vivamus sit amet libero turpis, non venenatis urna. In blandit, odio convallis suscipit venenatis, ante ipsum cursus augue.

Et mollis unc diam eget sapien. Nulla facilisi. Etiam feugiat imperdiet rhoncus. Sed suscipit bibendum enim, sed volutpat tortor malesuada

Integration Options

The **Integration Options** are only relevant when you use news feeds (RSS feeds) on your website.

Show Feed Link	The **Show Feed Link** option allows you to show or hide an RSS Feed Link. This will display a feed icon in the address bar of the web browser.
For each feed item show	This option allows you to control what to show in the news feed; the intro text of each article, or the full article.

Link Type Options

The **Link Type Options** allow you to set the display of the menu link to this page (in this case the **Home** link).

Link Title Attribute	Here you can add a description that is displayed when the mouse cursor hovers over the menu link to this page.

Link CSS Style	Only relevant if you are familiar with CSS and want to apply a custom CSS style to this specific menu link. If you've added a specific style in the CSS stylesheet, in this box you should fill in the name of that special style. Joomla will adjust the HTML and add the CSS style to the current menu **Home** link, as follows:
	
	`<a class="specialstyle" ref="/index.php">`
	`Home </a>`
	
	To find out more on using CSS, see *Chapter 11, Creating an Attractive Design: Working with Templates*.

| Link Image | Should an image be shown in the **Main Menu** link next to the **Home** link? Menu images (icons) can make a menu more attractive and easier to scan. Following is one of countless examples from the web: |

| Add Menu Title | When you use a **Link Image**, should the menu link text be displayed next to it? Select **No** only if you want a completely graphical menu, using just icons. |

Page Display Options

Under **Page Display Options**, you'll find some options to customize page headings and an option to control the general design of the page.

Browser Page Title	An HTML page contains a **title tag**. This doesn't appear on the page itself, but it's is displayed in the title bar of the browser. By default, Joomla will use the menu item title as the title tag. Here, you can overrule this default title. You can read more about this functionality in *Chapter 12, Attracting Search Engine Traffic: SEO Tips and Techniques*, on attracting search engines.
Show Page Heading	Here you can determine if a page heading appears at the top of the page (that is, in the mainbody). By default, this option is set to **No**. Select **Yes** to show the **Menu Item Title** as the **Page Heading**.
Page Heading	If you want to customize the **Page Heading** (instead of using the default **Menu Item Title** as the heading text), enter a text here.
Page Class	This is only relevant if you want to get more control over the page design: font size, colors, and so on. Using the **Page Class** field, you add a suffix to the name of all CSS styles used on this page. To use this feature, you have to know your way around in CSS. You can read more about CSS in *Chapter 11, Creating an Attractive Design: Working with Templates*.

Metadata Options

The **Metadata Options** allow you to add description and keywords to describe the web page's content.

Meta Description, **Meta Keywords**, **Robots**, **Secure**	Metadata information is used by search engines. You can add an article description, meta keywords, and enter instructions for **Robots** (web search engine spiders) and select whether this link should use a specified security protocol. You'll read more on metadata in *Chapter 12, Attracting Search Engine Traffic: SEO Tips and Techniques*.

Module Assignment for this Menu Item tab

Click the **Module Assignment for this Menu Item** tab to see links to all modules that are assigned to the current menu item. Modules in Joomla are always assigned to one or more menu items. When the visitor clicks a menu link, a page is displayed consisting of (among other things) specific module blocks. This overview of (links to) assigned modules makes it easier for administrators to jump directly from the menu item to all related modules and change their settings. You'll find more on modules in *Chapter 10, Getting the Most Out of Your Site: Extending Joomla*.

Creating more than one page containing featured articles

By default, the **Featured Articles** Menu Item Type is used only once on your site. All articles that have the **Featured** status, are shown on the homepage. This is because the **Home** link in the **Main Menu** is created using the **Featured Articles** Menu Item Type.

However, you can create as many **Featured Articles** pages as you like, each one showing featured articles from different categories. Let's say you want to create a page called "News Highlights", containing featured articles only from the **News** category. To do this, create a new menu link of the **Featured Articles** Menu Item Type and instead of **All Categories** select only the **News** category:

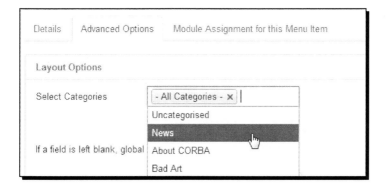

The output would be a separate featured articles page containing news highlights. To avoid the same featured news showing up on both the homepage and the News Highlights page, you would probably want to change the home page settings (currently set to show all categories) and get it to display featured articles from all categories except for the **News** category.

Another type of home page: using a single article

So far you've used Joomla's **Featured Articles** layout for your site's home page. But what if you want a completely different home page layout? That's easily achieved, since Joomla allows you to set any menu item as the default page.

Time for action – creating a different home page

Let's *not* use the **Featured Articles** and create a simple home page that only shows one single, full article:

1. Navigate to **Menus | Main Menu**. As you can see, there's a star in the **Home** column of the **Home** link. This indicates that this is the default page; the visitor will see this page in the mainbody when accessing your site.

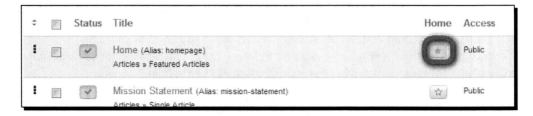

2. In this example we'll select the **Mission Statement** menu item as the new home page. Locate this article in the list and click on the grey star in the **Home** column.

3. Clicking the grey star will turn its color into orange, indicating this is now the default page. Click on **View Site**. The results are shown in the following screenshot. An ordinary article is now the home page:

If you want to update the **Main Menu** to reflect these changes, you can hide the existing **Home** link in the **Article Manager**, which is still pointing to the "old" homepage. To do this, in the **Menu Manager** you would click on the **Unpublish item** icon next to the **Home** link and rename the existing **Mission Statement** menu link to **Home**.

What just happened?

You've changed the default view of the home page to a fresh look, showing one article. Of course, you can dress up such a basic home page any way you like. For some sites (a simple "brochure site" presenting a small company or a project), this may be a good solution.

The consequence of this approach is, of course, that the **Featured** status (that you can set in the **Article Manager** and in the article edit screen) no longer determines what's published on the home page.

Have a go hero – undo!

For our example site, a single article home page doesn't fit the bill. You can easily revert to the home page you created earlier. In the **Main Menu**, set the **Home** link to be the **Default** item again and click on the cross in the **Status** column to unhide the **Home** link in the menu. Everything is back to normal now.

Creating category overview pages

In the previous chapter, you've seen how you organize content with categories and subcategories. By creating categories, you tell Joomla how to group things. However, you will also want to present category contents on the website in one way or another. That's where Joomla's category overview pages come in. They provide an intermediate level between the home page and content pages, presenting hyperlinks to category contents. They're a bit like second-level home pages. Joomla has no name for these pages; we'll call them overview pages or just category pages.

You've already seen some basic examples of Joomla's overview page when you created menu links of the **Category Blog** Menu Item Type to display categories (see the *Displaying main categories and subcategories on your site* section in *Chapter 5, Small Sites, Big Sites: Organizing your Content Effectively*). Now, we'll go beyond the basics and make category pages that exactly fit your (client's) needs.

Two main choices: Blog Layout and List Layout

Of course, being a somewhat advanced Joomler, you already know that you can create category overview pages through specific menu link settings. Creating a link to a category takes just the following steps:

1. Navigate to **Menus | Main Menu | Add New Menu Item**.

2. In the **Menu Item Type** section, click on **Select**. In the pop-up screen, click **Articles**. To display categories, you have two main options:

   - **Category Blog**
   - **Category List**

3. Select the appropriate layout, select the category the menu link should point to, and add a link—that's all there is to it.

There's a small catch to step 3. How do you choose between a **Blog** layout and a **List** layout? How do you create the type of overview page that fits the content of a specific category? That's what we'll find out now. Let's first have a look at the **Blog** layout; it's more common and more flexible than the **List** layout.

 Among the available Menu Item Types, you'll notice there's another one that has to do with categories: **List All Categories**. This has a specific use—as you may have guessed, it generates a page that lists hyperlinks to all article categories on the site. You can use this to generate a simple site map. We'll see an example in *Chapter 12, Attracting Search Engine Traffic: SEO Tips and Techniques*, on search engine optimization.

The first type of overview page: creating Category Blog layouts

The **Category Blog** layout is quite flexible and offers you very different ways of presenting your content. Time to start experimenting!

Time for action – create a facebook using the Blog layout

Let's use the **Blog** layout to create a small facebook, a collection of pages presenting the CORBA team.

1. For this purpose, create a new category (via **Content | Category Manager | Add New Category**) named **Who are CORBA?**. Under **Details**, select **About CORBA** as its parent category and click **Save & Close**.

2. Navigate to **Content | Article Manager** and create three new articles in the **Who are CORBA?** category in the **About CORBA** main category. In this example, we've used these titles: **Ms. Daiping Suraba, Dr. T. Phaedratski**, and **Dr. A. Fienstein**. Create articles with an intro text, a **Read more** link, and a main article text (if you're unsure how this works, refer back to *Chapter 4, Web Building Basics: Creating a Site in an Hour*).

3. Now let's create a category page. Make a new menu link by navigating to **Menus | Main Menu | Add New Menu Item**. In the **Menu Item Type** field, select **Articles| Category Blog**.

4. In the **Details** screen, select the appropriate category: **About CORBA > Who are CORBA?**. Enter a name (**Menu Title**) for the the new link: **Who are CORBA?**.

5. Click on **Save** and click on **View Site**. So far so good! There's a new link, showing a new category page:

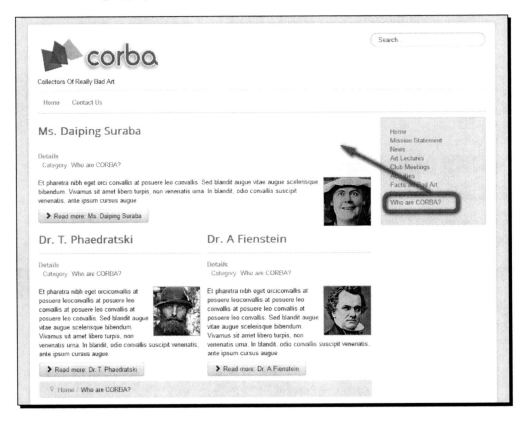

6. The page looks OK, but there's room for improvement. We don't want to display the first founding member in one wide column and the others in two narrow columns. Let's divide the article intros evenly over the page. Change the **Blog Layout Options** of the **Who are CORBA?** menu link as follows:

- ❏ **# Leading Articles: 0**
- ❏ **# Intro Articles: 3**

□   **# Columns**: 3

□   **# Links**: 0

7. Click on **Save** and click on **View Site**. The following screenshot shows the new outcome:

8. Looks alright, but the three-column layout doesn't fit with the overall site design.

9. Let's try one final alternative. Set **# Leading Articles** to **3**, **# Intro Articles** to **0**, **# Columns** to **0**, and **# Links** to **0**. Click on **Save** and click on **View Site**. Voila! A simple and clean one-column layout:

The resulting page looks balanced, so let's keep it this way.

What just happened?

You've tried out different ways in which category pages can show article content. You've added a facebook to the **Who are CORBA?** category by displaying the intro texts of the articles in a category overview page, and you've seen how the magical **Blog Layout** numbers determine what the page looks like.

Have a go hero – add a category description

Category content doesn't always speak for itself, so you may want to give your visitors a short introduction to a category page. We've already mentioned the possibility of entering category descriptions in *Chapter 5, Small Sites, Big Sites:Organizing your Content Effectively*. They allow you to show a few descriptive lines at the top of any category page. Why not add one to the **Who are CORBA?** category page?

4. Navigate to **Menus | Main Menu** and open the **Who are CORBA?** menu link to edit it. In the **Edit Menu Item** screen, click the **Advanced Options** tab and navigate to the **Category Options** panel. Make sure **Category Description** is set to **Show**. You may also want to set the **Category Title** to **Show**: this way the page will have a heading that reflects the menu link title. Save and close the menu link screen.

5. As yet there's no category description to display, so let's add a few lines. Navigate to **Content | Category Manager** and click on the **Who are CORBA?** category title to edit the category properties. In the **Description** field, add a little intro text:

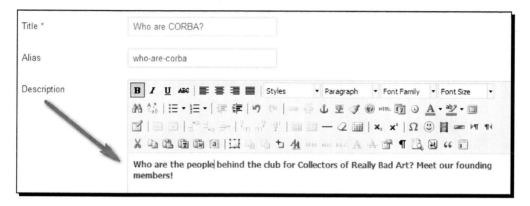

6. Click on **Save** and click on **View Site**. On the **Who are CORBA?** page, the category title and category description are displayed:

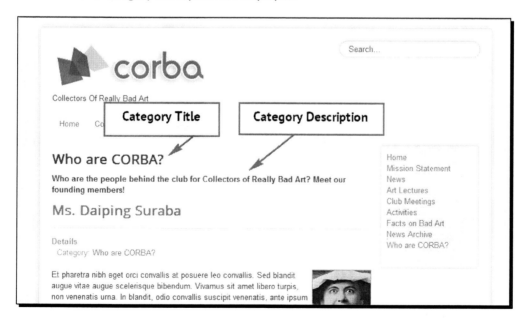

The more menu items you create, the longer and messier the main menu gets. You'll probably want to change the order of menu links—or create submenus to better arrange the long list of menu links. Don't worry, we'll get to building and customizing menus in *Chapter 8, Helping Your Visitors Find What They Want: Managing Menus.*

Showing full articles on a category overview page

So far, you've seen how you can show intro texts and links to articles on a category page. However, you can also use category pages to show a list of full articles. In fact, this is probably why this layout is called a **Category Blog**. A typical page on a weblog consists of a number of short articles ordered by subject or by date.

Here's an example of how you can get a category page to show three full article texts:

To achieve this in Joomla, you use a **Category Blog** page like the one you created just before. To show full articles instead of intro texts, change the article texts themselves. Up to now, they contain a **Read more** division telling Joomla to display no more than the intro text on overview pages. Navigate to **Content | Article Manager** and select the article you want to edit. In the editor screen, select the red dotted line indicating the separation between intro text (with a **Read more ...** link) and the rest of the text. Now delete this red line. This will tell Joomla not to split the article. On any overview page it will now show the full article instead of just its intro text.

When you create a page like this, you probably don't want to display the **Category: Who are CORBA?** information with every article. There's no use for this, as there are no additional articles in this category; all articles are already displayed on this one page. Again, you tweak these details through the settings of the menu link pointing to the page. In this case, to hide the link to the category name, edit the menu link settings of the **Who are CORBA?** link: under **Article Options**, set **Show Category** to **Hide**.

Have a go hero – experiment with Category Blog layout settings

Just like the **Featured Articles** layout, the **Category Blog** layout offers a huge array of settings that allow you to adjust the target page. You set them through **Menus | Main Menu | [name of link to category page]**. Here you'll find a number of option panels that you'll be familiar with; after all, you've already tried out the **Featured Articles** settings earlier in this chapter and the available options are very similar. The following table is a short overview of the options, particularly of those specific for the **Category Blog** layout. See the *The Featured Articles Menu Item Type – an overview of all options* section earlier in this chapter for a full listing.

Setting the options of the Category Blog Menu Item Type

Most of the settings of the **Category Blog** Menu Item Type are identical to those available for the **Featured Articles** layout. This holds for the **Article Options, Integration Options, Link Type Options, Page Display Options**, and **Metadata Options**.

There's just one slightly differently named heading: what's called **Blog Layout Options** here is similar to what's called **Layout Options** in the **Featured Articles** settings screen.

Category Options

The only settings specific for the **Category Layout** are found in the **Details** panel (where you select the category you want to display) and in the **Category Options** panel (under the **Advanced Options** tab). In the following listing you'll find an explanation of the options available in the **Category Options** panel.

Category Title	Show the category title as a heading on the category page?
Category Description	Shows the category description as an introductory text on the category page?
Category Image	If the category has an image added to it (under the **Basic Options** of the category edit screen), should this be displayed on the page?
Subcategory Levels	If the selected category has subcategories, enter the maximum number of subcategory levels that should be displayed on the page.
Empty Categories	Should empty categories be hidden or not? It's best to hide these categories, as there's little need for visitors to explore categories that have no content.
No Articles Message	When **Empty Categories** is set to **Show**, a message can be displayed telling the visitor there are no articles.
Subcategories Descriptions	Should the descriptions of subcategories be displayed?
# Articles in Category	Should the number of articles in the category be displayed?
Page Subheading	When you set **Category Title** not to show, you can enter another text here that will be displayed as the page heading. If you were to enter the text **Meet the CORBA team!** here, this would result in the following output:

The second type of overview page – Lists

Compared to the **Category Blog** layout, the **Category List** layout provides a more basic view of category contents. Instead of a series of intros and links, the visitor is shown only a number of links to categories and/or articles.

How do you make a such a list page? The steps are basically the same as the ones involved in creating **Category Blog** menu links. Navigate to **Menus | Main Menu | Add New Menu** Item and select **Category List** as Menu Item Type. Provide the necessary details (select a target category and type a link title) and you're done. In this section we'll find out in more detail how this works and how you can customize the default **List** layout.

Time for action – add a link to a Category List layout

een a **Category Blog** and a **Category List**. Earlier,
to the **News** category. Let's now create a list

Add New Menu Item.

lect button next to the **Menu Item Type**
ype pop-up screen, click on **Category List**:

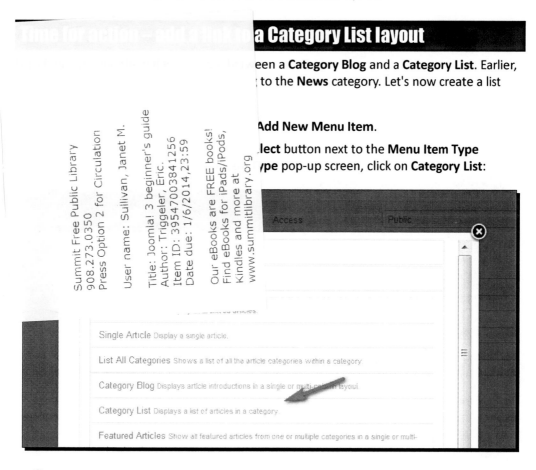

Single Article Display a single article.

List All Categories Shows a list of all the article categories within a category

Category Blog Displays article introductions in a single or multi-column layout.

Category List Displays a list of articles in a category.

Featured Articles Show all featured articles from one or multiple categories in a single or multi-

3. In the **Select a category** drop-down box, select **News**. In the **Menu Title** field, add a descriptive menu link text: **News Articles Overview**.

4. Click on **Save**. Done! Click on **View Site** to see the home page of your site; click on the **News Articles Overview** link to see the new list page. It should look similar to the following screenshot:

What just happened?

You have created a category page that displays a list of hyperlinks to articles instead of a series of teaser texts. Clicking on an article title takes the visitor to the actual article page.

The **Category List** layout can be useful for categories that are crammed with articles. If the **News** category would contain hundreds of articles, this layout could provide a quick overview to all articles, allowing visitors to scan or search for article titles. You can also consider using **List Layouts** on a site with many articles on related subjects, such as elaborate FAQ sections or large numbers of articles in a site section featuring product reviews. Lists enable visitors to quickly find information they search for. It's not really suited to attract casual surfers to explore the site's content. For that purpose you'll probably want to use the **Category Blog Layout**.

Customizing lists: Exploring Category List options

You can customize the look of **Category List** pages just like you change **Category Blog** pages: by changing the settings available in the menu link screen. Navigate to **Menus** | **Main Menu** | [name of menu link to the category]. In the **Details** tab, you'll enter required settings, such as the **Menu Title** (the link name) and the category you want to display. Click on the **Advanced Options** tab to see the other available options. Here's an overview.

Category Options

These are identical to the **Category Options** of the **Category Blog Layout**. To find out what options are available, have a look at the previous section on **Category Blog** layouts (see the section *Have a go hero – experiment with Category Blog layout settings*).

List Layouts

This panel contains the settings that are relevant to this specific Menu Item Type. They allow you to customize the list display.

Display Select	Select **Show** to display a select box allowing the visitor to choose how many items they want to see on the page. This option is turned off by default, because it's only useful if the list contains at least a few dozen hyperlinks.

Filter Field	The **Filter Field** is in fact a search box that appears at the top of an article list, allowing the visitor to quickly find content that matches the search criteria entered. The **Filter Field** setting allows you to specify that the search filter works by title, author name, or number of hits. You can also set the **Filter Field** to **Hide**.

Table Headings	Here you can select if you want to show or hide column headers (**Article Title**, **Author**, and so on) above the article listing. The output will look as follows:

The preceding screenshot shows the table view using the Beez3 template that comes with Joomla 3. At the time of writing, the Protostar template didn't (yet) support displaying table headings.

An advantage of showing table headings is that the visitors can sort the table list (as this is done by clicking the column heading).

Show Date	Do you want to show or hide the **Date** column (showing publication dates)? You can choose to show the **Create Date**, **Modify Date**, or **Publish Date**.
Date Format	By default, Joomla displays the date as in the following example: **Wednesday, 19 August, 2011**. If you want to format the date differently, enter a date format code here. For example, entering the code %Y-%m-%d will change the article date format to 2011-09-19. To find out which codes are allowed, check http://php.net/manual/en/function.strftime.php.
Show Hits in List, **Show Author in List**	These options allow you to hide the author name column and the column with the number of hits. By hiding both, you can display a basic hyperlink list that consist of only article titles:

Category Order	If the menu link points to a category and its subcategories (as set in the **Category Options** of this menu link), in what order should these multiple categories be displayed? You can order them alphabetically by title, reversed alphabetically, or in the default order that the categories have in the **Category Manager**.

Article Order	The order of the list of articles. This **Article Order** doesn't have an effect on the category list page itself (which contains no articles), but on the next page.
Date for Ordering	If articles are ordered by date, select what date you want to order them by? The options are: **Create Date**, **Modify Date**, or **Publish Date**.
Pagination	**Auto**: When there are more items available than it can fit on the first page, Joomla automatically adds pagination links (**<<Start <Previous 1 2 3 Next> End>>**).
Pagination Results	If pagination links are shown, Joomla can also display the **Pagination Results**: the total number of pages (as in Page 1 of 3).

8
Helping Your Visitors Find What They Want: Managing Menus

Menus and content in Joomla are closely intertwined. In the previous chapters, you have seen that menu links don't just point to existing pages, as you might expect if you have experience building websites the old fashioned way. When adding a menu link, you don't just tell Joomla what page the menu link should point to, but you rather instruct it to make that page. You've seen how this works when you added content to your site. By adding menu links, you created category pages and other types of pages.

However, to your visitor, Joomla menus are no different from other website menus. To them, menus should provide an easy means of navigation. In this chapter, we'll concentrate on menus as a means to navigate. We'll focus on how you can make and tweak menus to design clear and intuitive navigation, and also on how you can help the visitors find what they want without difficulty.

Up to now, you've added menu links using mainly the default settings. Let's find out how we can enhance menus and improve the navigability of the site.

The following is what you will learn to do in this chapter:

- ◆ Adding a new menu
- ◆ Creating submenus
- ◆ Adjusting menu module settings
- ◆ Creating hyperlinks in article texts

How many menus can you have?

On any Joomla website you can create as many menus as you want. The default sample site that you installed in *Chapter 2, Installation: Getting Joomla Up and Running*, is an example, as it contains no fewer than six menus. On the home page, four of them are shown—the **User Menu** (only displayed when a registered user has logged in to the site), the horizontal **Top Menu**, the **About Joomla** menu, and the **Main Menu** (titled **This Site**). In the following screenshot, you can see how the frontend menus are reflected in the administrative interface:

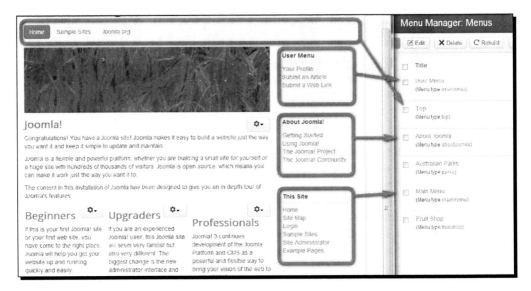

The **Australian Parks** menu and the **Fruit Shop** menu have been added to the sample data for demonstration purposes; they're only used on the Parks and Fruit Shop example site pages.

At least one menu is needed for Joomla to function properly—the menu containing the link to the home page. By default, that's the menu called **Main Menu**. The other ones are only there to showcase Joomla's menu possibilities. In real life, using this many menus would be confusing for both your site visitors and those who need to maintain the site.

However, it's great to be able to create as many menus as you like. This allows you to set up different menus for different functions and different users. You can, for example, have a main menu (at the top of the page) containing primary links, and another menu (somewhere down the page) containing secondary links. You may also want to have a special menu with action links (such as Login, and Register) and another menu that's only shown to visitors who have logged in.

Menus are modules (and why that's important)

You've already seen some examples of modules in action, such as the Custom HTML module. Remember, modules are Joomla's magic building blocks that can contain all kinds of functionality. Menus are modules too. In fact, every new menu you add is a new instance of the Menu module. This makes menus very flexible. Not only can you have as many menus (menu modules) on your site as you like, but you can also tell Joomla exactly where (on what part of the screen, in which module position) and when (on which specific pages, for which specific users) you want these menus to show up.

Sounds confusing? Don't worry, we'll practice adding and customizing menus in this chapter—and once you get the hang of it, you'll really appreciate Joomla's amazing menu flexibility.

Creating user-friendly navigation: cleaning up the Main Menu

When building a site, you'll start by adding links to the Main Menu. This menu is always part of the Joomla installation, even if you don't install sample data. But as your site evolves, it can become a long and cluttered list of hyperlinks. Even the menu of our small CORBA example site already contains too many links. When you find the Main Menu gets long and messy, what options do you have to improve site navigation?

Option 1: changing the order of menu items

By default, a new menu item is added to the end of the existing menu. If you add a new link to any menu, it will always show up as the last item:

This is probably not what you want. The order in which you add items isn't necessarily the order in which you want them to be displayed to your visitor. It's a good idea to rearrange links as soon as you've filled the menu with hyperlinks.

Deleting unnecessary menu items

In the previous chapters, we've added a few links for demonstration purposes or just to try things out. To get rid of redundant menu links, go to **Menus | Main Menu**, select the desired items and click on the **Trash** button. In our example site, we can trash a couple of links that are no longer needed (as there are other links present to get to the same content): **Art Lectures**, **Club Meetings**, **News articles overview**, and **Activities list**. Trashing a menu item can always be reverted by changing the **Status** to **Published**. To definitely delete menu items, select all items with **Status: Trashed** and click **Empty Trash**.

Time for action – changing menu item order

On the CORBA example site, let's move main menu items around to present them in a more logical order. The items that we want to get most attention should be in the top half of the menu; links to less important or static content should be placed down below. Below, the original menu is shown on the left-hand side; a more logical order—from most important to less important—is shown on the right-hand side.

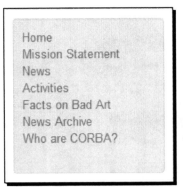

It takes just a few steps to adjust the order of menu items:

1. Navigate to **Menus | Main Menu**.

2. In the **Sort Table By:** drop-down list above the menu items list, select **Ordering**. Now click on the three vertical squares on the left-hand side of the menu item you want to move and drag-and-drop the menu item to its new position:

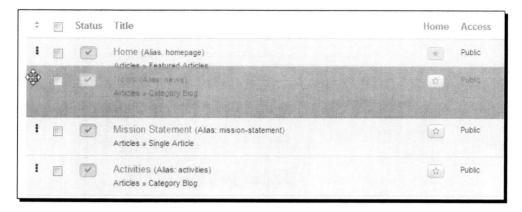

Repeat the previous step until you're happy with the sequence of menu items.

What just happened?

The menu items now show up in the order that you've chosen. **News** and **Activities** have been moved up from their humble positions.

Option 2: creating submenu items

There's still room for improvement in our **Main Menu**. Although there are now only five links left, the way they're organized may still confuse visitors. Having a **News** link and a separate **News Archive** link, both on the same menu level, is odd. **News Archive** probably shouldn't be a top-level link, so let's change it into a secondary link that will only be displayed after the **News** link has been clicked.

Time for action – creating a secondary menu item

This is how you remove the **News Archive** link from the primary level in the **Main Menu** and show it as a sublevel link:

1. To edit the **Main Menu** contents, navigate to **Menus | Main Menu**.
2. Click on the title of the item you want to edit, **News Archive**.

3. In the **Details** section, the **Parent Item** is set to **Menu Item Root**. This indicates it's a top level link. Change the **Parent Item** to **News**:

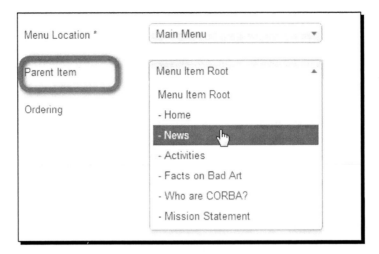

4. Click on **Save & Close**. In the list of menu items in the **Menu Manager**, the new sublevel menu item is shown indented:

5. To make sure the menu will display sublinks as intended, let's check a setting of the current menu module. Go to **Extensions | Module Manager**. In the **Select Type** drop-down list, select **Menu**. Click on the **This Site** menu module to edit it.

6. Click on the **Options** tab and under **Basic Options**, check if **End Level** is set to **All**. This indicates all submenu levels will be displayed. Leave **Show Sub-menu Items** set to **No**, unless you want to always display the submenu items (even if the main menu link hasn't been clicked).

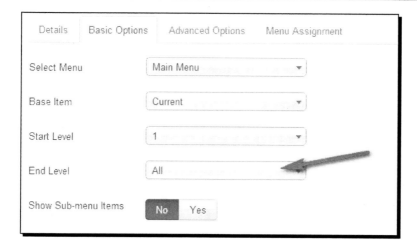

7. Click **View site** to see the output on the frontend.

8. The **Main Menu** now shows six primary links. When the visitor clicks on **News**, a secondary link **News Archive** is displayed:

What just happened?

By assigning a parent item to it, you turn a menu link into a submenu link. Using main ("parent") links and secondary ("child") links can clarify the coherence of the site.

Of course, submenus aren't the only way to make secondary content visible. In *Chapter 7, Welcoming Your Visitors: Creating Attractive Home Pages and Overview Pages*, you've seen that main links can point to overview pages with links to category content. Both submenu links and "secondary home pages" can be used to help the visitor drill down to the site contents.

To change the contents of a menu, you use the Menu Manager. To change the menu location and the menu behavior—such as the display of submenu links—you change the menu module settings. This combination of Menu Manager and Menu Module settings may seem confusing, but we'll practice using both sides of the Joomla backend in the next section, where we'll add a whole new menu.

Option 3: adding a separate new menu

You've seen how you can rearrange menu items and add different levels within a menu. Another way to improve a menu is by removing links that don't really fit in, and create a separate menu for these links that you can show somewhere else on the page. This way, you can either emphasize those links in the visual hierarchy of the web page—or you can choose to make them less prominent.

Let's have a look at the CORBA Main Menu items. Imagine your client has asked you to reorganize the navigation to enable visitors to quickly find the information on ugly paintings that this site is about. It's difficult for the visitor to distinguish between links on actual bad art contents and links on the organization behind the site. A good solution would be to create a separate menu on CORBA-related contents.

Time for action –creating a new, empty menu

In the main menu of the example site, three items are suited to be shown in another menu. These links are of interest to visitors who want to know more about the CORBA organization. Let's create a new menu named **About CORBA**, so that we can move the menu links **Who are CORBA?**, **Mission Statement**, and **Contact** there.

> *1.* Navigate to **Menus | Menu Manager**. Click on **New**.

> *2.* In the **Menu Manager: Add Menu** screen, enter the **Title**; this is the name that can be displayed with the menu. Enter the **Menu Type** too; this is the name that Joomla uses to identify the menu; it won't be visible on the frontend. When you enter a name, Joomla will save it without spaces or special characters. In the following example, we have entered **About CORBA** both as the menu title and the menu type. After clicking **Save**, you'll notice that the **Menu type** text has automatically changed to **about-corba**:

3. The **Description** is optional, although it can be useful to help you distinguish between different menus in the backend. For now, let's enter Menu about CORBA and click on **Save & Close**. You'll be taken to the **Menu Manager**. At the bottom of the list you can see a new entry. The **About CORBA** menu has been created:

If you were to click the **about-corba link** now, you would see all the **Menu Details** again: **Title**, **Menu type**, and **Description**.

What just happened?

In the **Menu Manager** you've created a new menu. It's visible in the Joomla backend—but of course it's still empty.

Time for action – moving hyperlinks to the new menu

One way to fill a new menu is by creating brand new links (**Menus | About CORBA | New**). In this case, however, we'll move three existing links from the main menu to our new menu:

1. In the **Menu Manager**, locate the **Main Menu**. Click on the name **Main Menu** to edit it.

2. Select the menu items you want to move to the new menu. In this example, we've selected **Who are CORBA?** and **Mission Statement**. At the top of the screen, click on the **Batch** button to move the menu items:

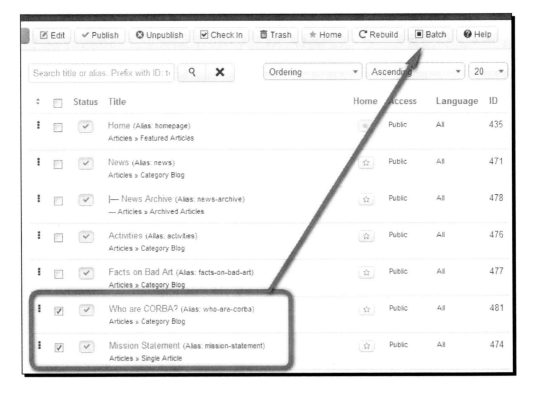

3. A popup screen called **Batch process the selected menu items** appears. In the **Select Menu or Parent for Move/Copy** drop-down list, scroll to **About CORBA | Add to this menu**. The text in the drop-down list changes to **Add to this menu**:

4. Click on the **Process** button. A message is displayed saying **Batch process completed successfully**.

5. Click on **Menus** in the left-hand menu to switch to the **Menu Manager: Menus** screen. This now displays two items in the **Published** column of the **About CORBA** menu

6. Click the number **2** to see the actual menu items. The contents of the **About CORBA** menu are shown:

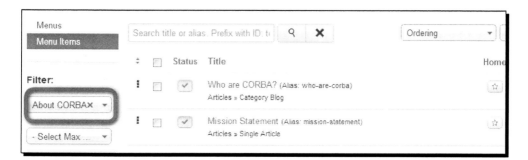

What just happened?

Everything is set up fine now; the new **About CORBA** menu contains the desired hyperlinks. There's just one thing left to do now—make it visible on your website.

Time for action – telling Joomla where to display the menu

To actually get the new menu to show on the site, you have to create a menu module. The module is the *functionality block* that contains your menu and that's needed to be able to display menu contents. Let's tell Joomla where you want it to show:

1. Go to **Menus | Menu Manager** to see all menus. Locate the **About CORBA** menu. Click on the **Add a module for this menu type** link, found in the **Modules linked to the Menu** column. (Actually this is a shortcut to the **Module Manager**—it saves you a few clicks navigating to to **Extensions | Module Manager**, clicking **New** and selecting **Menu**.)

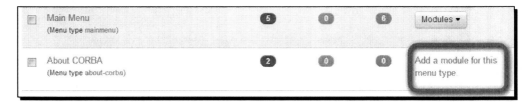

2. In the **Module Manager: Module Menu** screen, enter a title for the **About CORBA** menu. Select **Position: Right [position-7]**. This will make the new menu appear in the same column as the **Main Menu**.

3. Click on **Save** and click on **View site**. There you are! A separate menu appears. The new **About CORBA** menu is displayed in the right-hand side column:

4. You're almost there! We've got our new menu showing up in the left column, but we obviously want it to appear below the **Main Menu** to establish a better visual hierarchy. This takes just one extra step. If you've clicked out of the module editing screen, navigate back to **Extensions | Module Manager** and select the **About CORBA** module to edit the menu again.

5. In the **Details** section, there are two settings that control where the menu will turn up on the frontend. We'll leave **Position** unchanged (to keep the menu in the right-hand side column). In the **Ordering** drop-down box, the current value is **1**. The number indicates that the menu is now the top item in this module position. To change this value, select a lower position (in this example it's **5: This Site**). This will position the new menu below the current position of the **Main Menu**.

6. Click on **Save & Close** and then on **View Site** to check that the secondary menu is now published in the proper position:

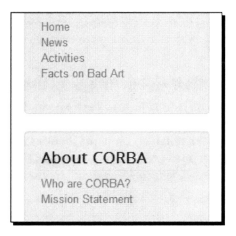

What just happened?

In this example, we've chosen to take two links out of the main menu and show them in a separate menu. We've succeeded in cleaning up the previously overcrowded main menu; it now shows just four main links. All links that point to content about the CORBA organization have been moved to a separate menu.

Don't worry if you don't like the default formatting of the Joomla Main Menu and submenu. Many templates allow for attractively styled menus. If you have some CSS coding skills, you can edit the menu styles yourself. You'll see examples of styling with CSS in *Chapter 11, Creating an Attractive Design: Working with Templates*.

Have a go hero – change menu settings

You may want to experiment with menu module settings (go to the **Module Manager**: **Module Menu** screen of the **About CORBA** menu) to adjust the position of the menu on the web page. Try out a few different menu module positions, for example, **Left (position-8)**. In *Chapter 10, Getting the Most Out of Your Site: Extending Joomla*, we'll explore the available module positions in greater detail.

Apart from the position setting, there are many other menu module settings that you can tweak to your liking. See the *Exploring menu module settings* section later in this chapter for a full overview.

Menu Manager or Module Manager?

To customize a menu, you'll sometimes use the Menu Manager, and sometimes use the Module Manager. What's the difference? The Menu Manager is used for everything that has to do with the *contents* of the menu. Anything to do with the *display* of the menu module you control through the module settings.

Using the horizontal drop-down menu as the main menu

In Joomla 3 the horizontal top menu is in fact the most important site menu. Not only is it visually prominent, it's also the menu that will remain visible even if the website is shown on the small screen of a smartphone or tablet computer. Joomla's default template, Protostar, is set up to automatically adapt to such small screens. However, the content layout does change when the site is displayed on a smaller screen—you can try that out now by resizing the browser window.

As you can see in the preceding screenshot, the top menu remains visible, but the right column (containing the **This Site** menu) has disappeared. In fact, the right column content is still there, but you need to scroll down all the way to the bottom of the screen to see it.

This means that in our current site (using the default site template) it would be better if we were to use the top menu as our default site menu. Right now that's not the case, but it's easy to assign the contents of the Main Menu to the Top Menu (and vice versa).

Time for action: displaying Main Menu links in the Top Menu

Let's set the Top menu module to show the Main Menu contents:

1. Go to **Extensions | Module Manager**. Locate the menu module named **Top** and click its name to edit it.

2. Click on the **Options** tab and under **Basic Options**, click the **Select Menu** drop-down box to select **Main Menu** (instead of the current selection, **Top**):

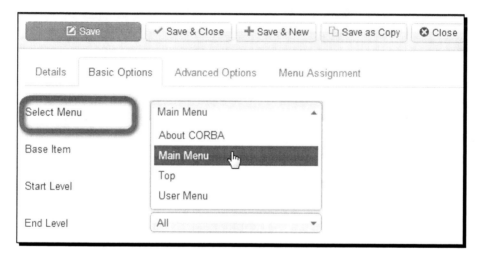

3. Make sure **End Level** is set to **All** and set **Show Sub-menu Items** to **Yes**. This way, the menu will display submenu links, not just the main level links. Save your changes.

4. Have a look at the frontend to see the output. As you can see, the top menu now displays the contents of the main menu. Hover your mouse over the **News** link to see the drop-down links working—even if there's only one submenu link (that is, the **News Archive** link) right now.

Have a go hero – clean up menus and menu links

At this moment the site contains two menu modules displaying the same menu contents. Both the **Top** menu module and the menu module called **This Site** display the contents of the **Main Menu**. You can easily correct this by assigning the **Top** menu contents to the **This Site** menu module. To do this, navigate to the **Module Manager**, open the menu module called **This Site**, and under **Options | Basic Options | Select Menu**, make sure the **Top** menu contents are selected:

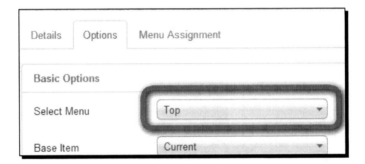

Save changes and have a look at the frontend of the site. The contents previously assigned to the top menu—just two links—are now shown in the **This Site** menu:

We could leave this menu as it is, but is doesn't serve a purpose—the **Home** link is already present in the horizontal top menu, so why not move the **Contact Us** link to another menu and unpublish the superfluous menu altogether? To to this, navigate to **Menus | Top**, select the **Contact Us** link and click **Batch** to move it to the **Main Menu**. Next, navigate to **Extensions | Modules**, locate the **This Site** module and click the green tick in the **Status** column to unpublish the menu module. Now the top menu displays all main links, including **Contact Us**:

Creating split submenus

Earlier in this chapter, you've seen that you create submenu links by selecting the appropriate **Parent** Item for any menu link. By default, every new link is a top level link—its **Parent Item** is set to **Menu Item Root**. Changing the **Parent Item** to another menu link turns the current menu link into a submenu link.

Usually, submenu links will be displayed within the same menu as parent links. You've seen how this works in both the vertical **This Site** menu (where submenu items become visible after the visitor has clicked a main menu item) and in the horizontal **Top** menu (where submenu items become visible as drop-down items when the mouse cursor hovers over a main menu item).

However, you can also choose an altogether different presentation. A common practice is to put main navigation links horizontally along the top of the page and display second level links in a *separate* menu module (for example, in a vertical menu in the left-hand side column). This creates a clear visual distinction between the main menu items and their submenu items. At the same time it's clear that the two menus share some relationship. The parent item can be marked as "active" (using a different style or color) when the related submenu is displayed.

An example is shown in the following screenshot. A primary link, **Activities**, is shown in a (horizontal) main menu bar. When this link is clicked, a separate submenu shows secondary links (submenu links) to **Lectures**, **Meetings**, **Exhibitions**, and **Seminars**:

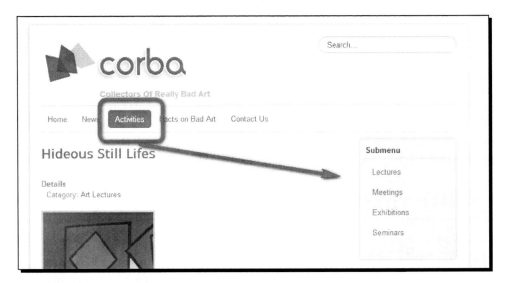

This menu setup can be useful if you've got a lot of submenu contents. Instead of displaying all links within the same menu, you can use a column or any other part of the page to display a list of submenu links.

How do you build this kind of menu system in Joomla? In short, you create a copy of the main menu, set the original main menu to show only the top-level links, and set the copy to show only the second-level links. Joomla will automatically display the appropriate submenu when the parent item is chosen in the top menu. We won't add a split menu system to our example site, as it doesn't have the amount of content that would justify an elaborate multilevel navigation. However, feel free to experiment on your own website, as this is a very powerful technique. The following are the required steps:

1. Suppose you have created a **Top** menu with two or more submenu links. Navigate to **Extensions | Module Manager**. Select the **Top** menu module and click on **Duplicate**:

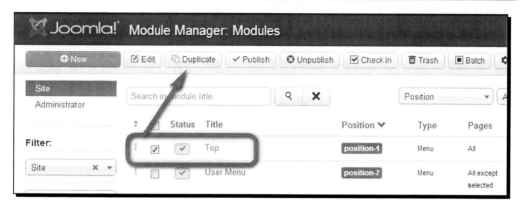

2. The same list now contains a copy, called **Top (2)**. Open the copy and enter a new title (for example, **Submenu**). Select a **Position** (for example, **position-7**).

3. Set the **Status** of the module to **Published**.

4. Under **Basic Options**, set the **Start Level** to **2** and the **End Level** to **2**. This will make the menu display only second-level menu items:

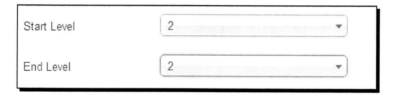

5. Click **Save & Close**. The menu copy is ready.

6. Now edit the original **Top** menu module to show only the top-level items. Set **Start Level** to **1** and **End Level** to **1**. This indicates the menu will only show primary links.

7. The submenu is done! By default, the submenu links are hidden. Only when the visitor clicks the top menu **Activities** link, is the submenu displayed elsewhere on the page.

Have a go hero – arrange menus any way you like

Joomla's split menu capabilities allow you to design exactly the type of navigation that's appropriate for your site. You can place a row of main menu links at the top of the page and position secondary (submenu) links in the left-hand side or right-hand side column. Try to figure out what arrangement of main and secondary links fits your site best and how you can realize this in Joomla. Here are a few suggestions (some common arrangements of site navigation) to get you going:

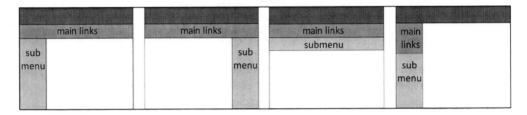

Joomla's default template allows for simple drop-down menus. However, there are many extensions available that are specifically designed to support more advanced horizontal drop-down menus. There are also many menu extensions available that support horizontal drop-down menus in any template. We'll see an example of this in *Chapter 11, Creating an Attractive Design: Working with Templates*.

Exploring menu module settings

When creating or editing a menu module, the module details and options allow you to control exactly where the menu is shown and how it displays. In many cases, the default settings will do—but if you really want control over your menus, it's a good idea to explore the wide range of additional possibilities. In the **Module Manager**, click on the menu name (such as **This Site** or **About CORBA**). The **Module Manager: Module Menu** screen appears:

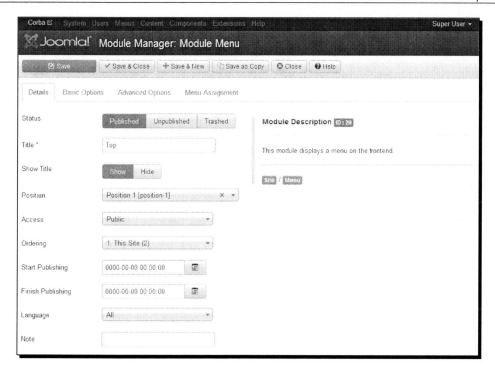

Switching to the menu module screen

You can customize menu properties by navigating to **Extensions** | **Module Manager** and finding the appropriate menu module. However, we've seen there's also a shortcut available, which takes you straight from the **Menu Manager** to the corresponding menu module settings:

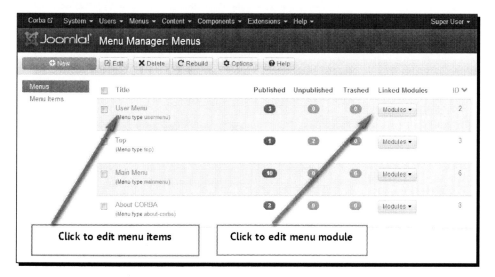

In the **Modules linked to this menu** column, click on the link to the menu module. Usually, there will be just one linked module available; however, if you use more instances of the same menu in different module positions, these will be listed here. The shortcut in the **Modules linked to this menu** column will display a pop-up screen with (almost) all the same module options as found through the **Menu Manager**.

Let's have a close look at all the menu module options available in the **Module Manager: Module Menu** screen.

The Details tab

The settings in the **Details** section control basic properties, such as the menu title and the menu position:

Properties	Description
Status	Select **Published** to show the menu module on the site, select **Unpublished** to hide it, or **Trashed** to send it to the trash can.
Title	Enter the title of the module that can be displayed on the frontend.
Show Title	In many cases, you can set the **Title** to hide. After all, why should a main menu be called Main Menu or This Site? Web visitors recognize a menu when they see one. Only special function menus (Login) may display a title.
Position	Select the predefined position where you want the module to be displayed. The options you have here depend on the template you're using. Template designers can add as many positions as they like, giving you maximum flexibility in assigning positions to menus and other modules.
Access	When you apply different access levels to different parts of your site, here you can determine who has access to this menu. When set to **Public**, every visitor can see the menu. Choose **Registered** to only give registered users access and **Special** to give only users with author status or higher access.
Ordering	You can put more than one module within a **Position**; by changing the **Ordering** setting, you control the order of the modules in the **Position** selected. The drop-down box shows all modules in the current **Position** (for an example, see *Time for action – changing menu item order*, explained earlier in this chapter).

Properties	Description
Start Publishing, Finish Publishing	If a (menu) module should be displayed for a limited period of time, enter the start and end dates here. If you just want to postpone publishing, only enter a start date.
Language	If you have a multilingual site, assign the appropriate language to this module.
Note	Room for a short note about this module for yourself or for others that have access to the administrative interface.

The Basic Options tab

The **Basic Options** tab contains a couple of essential settings:

Option	Description
Select Menu	Select the menu (found through **Menus | Menu Manager**) from which this menu should draw its contents.
Base Item	Usually, Joomla will only display submenu items related to the current menu item. Use the **Base Item** feature to display submenu items that are not related to the current active menu item. You can select a specific **Base Item** and the corresponding **Start Level** and **End Level** to display submenu items that would not normally show on the current page.
Start Level, End Level	**Start Level** and **End Level** allow you to split a menu showing primary links (level 1) at the top of the page and secondary links in (level 2 and further) a split menu in some other position. See the *Creating split submenus* section in this chapter for an example.
Show Sub-menu Items	Should submenu items be displayed even when the parent is not active (not selected)? Select **No** to have submenu items display only when the parent menu item is clicked. If the site template supports drop-down menus, select **Yes** here to get the menu to display drop-down submenus when the user hovers over the main menu items.

The Advanced Options tab

You'll probably only adjust the **Advanced Options** tab in certain specific situations.

Option	Description
Menu Tag ID, **Menu Class Suffix**, **Module Class Suffix**	You can set the **Menu Tag ID**, **Menu Class Suffix**, and **Module Class Suffix** to tweak the layout of the menu. These options are only relevant if you want fine control over the layout of your menu through the CSS stylesheet. In the default Joomla 3 template (called Protostar), the horizontal menu uses " nav-pills" (without quotes, but with a starting space) as the **Menu Class Suffix**. The vertical **This Site** menu in Joomla 3 uses a **Module Class Suffix**: "_menu" (without quotes).
Target Position	This is only relevant in some templates to specify the location of drop-down or pop-up menus.
Alternative Layout	Here you can select a custom layout for the current module, provided the selected template (or module) allows for these additional layout options.
Caching, **Cache Time**	If you have set a caching value in the Global Configuration, you can override it here for this module.
Module Tag, **Bootstrap Size**, **Header Tag**, **Header Class**, **Module Style**	These options allow you to customize the module layout, that is, by specifying the HTML tag used for the module title and the module itself.

The Menu Assignment tab

The **Menu Assignment** section allows you to control on which pages (through which menu links) the menu module will be accessible.

Option	Description
Module Assignment	On what pages should the module be displayed? By default, a module will be shown on all pages. Choose between **On all pages**, **On no pages**, **Only on the pages selected**, or **On all pages except those selected**. The actual selection is made in the next step.
Menu Selection	When you select any other **Module Assignment** than **On all pages** or **On no pages**, this option appears. Here you can select menus and the menu links they contain. This selection controls on which pages (that are linked to through the listed menu Items) the module is displayed.

What types of menu links are available?

Up to now, we've focused on creating menus and tweaking menu display and settings. Of course, menus are about the hyperlinks they contain, so let's have a closer look at the way these are created and modified. As creating menu links is an essential activity in Joomla, you're already familiar with the basic steps it takes to create these—navigate to **Menus**, click on the name of the menu, and click on **New**. Alternatively, click on the **Add New Menu Item** fly-out menu.

Every time you create a new link, you first have to select the **Menu Item Type**. You're presented with a pop-up screen containing an impressive list of available types. Click any of the headings to reveal all the available options:

 This list of Menu Item Types can be different in your particular Joomla installation. After you've installed a component that contains its own new page types, these can show up in the Menu Item Type list too.

When building the example site you've added links using a few of the available Menu Item Types. For example, you've already created links pointing to articles (**Articles| Single Article**) and others pointing to article overview pages (**Articles | Category Blog**). You've also added a link through **Contacts| Single Contact** to add a special function page—a contact form.

However, there are many more menu item types to choose from. Remember, Joomla menu item types are not about different types of menu navigation, they are about creating different types of content. They represent different preset ways of displaying all kinds of content.

The following table provides a short overview of what the available Menu Item Types mean and how you can deploy them. We won't go into the details here (as Joomla's Menu Item Types are really not about navigation, but about creating content). However, it's a good idea to browse the menu options mentioned next to get an idea of what they have to offer. We'll cover relevant Menu Item Types in more detail in other chapters about adding content (the references to these chapters are shown in the table):

Name	What kind of menu link is this?
Contacts	These menu links take the site visitors to a page with data on one or more contacts. They are part of the Joomla Contacts component (see *Chapter 4, Web Building Basics: Creating a Site in an Hour*).
Articles	You will probably use these links the most. These are menu links pointing to an article, or to overview pages (category pages), or to pages containing featured articles (see *Chapter 6, Chapter 6: Creating Killer Content: Adding and Editing Articles* and *Chapter 7, Welcoming your Visitors: Creating Attractive Home Pages and Overview Pages*). The **Create Article** link is used for registered users who have permission to add articles. You'll learn more about this in the next chapter.
Smart Search	A link to an alternative site search page, replacing the standard Search system found further down in this list. Smart Search features auto-completion and suggests alternative search phrases. It works in conjunction with a plugin and component, both called Smart Search. To be able to use this system, first enable the Smart Search plugin and use the Smart Search component to index all content.
Newsfeeds	Link to a page with one or more RSS feeds, news from other sites.
Search	Link to a page displaying the search engine of the site and listing the search results. Search is the "old" Joomla search engine system. It's still available just in case the new Smart Search system doesn't function properly (which, for example, can happen on very large sites).
Users Manager	Links to special pages for users with additional permissions, for example, a registration and login page.

Name	What kind of menu link is this?
Weblinks	Link to pages with links to other sites. The Web links you want to show, you must first enter via the Weblinks component.
Wrapper	Link to a page that shows an external web page within this site (in a frame).
System links	External URL: Link to an external site. Menu item alias: a copy of an existing menu link. Separator: Not a link, but a line used to visually separate different parts of the menu.

Have a go hero – try out Menu Item Types

The extensive list of Menu Item Types looks inviting; why don't you have a go at the different types of menu items? Add a new menu link to the main menu and choose a menu item type you haven't used yet. Check out the **Search**, **External Link**, or the **Separator** menu item types; they're pretty straightforward. Some others, such as the **User** link, are quite complex and won't make sense at first glance—but don't worry, they won't mess up your site permanently and you can easily change or delete unwanted menu items again. In the course of this book, you'll learn to use many of these menu item types.

Why do you have to create menu links manually?

You may wonder why Joomla doesn't automate the process of adding menu links as soon as you create new content. Manually creating menu links gives you much more control. You determine what type of page a menu link points to, in what order menu links appear, on what pages they show up, and so on. And don't worry, you'll only make menu items pointing to the main pages and content groups—not to each and every page. Menus usually point to overview pages, a couple of selected articles, and special function pages (such as a search page). Joomla will automatically create links to any amount of articles below the main levels, using overview pages, as you've seen in *Chapter 6, Creating Killer Content: Adding and Editing Articles*.

Creating plain text links

Sometimes you'll want to show hyperlinks that are not part of a menu, but are embedded in an article text. To create these, you use the **Article** button at the bottom of the article editor screen:

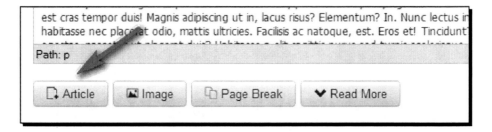

This makes adding links very straightforward. Let's find out how it works.

Time for action – creating text links

We'll create an internal hyperlink, a text link from one page to another page on the same site.

1. Go to **Content | Article Manager** and open the article that you want to add a link to.

2. Place the mouse cursor in the article text, on the position where you want to insert the hyperlink.

3. Now click on the **Article** button at the bottom of the editor screen. A pop-up screen appears, listing all articles on the site. Click the title of the article you want to link to (in this example, **Bad Art Exhibition Coming Up**):

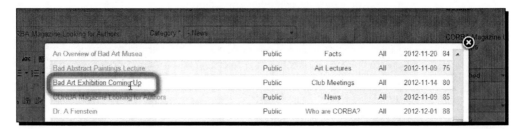

4. The pop-up screen is closed. You're done! A link to the target article is inserted:

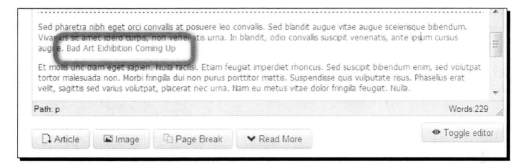

5. Let's tweak the link text a little. By default, it consists of the target article title. To change this, you can edit the hyperlink text just as you would any other text in the article editor screen. However, if you want to replace the whole hyperlink text, it's easiest to switch to HTML code view. Otherwise, you could inadvertently remove the hyperlink by changing it to plain text. To edit the text, click on the **Toggle editor** button.

6. Now the HTML code of the text is displayed. Locate the hyperlink code, the code starting with `<a href`. It should be similar to the following:

```
<a href="index.php?option=com_content&amp;view=article&amp;id=80&amp;catid=80&amp;Itemid=476">Bad Art Exhibition Coming Up</a></p>
```

7. To replace the link text to **Visit the exhibition**, change this as follows:

```
<a href="index.php?option=com_content&amp;view=article&amp;id=80&amp;catid=80&amp;Itemid=476">Visit the Exhibition</a></p>
```

8. Click on **Save & Close** and click on **View site**. Browse to the article you've edited; it now contains a text link.

What just happened?

You've created a text hyperlink from an article to another page in the same site. You can create a hyperlink to any page on the site, providing there is already a menu link pointing to it.

 If you often need to add text links to articles, there's another editor available which gives you even more flexibility—the **Joomla Content Editor** (**JCE**). It allows you to just click and select any item on the site, not just articles. To know more about the JCE editor, see *Chapter 10, Getting the Most out of Your Site: Extending Joomla*.

Pop quiz – test your menu knowledge

Q1. How many menus can you add to your website?

    a.   Six menus (the Main Menu and five other menus).

    b.   As many as you want.

    c.   You can only have one Main Menu.

Q2. How can you add submenu items to a menu?

    a.   By creating "parent links" and "child links".

    b.   By assigning a different Parent Item to a menu link than the default (Home).

    c.   By creating a new menu.

Q3. When you create a new menu link, why does Joomla show such a big list of Menu Item Types?

    a.   To enhance navigation.

    b.   To enable you to create new menus.

    c.   To enable you to create different types of target pages.

Summary

In this chapter, we learned a lot about creating user-friendly navigation through Joomla menus. This is what we covered:

- New menu links are added to the bottom of the list. To change a menu item's order, you move links up or down in the Menu Item Manager.

- Menus can be more than one level deep. By assigning a parent item to a menu link, you create a submenu item.

- You can move links that don't fit the main menu to a separate menu. You can also create interrelated menus, such as a main menu showing parent links and a secondary menu that automatically shows child links.

- Submenus aren't the only way to make secondary content visible. Main links can point to overview pages with (automatically generated) links to category content.

- To create hyperlinks in an article to another article, use the **Article** button in the editor screen.

You've now finished making a basic, functional, and easy-to-navigate website.

In the next chapters, we'll take things further—after all, dynamic database-driven CMS magic doesn't stop at creating basic sites. In the next chapter, you'll learn how to add extra functionality, such as the ability for your visitors to contribute content or to register as site members.

9

Opening Up the Site: Enabling Users to Log In and Contribute

In the last few chapters, you have set up a great little site, but still there's something quite old fashioned about it. You're the only person who has access to it and who is allowed to add and manage content. This means you haven't yet benefited from Joomla's built-in tools to create a team of specially designated power users who can log in to the site to add or edit content. In Joomla, you're allowed to add as many content contributors as necessary and you can give them permission to create or edit articles, or to do even more.

But opening up your site to the world doesn't end there; Joomla offers some powerful methods to engage your web visitors and turn them into active users. You can enable visitors to register and give them exclusive access to premium content. Also, you can allow them to rate articles, giving others a good indication of must-read content.

In this chapter, you'll learn about:

- ◆ Creating and managing user accounts: enabling web team members to log in and maintain the site contents
- ◆ Configuring self-registration for site visitors and creating content for registered users only
- ◆ Creating user groups and permissions: a practical example of how you can use ACL

One of the biggest recent changes in Joomla is the introduction of a new system to manage user permissions, usually referred to as **Access Controls Lists (ACL)**. Currently, Joomla offers you almost infinite control of what users can see and do on the site. However, out of the box the ACL system comes with a set of basic user groups and default permissions—and in many cases these may offer all the features you need. We'll first have a look at the basics; later in this chapter we'll cover an example of more advanced ways to deploy the ACL system by crafting made-to-measure user groups and their distinctive permission settings.

What are the default user groups and their permissions?

After you've installed Joomla, a series of users groups is already present, each with their own permissions applied. Let's have a look at the default setup.

To view the default groups and their permissions, go to **System | Global Configuration** and click on the **Permissions** tab. The **Permissions Settings** screen is displayed:

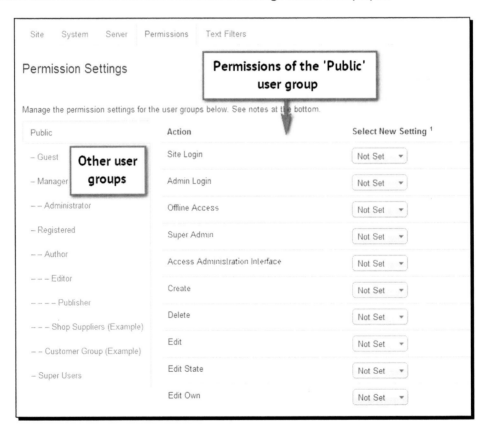

Here, all currently available user groups are displayed in a set of panels. A **user group** is a collection of users sharing the same permissions, such as **Public**, **Manager**, or **Administrator**. The panel showing the permissions of the current group is displayed expanded (by default this is the top group, **Public**).

In the expanded panel for the **Public** group, their generic (site-wide) permissions are shown: **Site Login**, **Admin Login**, and so on. These permission settings control the things users are allowed do on the site. For the default user groups, these permissions have already been set.

When adding new user accounts to the site, you assign users to one of these **User Groups**, granting them various levels of access to the site. If you need tailor-made sets of permissions, you can create your own user groups with specific sets of permissions. However, it's best to start using the default groups and their permissions. Here's an overview.

Public and Guest users – the site visitors

The Public level is the very basic level; anyone visiting your site is considered part of the Public group. Members of this group can view the frontend of the site, but they don't have any special permissions.

By default, the **Access** level of content in a Joomla site is set to **Public**. The site administrator can set the Access level for different types of content, ranging from modules and menu items to individual articles (shown in the following screenshot):

When the **Access** is set to **Public**, this indicates that anyone belonging to the Public group (your site visitors) will be able to see that content. When the Access is set to any of the other available levels (covered later in this chapter), specific "viewing rules" apply for specific user groups.

At first glance, the **Guest** group seems similar to the Public user group—Guests are users who have not logged in. However, the presence of the Guest group serves a specific purpose. Other than Public content, Guest content is hidden once users have logged in. In other words, assigning the Guest access level allows you to show content to non-logged in users and to *hide* content for logged-in users. For example, if you have a banner module on your site that says **Sign in now**, you can hide this module for people who have already logged in by setting its access level to Guest.

Registered users – the user group that can log in

These are regular site visitors, except for the fact that they have registered and activated their account. After they have logged in with their account details, Registered users can view content that may be hidden from ordinary site visitors (Public users) because the **Access** level of that content has been set to **Registered**. Setting **Access** to **Registered** allows you to present all kinds of content to logged-in users that ordinary (Public) users can't see.

Although **Registered** users have special access rights, they can't contribute content. They're part of the user community, not of the web team. We'll discuss user registration later in this chapter (see the *Allowing visitors to register* section).

Author, Editor, and Publisher – the frontend content contributors

Up to now, you've only experienced Joomla's backend editing capabilities. To change anything on the site, you log in to the backend to access the administrative interface. However, it is also possible to log in to the frontend and edit or add articles straight away, through a frontend content editor screen. We'll see how that works in a moment.

The idea behind having frontend editing possibilities is to lower the threshold for non-technical content contributors. They don't have to bother to learn the backend interface and can edit, and add, articles directly in an interface that they already know—the public frontend of the site.

Authors, Editors, and Publishers are allowed to log in to the frontend, to edit or add articles. There are three types of frontend content contributors, each with their specific permission levels:

- ◆ **Authors** can *create* new content for approval by a Publisher or someone higher in rank. They can edit their own articles, but can't edit existing articles created by others.

- **Editors** can *create* new articles and *edit* existing articles. A Publisher or higher must approve their submissions.

- **Publishers** can *create*, *edit*, and *publish*, *unpublish*, or *trash* articles in the frontend. They cannot *delete* content.

Authors and editors can't publish content. Only after approval by a Publisher (or someone higher in rank) will the content they submit be visible. Although this has its advantages—someone will be double-checking all content before it's published—having to review all of the new articles can create an extra workload for those with publishing permissions, and it could possibly turn into a bottleneck impeding a steady flow of new content. That might be a reason to instead assign Publisher (instead of Author) permissions to your web team members. Publishers have the same permissions as authors and editors, but they are the ones who can also actually publish content.

Generally, assigning a user to the Publisher group will be a good choice when you want web team members to be able to individually add and publish content, without you having to grant them access to the (more complex) backend of the site. Publishers can easily create new content without having to learn their way around in the backend—or being able to create havoc by changing things they shouldn't.

Manager, Administrator, Super User – the backend content contributors and administrators

Finally, there are three types of backend users. They have all the permissions of the frontend group, but they are also allowed to log in to the backend to add and manage content and to perform administrative tasks.

- **Managers** can do all that Publishers can, but they are also allowed to log in to the backend of the site to *create*, *edit*, or *delete* articles. They can also create and manage categories. They have limited access to administration functions.

- **Administrators** can do all that Managers can and have access to more administration functions. They can *manage* users, edit, or configure extensions, and change the site template. They can use manager screens (**User Manager**, **Article Manager**, and so on.) and can create, delete, edit, and change the state of users, articles, and so on.

- **Super Users** can do everything possible in the backend. When Joomla is installed, there's always one Super User account created. That's usually the person who builds and customizes the website. In the current example website, you're the Super User.

Shop Suppliers and Customers – two example user groups

If you've installed Joomla with sample content, you'll notice two groups in the **Permissions Settings** screen that we haven't covered yet—**Shop Suppliers (Example)** and **Customer Group (Example)**. These user groups have been added as part of the sample data, to show how you can create customized groups.

Enabling users to log in and contribute content

Let's find out how you can use the default user groups to add a couple of people allowed to log in to the site and contribute content. After you've installed Joomla, there's just one user present—the Super User. By navigating to (**Users | User Manager**), you can check the account details of the Super User—the **Name** (by default this is Super User), the **User Name** (this is **admin**, unless you've changed this yourself when setting up your account), whether this user account is **Enabled**, the user's **Email** address, the user's **Last Visit Date** and **Registration Date** and the user's **ID** (an identifying user number that's used by the system):

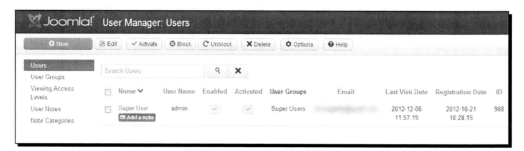

Click the **Name** of the user to edit their account details. For example, for security reasons you'll probably want to change the default **User Name** (admin) to something that's harder to guess. Just enter a new name and save changes. The next time you log in, use your updated credentials.

There's also a shortcut available to take you to your own user settings—the **Edit Profile** quick icon link in the Control Panel. In this screen you can change your **Name**, **Login Name**, **Password**, and other details. However, you can't manage all account details here. For example, you can only change the user groups this account is assigned to via **Users | User Manager** and clicking on the account **Name**.

Let's find out how you can make use of the User Manager, Joomla's backend manager where you can view, edit, and create site users. We'll add a few other people to the site who, apart from the Super User, are allowed to add content.

Time for action – adding a user with frontend authoring permissions

Let's create user accounts for a couple of club members who'll become content contributors.

1. Navigate to **Users** | **User Manager**.

2. There's just one user, you. By default, Joomla calls this first user **Super User** (and this user belongs to the **Super Users** group). To add another user, click on the **New** button in the toolbar.

3. In the **Add New User** screen, add **Account Details** as desired. In this example, we've entered `Jim Van Gogh` in the **Name** field. In the **Login Name** field we've entered `jvgogh`. Enter a **Password** and a valid **Email** address for the new user:

4. Click the **Assigned User Groups** tab and, select **Author**. This will allow the new user to submit and edit content (after logging in to the frontend of the site):

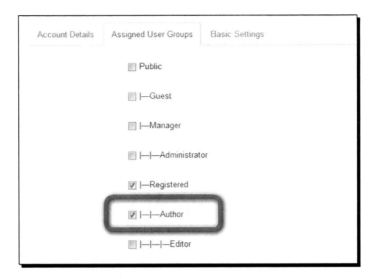

5. Click on **Save & Close**. The **User Manager** screen now shows the new **User**:

What just happened?

In the site user list in the **User Manager**, you're no longer on your own. As Mr. Van Gogh has been assigned to the **Author** user group, he is now permitted to log in to the frontend of the site and add content. However, to enable the new user to do anything, we'll have to create a way for him to log in to the frontend. After all, the method of logging in that you yourself have been using (through a separate backend URL such as `http://www.yoursite.com/administrator`) is only accessible to users with backend access—and Mr. Van Gogh doesn't have those permissions.

Enabling content contributors to log in to the frontend

Once you've assigned users to the Authors, Editors, or Publishers group, there has to be an entrance to the site frontend. In Joomla, the frontend entrance is the login form. After you've installed Joomla, the Login Form module is already enabled and it's displayed on the home page. If you haven't changed this default setup, you can skip the next step. If you've disabled or removed the login form, enable the login form as described in the next section.

Time for action – put a Login Form on the home page

The Login Module is part of the Joomla default installation. Here's how you make sure it's visible on the home page.

1. Navigate to **Extensions | Module Manager**. Locate the **Login Form** module and click its name to edit the module settings. Select **Status: Published** to publish the module. The **Position** is set to **position-7** to display the **Login** module in the right-hand side column in the current site template.

2. Make sure **Menu Assignment** is set to **Home** only; this way, the **Login** module will only show up on the home page. We can safely assume that users will probably want to log in to the site directly from the home page, so there's no need to clutter valuable screen real estate with a login form on other pages.

3. In this example, we'll leave the **Basic Options** unchanged. You could enter some **Pre-text** or **Post-text** here—a text shown before or just below the **Login** module.

4. Click on **Save** and click on **View Site** to check the output on the frontend. In the left-hand side column, the **Login Form** is now shown below the **Main Menu**:

What just happened?

You've now enabled users to access your site through a **Login Form**. Maybe you've noticed that as soon as you add this form, it also displays a **Create an account** link. By default, Joomla is configured to allow user self-registration. You'll read more about user registration later in this chapter.

Time for action – logging in as a frontend content contributor

There's a user assigned to the **Author** group, there's a **Login Form** to enable this user to enter the site—so why don't we
try out how our Author logs in and submits content?

> **1.** Navigate to the frontend of the site and use the **Login Form** to log in as the new user (in this example **jvgogh**).
>
> **2.** In the right-hand column, a **User Menu** appears. This is part of the Joomla default installation and it's set to be only visible when a user has logged in—that's why it turns up all of a sudden. The **User Menu** provides links to functionalities only available to registered users. For example, it allows the Author to view and edit his or her user details. However, we're primarily interested in the possibility of entering new content, so let's click on the **Submit an Article** link. Now here's a surprise; the Joomla frontend turns into a live web page editor!

3. For testing purposes, enter a title, some article text, and select the appropriate **Category** (click on the **Publishing** tab to find the **Category** drop-down box). In this example, we've created a dummy article called **CORBA welcomes new members** in the **News** category.

4. Click on **Save** to submit the article. You'll see a notice: **Article successfully submitted**.

What just happened?

You've just logged in to your own site as if you were part of the **Author** user group. As an Author, you're able to submit content on the frontend of the site. The new article isn't published on the site yet—we'll get to that in a minute.

Have a go hero – create a frontend User Menu

In the previous example, you've seen a **User Menu** suddenly appear when a registered user has logged in. This **User Menu** is pre-installed when you choose to install Joomla with sample data. Now what if you haven't installed sample data? You'll obviously want your logged-in Authors to be able to submit content. To do this, create your own dedicated menu for frontend users.

The procedure is pretty straightforward; these are roughly the steps involved. In the **Menu Manager**, create a new menu and call it, for example, **User Menu**. You now have an empty menu—click on the menu name and click on the **New** button to add links. To enable authors (or higher) to submit an article, in the **Menu Item Type** list add a link of the **Articles | Create Article** type. Set the **Access** level to **Special**; this ensures the menu link is only visible for users with **Author** permissions or higher. Save your changes and add a menu module aimed at displaying the menu. In the **Menu Manager**, click **Add a module for this menu type**. Make sure to set your new menu module to be published. If you're a bit rusty on menu creating skills, please have a look again at *Chapter 8, Helping Your Visitors Find What They Want: Managing Menus*.

Allowing users to manage their own accounts

The default login form already enables users to log in, create a new account, and retrieve their password or username. However, instead of using the login form you can also create separate menu links to a login page, a self-registration page, or to a page enabling users to manage their account details (for example, to change their password). You'll find these particular link types in the **Users Manager** section of the **Select a Menu Item Type** screen. We'll try a few of these **Users Manager** links out later in this chapter, in the *Allowing visitors to register* section.

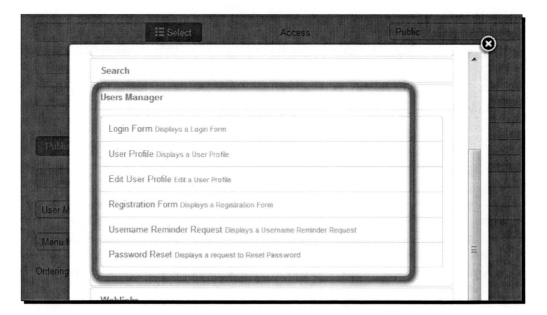

Reviewing and publishing team content submissions

Up to now, you've seen how you can create user accounts for team members on your site and how you can enable them to log in. You've also switched to another role to see your site through the eyes of a logged-in team member—an Author, someone who's able to submit (but not publish) content. Now let's see how you can get submitted content to show on the site.

Time for action – reviewing and publishing submitted content

Once again, switch back to your original role, the Super User. Now that an Author has submitted an article, you should review and approve the new content to publish it.

1. Log in to the backend of your site in your default role, Super User. In the **Info Bar** (in the bottom-left area of the screen) Joomla notifies you that you've got exactly one message:

2. Click the number **1** link. Alternatively, you can view messages via **Components| Messaging | Read Private Messages**. You'll see this screen:

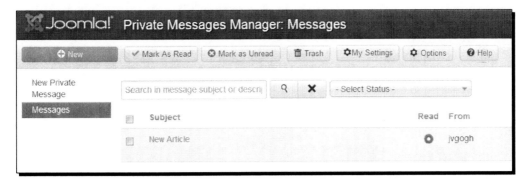

3. Click on **New Article** to read the message contents—**A new Article has been submitted by 'Jim Van Gogh' entitled 'CORBA Welcomes New Members'**.

Receiving submission reminders

Do you want to get an e-mail notification every time new content is submitted? Navigate to **Components | Messages | Read Private Messages** and click on the **My Settings** button in the toolbar. Select **Email New Messages: Yes**.

4. To review and publish the new article, navigate to **Content | Article Manager** and locate the new article. (Another way to find new articles is to navigate to **Site | Control Panel** and explore the **Recently Added Articles** panel.) You'll notice a red circle in the **Status** column indicating the article is still unpublished. Click on the title of the article to view and edit it as desired:

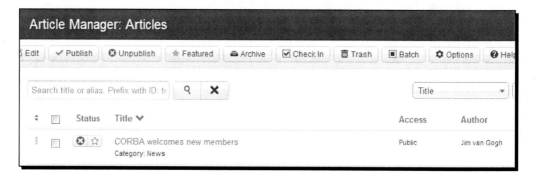

5. When you're happy with the article, click on **Save**. In the **Status** column of the **Article Manager**, click on the red circle. It will turn into a green and white check mark.

6. Click on **View site**. In the **News** section, the new article is shown:

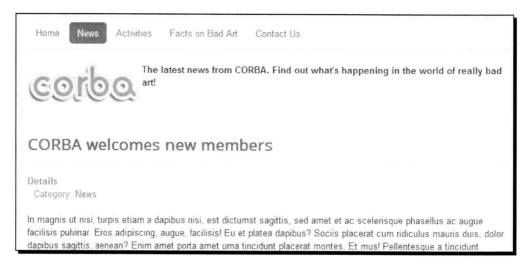

What just happened?

Logging in as the site administrator, you're able to check articles that have been submitted by authors. You can review an article, edit it, and publish it if you're happy with it.

Have a go hero – explore different User Group permissions

So far you've seen what Authors are allowed to do in Joomla. Why not explore other **User Groups** permissions? It's a good idea to change the new example user's permissions and log in as this user to get a grasp of the possibilities. Changing user permissions only takes a few clicks. The following are a few pointers to get you going.

Find out what editors and publishers can do

Navigate to **Users | User Manager** and click on the name of the test user (in our example, **Jim Van Gogh**) that you've added earlier and who's assigned to the **Author** group. Now, in the **Assigned User Groups** section, select **Editor** to give the user new frontend editing permissions. Click on **Save** and log in to the frontend with the username and password of Mr. Van Gogh. You'll notice a small difference—if you click on the wheel icon displayed next to the article title, you get access to a special **Edit** link:

This opens up a range of new possibilities. When clicking on it, the web page turns into an editor screen just like the one you've seen before when submitting an article (see *Time for action – logging in as a frontend content contributor* earlier in this chapter). As you can see, editors can change the text of existing articles by editing them in the frontend of the site—and immediately publish the edited article. Although they can't create and publish content on their own (without approval of a Publisher or higher), they are allowed to make changes to existing content on their own.

To find out what Publishers can do, change the **User Group** that Mr. Van Gogh is a member of to **Publisher**. After logging in to the frontend, at first sight there are no differences to this role and the Editor role. However, after you've edited or created an article, saving the article will immediately publish it. The article won't be submitted for review first.

Finding out what backend users can do

A final step in "upgrading" user accounts is assigning one of the three backend accounts: **Manager**, **Administrator**, or **Super User**. For example, change the existing **Publisher** user account and assign the user to the **Manager** group. You can now log in with this user's **Username** and **Password** to the backend of the site (via `http://www.yoursite.com/administrator`):

After logging in, you'll be taken to the backend Control Panel where you can add and edit content the same way you're used to in your role as site administrator. As the new user has been assigned the **Manager** role, he has permissions to do most things with content that site administrators can (creating new categories and articles, managing contacts, and so on). However, you'll notice a manager can't manage users, extensions, or templates. Compared to the backend options that you as a Super User are used to, only a limited number of menus, menu items, and shortcuts are available:

Enabling self-registration – allowing visitors to register

In the previous section, you set up new user accounts manually in the backend using the **User Manager**. Giving a team of content contributors access to the site is a great way to collaborate in maintaining the site and keeping its contents up-to-date.

Another way to open up your site is to enable user self-registration. That way, a user community can develop and any amount of users can register themselves without the site administrator having to do or approve anything (of course, the administrator is still in charge and has the ability to block or remove users).

Registered users don't contribute content, but they do have exclusive access to parts of the site where the **Access** level is set to—you guessed it—**Registered**. Let's first find out how to create "members only" content and enable visitors to join through self-registration.

How do you enable users to create their own account?

It may have skipped your attention, but when you set up a **Login Form** (see *Time for action – put a Login Form on the home page* earlier in this chapter), you've also enabled user self-registration. By default, the **Login** module not only allows existing users to log in, it also contains a link inviting visitors to create a new account:

 If you don't want users to be able to register, navigate to **Users | User Manager** and select the **Options** button. In the **Component** screen, make sure **Allow User Registration** is set to **No** (the default value is **Yes**). Now the **Create an account link** will disappear.

Displaying a Login menu link

Although Joomla by default is set up to display a small login
form on the home page, you may find this too big or too conspicuous. If you'd rather show
just a small **Login** link pointing to a separate login page, that's possible too.

To add a **Login** link, navigate to **Menus | Main Menu**, click on **New**, and in the **Select a
Menu Item Type** pop-up screen, select **Users Manager| Login Form**. Add a title for the link
(for example, **Login**), and click on **Save & Close**. Now a **Login Form** page will be displayed
after the visitor has clicked on the **Login** link:

As the **Login Form** on the home page left-hand column is no longer necessary, unpublish the
Login Form module via **Extensions | Module Manager**.

Time for action – register yourself and log in

Let's see what site visitors have to do to create an account. To test this, we'll create a dummy
user account ourselves. Log out of the site and navigate to the frontend.

1. On the frontend, click the **Create an account** link below the **Login Form** in the
    left-hand side column (if you've created a menu link to a separate login page,
    as previously described, then click on this menu link and click on **Don't have an
    account?**). This will take you to the **User Registration** page. Enter your details and
    make sure to use a valid **Email** address.

2. After clicking on **Register**, you are taken to the home page. On the home page, Joomla displays a system message confirming your account has been created.

3. Joomla will now send you an automatically generated e-mail. It contains a link you must click on to activate your new user account. You'll be taken to the home page and a confirmation message will be displayed—**Your Account has been successfully activated. You can now login using the username and password you chose during the registration.**

What just happened?

You're now officially a member of your own site! Try this out by using the **Login Form** on the home page. Enter your **Username** and **Password** and click on the **Login** button. You'll notice the **Login Form** confirms you're logged in and shows a **Log out** link. However, logging in as a registered user doesn't make much sense yet, since there's no special content that only registered users can access. We'll take care of that in a minute.

You can also enable users to register without having to enter a valid e-mail address. To do this, navigate to **Users| User Manager** and click on the **Options** button. Set **New User Account Activation** to **None**. However, be aware this can lower the threshold for spammers to create fake member accounts on your site.

Hiding content for non-registered users

Creating "members only" content doesn't take much more than setting the access level of an item to **Registered**. This item will be hidden for regular users, but it will show up for those who have logged in. Most of Joomla's building blocks can be set to a specific access level. Whether this block is just one specific page, a module, or all of the contents of a specific category, you can set it to be visible to registered users only. This basically means that you can make your site look very different to different types of users. Public users may only see a basic website; registered users have the same content plus a whole bunch of extra articles, menus, menu links, or modules.

Time for action – hiding content from non-registered users

Let's explore how hiding content works. By default, every menu item is visible—the **Access Level** is set to **Public**. We'll change that setting for the **Activities** link that's currently shown in the **Main Menu**:

Let's make this **Activities** link only visible for registered users that have logged in:

1. Go to **Menus | Main Menu** and click on the **Activities** link to edit it.

2. In the menu links **Details**, set the **Access** level to **Registered**, and click on **Save & Close**.

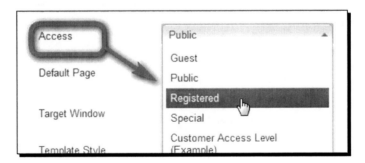

What just happened?

That's it! By changing a single menu item parameter, you've effectively hidden the menu item from non-registered users. The output is shown in the following screenshot:

The **Activities** link will only be displayed after a registered user has logged in.

Have a go hero – changing access level settings

You may want to explore the way you can change access levels for different items on your site. Take a look at the details of any article, menu item, or module—you'll find that there's always the same set of **Access** level choices available. For example, if you would like to make a whole menu visible for registered users only, you'd set the **Access** level of that particular menu module:

 What's the Special access level all about? You'll have noticed that there are four default access levels—not just **Public**, **Guest**, and **Registered**—but also **Special**. Whatever is set to **Special** is only visible for authors and higher. You'll read more about access levels later in this chapter, in the *What Viewing Access Levels are available?* section.

Getting your visitors to "register to read more"

It's great to be able to completely hide contents from non-registered users, but this approach does have one drawback. It doesn't encourage users to register as they simply can't see what they are missing out on. Sometimes, it's better to show non-registered users only part of an article and invite them to join (register) to read more.

On the example site, we'll do just that. We won't completely hide content from non-registered users, as this would leave a very sparse website for first time visitors, that wouldn't really persuade them to explore the hidden stuff.

Time for action – partially hiding content from non-registered users

Suppose your client wants to offer their site members some exclusive content; anyone registering to the CORBA site can read all about exclusive club meetings. Let's make sure the content shown through the **Activities | Club Meetings** menu link is displayed only partly—unless users register:

1. Make sure you're logged in to the backend of the site as the Super User. Open the current **Activities** menu link (**Menus | Main Menu**) to edit it. Make sure the link itself is visible for all—the **Status** should be **Published**, the **Access** should be **Public**.

2. Under **Advanced Options | Article Options**, set **Show Unauthorised Links** to **Yes**. This is the step that takes care of the "Register to read more" magic. Of all articles that have been assigned **Registered** status only the intro text will be displayed. **Save & Close** the menu link.

3. To set the access level of the desired articles to **Registered**, navigate to **Content | Article Manager**. In the **Select Category** drop-down box, select **Club Meetings**.

4. Select all **Club Meetings** articles by clicking on the checkbox in the upper-left row:

		Status	Title ❤		Access	Author
↕	☑	Status	Title ❤		Access	Author
⋮	☑	✔ ☆	Bad Art Exhibition Coming Up Category: Club Meetings		Public	Super User
⋮	☑	✔ ★	The Art of Bob Ross Category: Club Meetings		Public	Super User
⋮	☑	✔ ★	This Years Meeting Category: Club Meetings		Public	Super User

5. Click on the **Batch** button. In the **Batch process the selected articles** pop-up screen, there's a **Set Access Level** drop-down box. Select **Registered**:

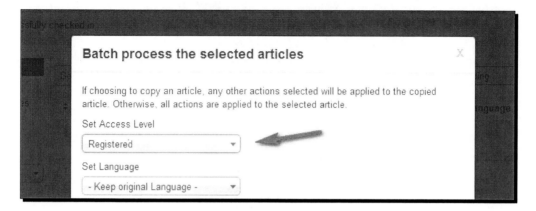

6. Click **Process**. In the **Access** column, you can see that all the articles are now **Registered**:

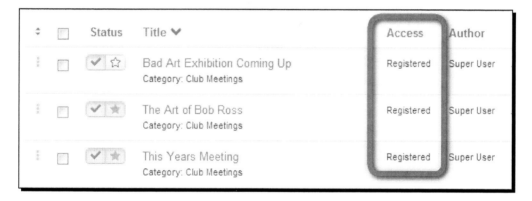

7. In the frontend of the website, navigate via the **Activities** link to the overview page containing articles from the **Club Meetings** (and **Art Lectures**) categories. You'll notice all **Club Meetings** articles are now only partially shown, with a **Register to read more** hyperlink:

What just happened?

You've created web pages that can be fully viewed by registered users only. Articles for **Registered** users are partially displayed with a **Register to read more...** link. This way, unregistered users get a taste of the registered content. When site visitors click on the **Register to read more...** link they are automatically taken to a separate login page.

Visitors that haven't yet created an account can click on **Don't have an account?** to do so now. If the visitors already have an account, they can log in here. You can check this out for yourself by logging in now with the dummy user account you created earlier.

Creating custom-made user groups

Up to now, we've used the user groups and their sets of permissions that are available in Joomla out of the box. However, you can also create custom-made user groups and assign them permissions to do and see just what you allow them. Instead of using the existing user groups and their predefined sets of permissions, you can create as many groups as you want and grant the people in those groups any combination of permissions. If you want, you can set permissions for specific parts of the site—permissions apply to either the whole site, or to specific components, categories, or items (such as a single article).

Creating a custom user group and assigning permissions involves the following four steps:

1. Create a user group (a group of people sharing the same permissions).

2. Tell Joomla what the group can see. What's visible on the site, what's hidden from them? In Joomla terms, this means you assign a **Viewing Access Level** to the group.

3. Tell Joomla what the group can do. What actions they can perform on the site. In Joomla terms, this means you set the **Permissions** for this user group.

4. Add users to the group.

First, we'll have a look at the types of **Permissions** you can assign and what **Viewing Access Levels** are available. After that, we'll find out how to set up a new user group with specific permissions using this four-step approach.

What are the permissions you can assign to user groups?

When assigning permissions (such as site-wide permissions found via **System | Global Configuration | Permissions**), nine types of permissions are available, such as **Site Login**, **Admin Login**, and so on. The following table outlines what the permission names mean:

Permission name	Allows user to do the following
Site Login	Log in to the frontend of the website
Admin Login	Log in to the backend administration interface
Offline Access	Log in to the frontend of the website when the site is offline (when the site is under construction)
Super Admin	Do anything on the site—these users have all **Super User** permissions
Access Administration Interface	Have administrative access to the Joomla backend
Create	Create new content
Delete	Delete content

Permission name	Allows user to do the following
Edit	Edit all content
Edit State	Publish, unpublish, trash, and archive content
Edit Own	Edit content they've created themselves

To allow or deny users to do things, each of the available permissions can be set to **Allowed** or **Denied** for a user group. If the permission isn't explicitly allowed or denied, it is **Not Set**.

Parent and child user groups

When creating a new set of permissions for a new group, you don't have to set each and every permission manually—permissions are inherited between groups. That is, a child user group automatically gets the permissions set for its parent. **Public** is the parent group, **Manager** is a child of **Public**, **Administrator** is a child of **Manager**. **Permissions** are inherited by all child groups (unless these permissions are explicitly set to **Allowed** or **Denied** to "break" the inheritance relationship). In other words, a child group can do anything a parent group can do—and more, as it is a child and therefore has its own specific permissions set. If you add a new group as a child of the **Registered** group, this means your new group inherits the right to log in to the site. In the **Permissions Settings** screen, the indentation of user group names indicates the permissions hierarchy.

What Viewing Access Levels are available?

We've just seen which things users can be allowed to *do*—through **Permissions** settings. However, determining what users can do is not all there is to setting up permissions. You'll also want to control what users can see on the site. This is where **Viewing Access Levels** come in. By assigning an access level, you control whether users can only see the public site, if they have access to special sections of the frontend, or maybe access the backend? What articles, menus, modules, or components can the user group actually view?

By default, four **Viewing Access Levels** are available: **Public**, **Guest**, **Registered**, and **Special**. The **Customer Access Level** is just an example used in the sample data. Go to **Users | User Manager** and click on the **Viewing Access Levels** tab to see the available levels.

This is what the default **Viewing Access Levels** mean:

- **Public** means that there are no special viewing permissions involved. It's the set of permissions for the Public user group, who are only allowed access to the public site.

- **Guest** is the set of permissions for **Guest Users**. These are users who have not logged in. The purpose of this access level is being able to give only non-logged in users access to certain content—in other words, to hide things from users once they have logged in. Content that has been assigned the **Guest** access level will be visible for guest users, but not for logged-in users—**Registered** or **Special** users.

- **Registered** is the set of permissions for **Registered Users**. These are allowed to log in to the site to view the site parts that are set to the **Registered** access level. Registered content is hidden from Public and Guest users.

- **Special** is the set of viewing permissions for all users involved in maintaining the site. In the default setup, this means Special content is accessible for Authors, Editors, Publishers, Managers, Administrators and Super Users.

Viewing Access Levels can be set for all kinds of content on the site, from modules and menu items to individual articles, by changing the value of the **Access** drop-down list.

Creating a custom user group to manage contacts

Let's find out how we can create a custom user group on our site. Our client wants to set up a contacts database on the site, using the Joomla **Contacts** component. This allows visitors to find specific contacts in the organization and view their contact details. To create this database, we would like to have a new type of user—someone who's able to administer the contacts database of your site, accessed through **Components | Contacts**.

Let's assume we want to allow the club secretary to manage and update contact details. This means we want him to access the backend, but we don't want him to be able to view or change anything other than the **Contacts** menu and functionality. Let's find out how to achieve this.

Time for action: Step 1 – create a user group

1. Go to **Users** | **User Groups** and click **New** to create a new group called **Contact Administrator**.

2. Set **Group Parent** to **Registered**. This way, the new group gets the login permission from the **Registered** group, but no other permissions.

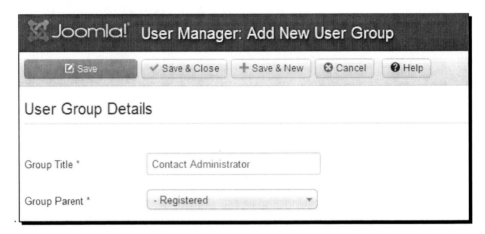

3. Click **Save & Close** to apply changes.

What just happened?

You've created a new user group. As they inherit **Registered** permissions, they can log in to the site, but as yet no specific permissions have been assigned to this group.

Time for action: Step 2 – tell Joomla what the group can see

To specify what the members of the new user group can see and do, we'll first specify which **Viewing Access Level** this user group has. This level defines what users can access and see on the site—but it doesn't give them the rights to do anything.

In this case, we want the new user group to be able to access the backend. For this, we can use an existing **Viewing Access Level**—the **Special** level. In the default Joomla setup, anyone with the **Special** level can access the backend controls.

1. Go to **Users** | **Access Levels**. The existing **Viewing Access Levels** are shown:

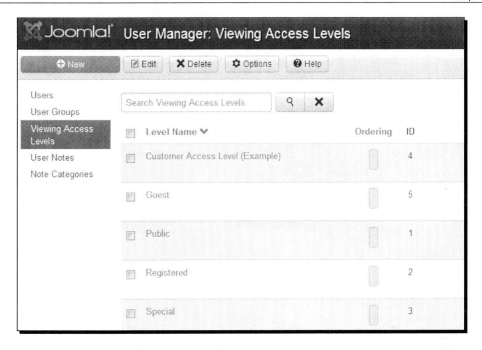

2. To add the new user group to the **Special** access level, click the **Level Name |
Special**. Add the new **Contact Administrator** user group to this level by clicking
the select box to the left of the name **Contact Administrator**:

3. Make sure to save your changes.

What just happened?

So far you've created a user group and made it possible for them to view the backend once
they've logged in by assigning them to the **Special** level. However, they still can't actually log
in to the backend. Logging in to the backend is an action—and that specific action permission
is set through the *Admin Login* permission in the **Global Configuration**.

Time for action: Step 3 – Tell Joomla what the group can do

Let's give the **Contacts Administrator** permission to log in to the backend:

1. Go to **System | Global Configuration** and click the **Permissions** tab. Select the **Contact Administrator** user group. The permissions for the group are shown.

2. For this group, change the **Admin Login** permission to **Allowed**:

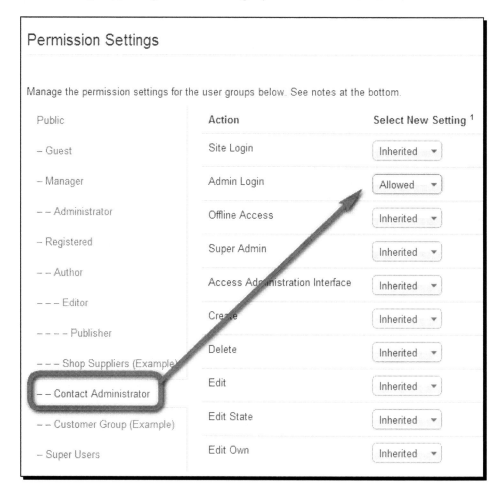

If you were to log in to the site as a **Contact Administrator** now, you'd be able to access the backend, but there would hardly be any functionality available at all—you'd just see the backend interface with just a few menu options (allowing you to edit your account profile).

So now that we've set the proper permissions on a site-wide level, it's time to set more specific permissions. We have to allow our new group to actually manage contacts in the backend. To do this, we customize the permissions of the **Contacts** component.

3. Go to **Components | Contacts** and click the **Options** button.

4. Click on the **Permissions** tab to change permissions to **Allowed** for this group for any action, as shown here:

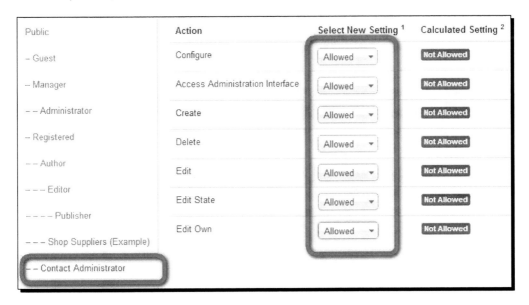

5. Click **Save & Close** to commit changes.

What just happened?

Setting permissions is done. Users in this group can now access the backend and manage contacts, but they won't be able to do anything else.

For what parts of the site can you set permissions?

You can set permissions at up to four levels on the website, ranging from site-wide permissions to permissions on the level of individual items, such as articles:

1. Site wide permissions, via **System | Global Configuration | Permissions**. You've seen these default site-wide permissions for each group earlier in this chapter.

2. Permissions for components. Joomla components are **Articles**, **Menus**, **Users**, **Banners** and so on. There's a **Permissions** screen in each of the Joomla components. For example, go to **Article Manager | Options | Permissions** to access the **Permissions** screen of the **Article Manager**.

3. Permissions for categories. In the screen where you create or edit a category (**Category Manager | Edit** or **New**), there's a **Category Permissions** section. Here you set permissions for all items (that is, articles) within a category.

4. Permissions for articles. Go to **Content | Article Manager | Options | Permissions** to set permissions for all articles or open any article to set specific permissions in the **Article Permissions** section.

Time for action: Step 4 – adding users to the new group

As yet there are no members assigned to the new group. One last thing to take care of! Let's create a new user.

1. Go to **Users | User Manager** and click **Add a new user**. Enter the required details: **Name**, **Login Name**, **Password**, and **Email**. Of course, instead of creating a new user you can also edit the permissions of the user you added earlier—**Jim van Gogh**.

2. In the **Assigned User Groups** section, assign the new user to the appropriate group by ticking the box to the left of the **Contact Administrator** group name:

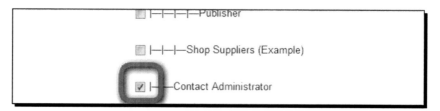

3. Save your changes. You're done!

What just happened?

You've set up a user group and assigned the appropriate access levels and permissions. You'll probably want to find out if everything is set up correctly, log out and log in to the backend as the new user. You'll notice the backend interface is almost empty. Most of the usual menus and shortcuts have disappeared or are dysfunctional. Only the functions relevant to the new user group are available; the only component the user can see and access is **Contacts**.

Click the **Components** | **Contacts** | **Contacts** submenu link. You'll notice all the functionality related to managing contacts is available for the new user:

Pop quiz – test your knowledge of Joomla user management

Q1. What's the difference between registered users and ordinary site visitors?

    a.   Registered users can add content to the site.

    b.   Registered users are able to view "registered" content.

    c.   Registered users are team members.

Q2. What's the use of displaying a login form on your website?

    a.   To allow users to log in or to register.

    b.   To allow anyone to log in to the backend.

    c.   To allow users to activate their account.

Q3. What's the advantage of using "Register to read more" links?

    a. Site visitors will feel encouraged to add content.

    b. Site visitors will feel encouraged to register to read partly hidden content.

    c. Site visitors won't be able to know what content is hidden.

Q4. On which levels of the site can you set permissions for user groups?

    a. Only for the whole site, through Global Configuration

    b. For components, for categories or for individual articles.

    c. Site-wide, for components, for categories, or for individual articles.

Summary

In this chapter, we've explored the exciting possibilities of the Joomla ACL system.

- You've seen how you can create new users and assign them to a specific Group, granting them various levels of access. Some users only have access to registered areas of the frontend; others can also log in to the backend of the site.

- The default user groups consist of seven levels, from guests (**Public**) to the most powerful (**Super Users**). However, you can also add custom user groups. By controlling user permissions you tell Joomla what parts of the site specific users can view and what they can do there.

You've steadily built a fine website. It looks good, it's organized clearly, easy to expand, and easy to navigate. Moreover, you've now added some advanced features to the site using Joomla's user management capabilities. What more can you want? Much more! Now it's time to look further and explore the vast range of powerful extras by extending Joomla. In the next chapter, you'll enhance your site and make it even better and much more fun to use.

10

Getting the Most out of Your Site: Extending Joomla

When you've got your basic Joomla-powered site up and running, and you've got all of your content and functionality covered, chances are you'll want more. Maybe your client has specific requirements, or maybe you just want to increase the wow factor of your site and add some visually attractive or slick effects. Doing more things with Joomla and making your site stand out from the rest of them—that's where extensions come in.

The real power of Joomla lies in its extensibility. If you need any functionality that's not built into the basic Joomla installation (or "core"), you'll very likely find it in the huge treasure house that's called the Joomla extension database. Extensions are little pieces of software that you can download and install to become part of the backend, extending Joomla's capabilities.

In this chapter, you'll:

- ◆ Try out Joomla's core extensions
- ◆ Download and install third-party extensions
- ◆ Put extensions to work to enhance your site or the administrative interface

Don't let the term *extension* confuse you; some extensions are part of the Joomla core. They are integrated into the basic Joomla package. Many of these provide essential functionality, so you can't even uninstall them. Joomla's search function, its menu system, or its **Contacts** functionality are examples of these pre-installed extensions. This means you already have some extensions experience. As soon as you start using Joomla, you deploy extensions.

In this chapter, we'll focus on the possibilities of some core extensions that we haven't covered yet and also on using third-party extensions. We'll install some must-have extensions and find out how they work.

Extensions in all shapes and sizes

Before digging into the wonderful world of extensions, it's good to know they come in different shapes and sizes. Basically, there are three types of extensions, the big ones, the medium ones, and the tiny ones. We'll look at each of them next.

The big ones – Components

You manage them through a special **Components** menu in the backend. They are the most comprehensive extensions, often providing lots of administration options and settings. Component output is usually displayed in the main content area. An example is the **Contacts** component (to manage a system of contacts, contact details, and contact forms). We'll have a more detailed look at this component later in this chapter.

The medium ones – Modules

Modules are "blocks" that contain special functionality. You've already seen examples at work, such as the menu module. You manage modules in **Extensions | Module Manager**.

Modules usually turn up around the main content area: in the left-hand side and right-hand side column, or in the header and footer. These module positions are predefined by the template designer. In the default template, positions have names such as "position-1"; in other templates, descriptive names such as "left", "right", and so on are used. In the following screenshot, you can see the main available module positions in the default template:

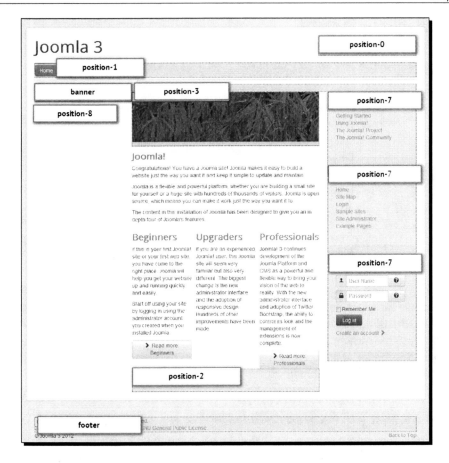

What module positions are available?

When creating modules, you place them in a specific module **Position**. To find out which module positions are available in the current template, go to **Extensions | Template Manager**. Click the **Options** button and make sure **Preview Module Positions** is set to **Enabled**. From now on, every template found through the **Template Manager | Templates** tab will contain a **Preview** link. Click this link to see the template including an overlay displaying all available positions and their position names (such as **position-7**). When switching to a different template, you'll probably have to re-assign modules to their new positions. You'll learn more about that in the next chapter on using templates.

The tiny ones – Plugins

The third type of extension is called **Plugins**. These are usually minor enhancements, such as an extra button in the text editor that makes it easy to insert hyperlinks.

In the **Extensions** menu you'll also find **Template Manager** and **Language Manager**. We won't cover them here, as they serve very specific purposes:

- Templates determine the site's layout, colors, and typography. See *Chapter 11, Creating an Attractive Design: Working with Templates*, on using templates.

- Language files allow you to set the default language for the frontend and the backend of the site. On the frontend, this will translate all preset texts (such as *Read more* and *Written by*) to a language of your choice. At the end of this chapter, we'll have a look at the **Language Manager** functionality.

Don't worry, you don't have to memorize this extensions topology. Although technically and practically there are important differences between these components, modules, and plugins, the bottom line is that they all extend Joomla's capabilities by adding extra functionality in the backend of your site. You just choose the tool that does the job— sometimes this means you'll use a component, sometimes a module, and sometimes a plugin (and sometimes a combination).

Where do you get extensions from?

Apart from the few dozen extensions that are part of the default Joomla installation, you can find thousands of additional extensions developed by third parties on the web. Most of these are listed on `http://extensions.joomla.org`, the **Joomla Extensions Directory** (or **JED**, as it is fondly called by the Joomla community):

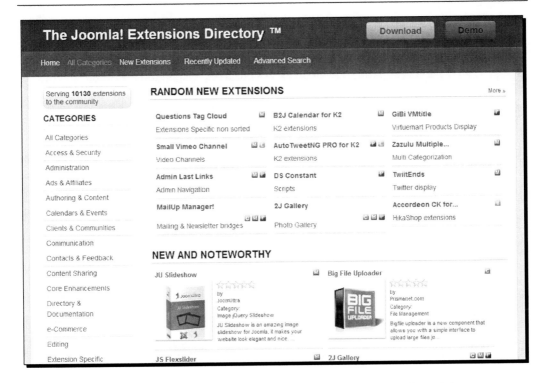

Here you'll see that extensions offer a wealth of new possibilities, whether it's better content presentation (through alternative menus, link lists, and galleries), user interaction (using forums and comments), or backend tools (interface enhancements).

Browse the JED categories (navigation systems, forums, and so on) every now and again and keep an eye on the **NEW AND NOTEWORTHY** section. Make sure to check out the **Editor's Picks** and the **Most Popular** extensions to find some true gems. It's a good idea to read other user's comments. They will often give you a good indication of whether an extension is mature enough and whether the support by the developer is up to standard.

The JED lists many extensions, but there are much more extension portal sites and developer sites. Just Google for "Joomla extensions" or "Joomla extensions must-haves" and make sure you've got enough coffee prepared to embark on a long and adventurous online treasure hunt. However, do make sure you only download extensions from reliable sources. The JED is the safest place to find extensions, as it unlists any extension as soon as security vulnerabilities are discovered.

What do extensions cost?

Many Joomla extensions are free or available for a reasonable fee. Sometimes, developers require registration before you can download the extension. Both free and commercial extensions are usually distributed under an open source license, the **General Public License (GPL)**. Joomla itself is also a GPL software. A major benefit of using GPL software and extensions is that, basically, anyone is allowed to use and modify the source code. This implies you're not dependent on the original software developer for updates or customizations. See also `http://www.gnu.org/licenses/quick-guide-gplv3.html`.

Enhancing your site using core extensions

Let's explore some extensions that are part of the Joomla core package. We'll put the **Newsflash** module to work and after that we'll have a closer look at the use of a more complex extension, the **Contacts** component.

Highlighting articles using the Newsflash module

When your site grows, it's important to make sure the home page properly reflects all of the content categories to prevent your valuable new content from staying unnoticed. By selecting **Featured Articles** (see the *Adding items to the home page* section in *Chapter 4, Web Building Basics: Creating a Site in an Hour*) you control what articles show up in the central area of the home page. But there are more ways to attract attention to specific articles.

Time for action – adding a Newsflash to the home page

Let's use the **Newsflash** module to show a random article intro text from a selected category each time the page is loaded. Every time the visitor returns, another item will be displayed in the **Newsflash** module position.

1. Navigate to **Extensions | Module Manager**. Click **New** and select **Articles – Newsflash**:

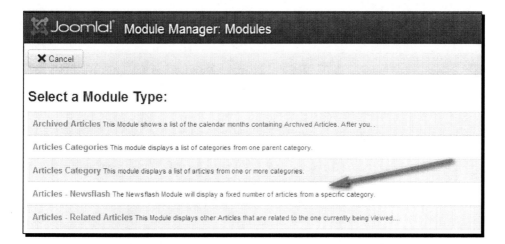

2. Make sure **Status:** is set to **Published** to get the module to display. This is the default setting.

3. In the **Title** box, type an appropriate title. In this example, we'll enter `Recent Lectures` as the module title. Make sure **Show Title** is set to **Show**.

4. Select **Position: position-7** to display the module in one of the boxes available in this template below the main content.

5. Click the **Menu Assignment** tab and select **Only on the pages selected**. Set the module to show on the **Home** page only.

6. Click on the **Basic Options** tab, select the **Category** from which Joomla should show one or more article intro texts: **Art Lectures**.

7. Set **Show Images** to **Yes**; this way the images in the article's intro text will be displayed. Images will only fit if they aren't wider than the available module position, as bigger images aren't resized automatically.

8. Set **Show Article** title to **Yes** to display the article title (and not just the intro text).

9. Set **Linked Titles** to **Yes** to turn the title of the newsflash articles into a hyperlink.

10. Select **'Read more...' Link: Show** to display a **Read more** link after the intro text.

11. In the **Number of articles** box, enter 1. This will make the module display one article from the selected category.

12. In the **Order Results** drop-down box, select **Random**. This will make the module display random articles from the selected category each time the visitor revisits this page. (You can also choose **Create Date** or **Modify Date** to order by Date, or **Ordering** to leave the order as it is in the **Article Manager**).

13. Click on **Save** and click on **View Site**.

The **Newsflash** module is shown in the main content column in the following screenshot:

What just happened?

The **Newsflash** module can help you attract attention to a specific set of articles; every time the page is revisited (reloaded in the visitor's browser), a new random article intro text from the selected category is shown. Don't let the name **Newsflash** fool you, as the module is obviously not just for news items. You can use it to show one or more items from any category. The fun part of using a random selection is that you can surprise the visitor with different content at every revisit, without having to actually refresh your site.

Have a go hero – change the Newsflash settings

As with almost any module, the settings and parameters greatly determine the output of the **Newsflash**. In the following screenshot, you can see what the output can look like if you change the position and layout settings:

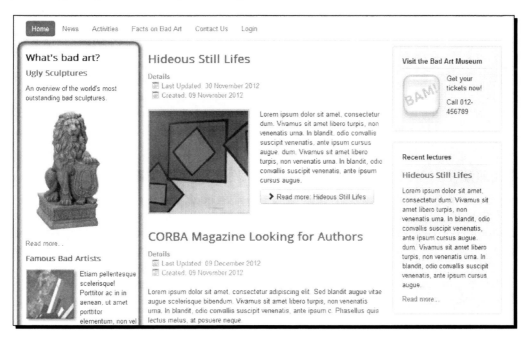

Here, the **Position** is set to **position-8**, the left-hand side column of the Protostar template (set to be displayed only if any content is assigned to it). We've chosen to display **2** random article intro texts from the **Facts on Bad Art** category in one column. This way, the **Newsflash** module allows you to display article intro texts from a selected category in a separate block on (for example) the home page.

Using the same module twice (or more)

Suppose you want to use the **Newsflash** module a few times on the same page. Is that possible? Yes, you can have multiple instances of any module on a page. You've already seen an example if you have installed Joomla with sample data, as the sample site shows various menus on one page (such as **Main Menu**, **Top Menu**, and **User Menu**). These are all copies of a single module type, **Menu**.

In the previous screenshot, I've used two instances of the **Newsflash** module to display content from different categories on different module positions (in the left-hand side column, you see intro texts from the **Facts** category and in the right-hand side column, you see one article intro from the **Lectures** category).

To do this, it's easiest to create a copy of the first module, so that you don't have to create the second instance from the ground up. Navigate to **Extensions | Module Manager**, select the module to copy, and click on **Duplicate** in the toolbar. In the **Module Manager**, a copy will show up named **[module name] (2)**. You'll probably want to give the copy a different **Title**, select another **Position,** and set the source to another **Category**.

Creating a list of contacts using the Contacts component

In *Chapter 4, Web Building Basics: Creating a Site in an Hour*, you've already deployed Joomla's built-in **Contacts** component to create a generic contact form. However, the **Contacts** component has much more functionality than what's needed for creating a simple form. Instead, you can set up a system of contacts, displaying as many contacts in as many categories as you need. Imagine you want to display a list of contacts to allow the visitor to select the specific department or staff member they want to get in touch with. The result would look as displayed in the following screenshot:

When the user clicks on any of the **Staff** names, the appropriate contact details are shown as in the following screenshot:

This system allows the visitor to find the appropriate contact, browse the contact details, and get in touch through a contact form for each contact. Let's find out how we can create a couple of contacts and create a list using the **Contacts** component.

Time for action – adding a series of contacts

We'll create a contacts category, add contact details, and finally make a menu link to point to the new set of contacts.

1. Navigate to **Components | Contacts | Categories**. If you installed Joomla using sample data, there may still be sample categories present. It's easy to remove them: select them all (make sure **All** is selected in the drop-down box on the right-hand side above the contact listing) and click on **Trash**.

2. Click on **New** to create a new contacts category. In the **Title** field, enter CORBA Staff. In the **Description** box, enter a short description that will be displayed above the contacts list. In this example, we've entered Are you interested in joining CORBA? Do you want to support us or organize bad art activities? Don't hesitate to contact our staff!. Click on **Save & Close**.

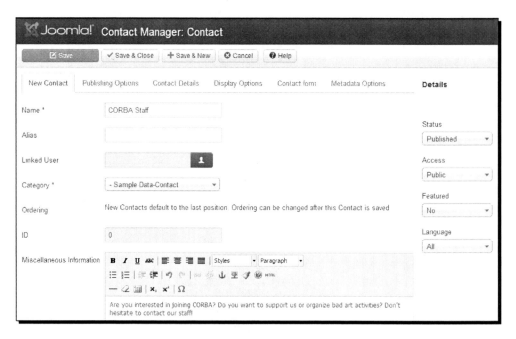

3. Click on the **Contacts** link in the menu on the left-hand side and click on **New**. Enter the details for a new contact. In this example, we've entered in the **Name** field: Pablo Warhol. Under **Contact Details**, enter information as necessary. Select an **Image** to display a portrait with the contact information, add a **Position** (such as **Secretary**). Enter a **Telephone** number and an **Email** address for the contact; even if we won't display the e-mail address, it will be used when the visitor uses the e-mail form for this contact. Click on **Save & New**.

4. Repeat the previous step to enter information for a couple of other contacts. When you're done, click on **Save & Close**.

We now have a new contacts category holding a set of contacts. Let's add a new menu link to display the list of contacts.

5. Navigate to **Menus | Main Menu**. Edit the existing **Contact Us** link (alternatively, if you haven't yet created a **Contact Us** link previously, just click **New** to create a new menu item). In the **Menu Item Type** section, select **Contacts | List Contacts in a Category**. Under **Required Settings**, make sure the **CORBA Staff** category is selected.

6. Click on the **Advanced Options** tab. In the **List Layouts** panel, set which details you want to display in the contacts list. Set **Phone**, **City**, **Suburb**, **State**, and **Country** to **Hide**. We don't want to show too much details in the overview list of contacts. Set **Display Select** to **Hide**: we have a short list of contacts, so we don't want to bother the visitor with a drop-down list enabling him to select the number of contacts displayed on the page.

7. Under **Contact Display Options**, select what details are displayed on the details page of each contact. Select **Display format: Tabs**. Set **Name**, **Contact's Position**, and **Telephone** to **Show**. Under **Mail Options**, select **Show Contact Form: Show**, to make sure every contact can be reached through their own contact form.

8. Click on **Save & Close** and then click on **View Site**. In the frontend top menu, click on the **Contact Us** link to see the results. The site should now display a menu link to a list of contacts as displayed in the previous two screenshots.

What just happened?

Using the **Contacts** component, we've created a little database of people and their details. When the visitor clicks the menu link pointing to the **Contacts** category, a list is shown. Clicking on any of the names on the list reveals the contact details and a tabbed link to a contact form, enabling the visitor to e-mail the selected person.

Have a go hero – try out contact component settings

You'll have noticed you can enter a huge number of details per contact and also select which details you want to show or hide in the contacts list and the contact details page. Go ahead an experiment with the settings and options. The **Options** found in the **Contacts** screen under **Components**, are general settings for all contacts and contact pages; you can overrule these by more specific settings through the menu link pointing to a specific contact.

What extensions are part of the Joomla core?

We've tried out how you can put a module or a component to use. However, the Joomla core package contains many more extensions. Let's have a look at the modules and components that are part of the default installation. Navigate to **Extensions | Module Manager** and click on **New** to see a list of available modules.

Module Name	What can you do with it?
Archived Articles	When you archive items in Joomla, you can use this module to display a list of links to the archived articles (sorted by date). We've explored archiving articles in *Chapter 6, Creating Killer Content: Adding and Editing Articles*.
Articles Categories	This module shows a list of links to the subcategories in a category. You can use it to allow people to draw attention to subcategories and allow visitors to navigate more easily to content one level lower in the site structure.
Articles Category	This module shows a list of titles and article texts (or intro texts) of articles in one or more categories. In fact, this is quite a powerful module that can be used to display selected articles that meet specific criteria in a module position.
Articles – Newsflash	You've read about this module earlier in this chapter. It's not just for news, but it allows you to display the intro texts of a set of articles in any category.
Articles – Related Articles	Shows a list of hyperlinks to pages with a subject matter related to that of the current page. The relationship is based on the meta tag keywords of the articles. If the current page and two other articles contain the keyword tutorial, then two items will appear in the link list.
Banners	This module displays banner ads created using the **Banners** component.
Breadcrumbs	This displays a set of hyperlinks that helps visitors understand where they are (that is, **Home | Category | Article**)
Custom HTML	This is a simple, but very flexible module to display content anywhere on the page. See *Chapter 4, Web Building Basics: Creating a Site in an Hour*, for an example of its usage.
Feed display	This displays a list of hyperlinks to news updates (newsfeeds) from another website.
Footer	This module you probably won't use. It displays a Joomla copyright notice on the site.
Language Switcher	Use this module if you are working with content in multiple languages on your site. Users can choose their preferred site language using this switch.

Module Name	What can you do with it?
Latest News	Shows a list of hyperlinks to show the most recently added articles in specific categories. The name can be a little confusing, because it is really about "latest content", not just news.
Latest Users	Useful if users are allowed to register and log in to the site: this module shows a short list of users that have logged in recently.
Login	This module shows a form that users can use to log in or create a new account. You've seen this in action in *Chapter 9, Opening Up the Site: Enabling Users to Log In and Contribute*.
Menu	This is Joomla's default menu module. All menus in Joomla are instances of this generic menu module.
Most Read Content	Displays a list of hyperlinks to the articles that have been accessed most often.
Random Image	Shows a random image from an image folder any time the page is reloaded; a simple way to surprise the visitor with a page that looks different on every visit, even when there's no new content added.
Search	Shows the site search field.
Smart Search Module	Use this module instead of the regular **Search** module together with the **Smart Search** component and the **Smart Search** content plugin. **Smart Search** is an enhanced search system for your site. See also the list of components, in the next table.
Statistics	Shows a set of website statistics, such as the number of articles and visitors hits.
Syndication Feeds	This shows a RSS Feed link; users can click on this to subscribe to updates for the current page and read them in a special application (a news reader).
Weblinks	If you use Joomla's **Weblinks** component, you can show **web** links from a specific category through this module.
Who's Online	Shows how many users are logged in.
Wrapper	Allows you to show an external page (a page from another site) within your site.

Every module that's listed in the **Module Manager** has a **Title** and a **Type**. The **Title** is the (customizable) name of the module that you can show on the frontend of the site. The module **Type** is the (fixed) name Joomla uses internally. As you saw previously, you can repeatedly use the same module type (for example, **Menu**), but you distinguish module copies with their name (for example, **Top Menu**, or **User Menu**).

Navigate to the **Components** menu to see which components are part of the Joomla core. The following is a short overview:

Component Name	What can you do with it?
Banners	Manage banner ads on your website. You can create new banners and manage banner clients.
Contacts	Add and manage contact information and link contacts to registered users. Earlier in this chapter you saw an example of its use.
Joomla! Update	Using the **Update** component, you can check whether there are updates available for the Joomla core software. If there are, updating is just a matter of clicking the **Update** button. You don't have to remember to check the **Update** component: there's a quick icon in the Control Panel that takes care of checking for updates and that will take you straight to this component if updates are available.
Messaging	Send and receive private messages (to and from other administrators having access to the site backend).
Newsfeeds	Add newsfeeds from other sites to your Joomla site.
Redirect	When URLs in your website change, you can redirect users that still use the outdated URL to the new page by entering old and new URLs here.
Search	Access search statistics to see how many searches were done for certain keywords or keyword combinations.
Smart Search	**Smart Search**, the enhanced search functionality, is a combination of this component, the **Smart Search** module and the **Smart Search** plug-in. You can use **Smart Search** instead of the default Search by enabling the plugin, creating a search index using the component, and using the **Smart Search** module (or menu link). **Smart Search** is faster and more user friendly, as it gives users suggestions and auto-completes search phrases. See also the documentation at `http://docs.joomla.org/Smart_Search_quickstart_guide`.
Weblinks	Add and categorize links to other websites (to display on your site through the **Web Link Menu Link** type).

Enhancing your site using third-party extensions

When you run into the limitations of the Joomla core extensions, it's time to check out some more sophisticated, dedicated extensions. Any functionality you can think of is likely to exist in the form of a component, module, or plugin (or a combination). It takes just a few steps to add a new extension to your website. First, you download the extension (as a ZIP file), then you install it through Joomla's Extension Manager, and finally you adjust its settings to get it to work the way you want to.

Trying out an alternative newsflash module

Earlier in this chapter, you've explored a module that comes with Joomla, Newsflash. This is great if you want to draw attention to a couple of selected articles. However, there are many "article teaser" modules available that offer added functionality and are much more versatile. Let's try out an example to find out what the differences are.

Time for action – downloading and installing an extension

We'll install an alternative module to show teasers on the home page, **BT Content Slider**:

1. Navigate to `http://extensions.joomla.org/extensions/news-display/articles-display/articles-showcase/19125` and click on **Download** to download the ZIP file containing the extension. You're taken to the developer site. After clicking the **Download** button there, click on **Register** to register for a free account and log in to the site. You're taken to the download page where you can download the ZIP file. Make sure to select the most recent version for Joomla 3.x.

2. In the backend of your site, navigate to **Extensions | Extension Manager**. You'll be taken to the **Install** screen of the **Extension Manager**.

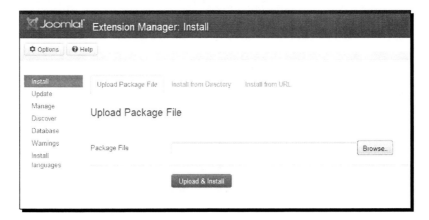

3. Now install the extension by clicking on **Browse** to select the extension ZIP file on your computer. Click on **Upload & Install**. Once the installation is complete, you'll see a message (Installing module was successful).

What just happened?

Congratulations, you successfully installed your first extension! The new module can now be found through **Extensions | Module Manager** and you can add one or more instances of the module to your site. We'll see how that works in a minute.

Time for action – putting the extension to work

Let's get BT Content Slider to display article teaser texts on the home page.

1. If you've followed along and installed the **NewsFlash** module earlier, you may want to hide that module now. To do so, navigate to **Extensions | Module Manager**. Locate the **NewsFlash** module that is titled **Recent lectures**.

2. Click on the green check mark in the **Status** column to unpublish this **Newsflash** module, that is, hide it on the frontend.

3. In the **Module Manager**, locate the **BT Content Slider** module (**mod_bt_contentslider**) and click on its **Title** to see the available options.

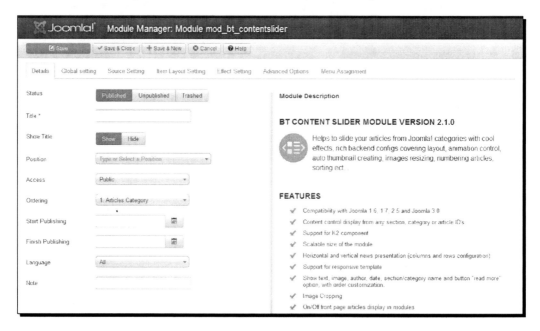

This looks quite different compared to the default **Newsflash** module—the **Content Slider** settings are divided into seven tabbed panels! In the options panels, dozens of settings are available to customize the extension. But don't despair, you'll only have to tweak a few settings to get this module to work.

4. Let's start with the **Details** tab. In the **Title** field, enter New from CORBA. We want to display this title in the frontend, so check that **Show Title** is set to **Show**.

5. Select **Position: position-3**. This will display the module contents between the header and the main content. A quick way to enter the desired position is to just type it in the **Position** field; Joomla will automatically suggest available positions. Set **Status** to **Published**.

6. Click on the **Menu Assignment** tab and set the module to display on the **Home** page only.

7. In the **Source Setting** panel, select the categories that should be the source of the module output. In this example, we've chosen to show content from the **News** and **Reviews** category. Of course, if you haven't added any dummy content to these categories, for this purpose any other category containing articles is okay. It's best to use articles that have images in either the intro text or in the **Images** and **Links** fields; the **Content Slider** will display thumbnails of these images.

8. Click on **Save** and then click on **View Site** to see the output on the home page. It should look like the following screenshot:

This is what the module output looks like using the default settings. Three article intro texts are displayed; they include a thumbnail of the article image. You'll notice the contents of the module changes automatically: every few seconds a new set of intro texts slides into place. Try the navigation bullets at the top-right of the module block: you'll notice these controls allow the visitor to manually browse the available teasers.

9. Let's change this basic presentation. Navigate to the module settings again and under the **Global Setting** tab, locate the **Number of Rows** option and change this to **2**. Under the **Item Layout Setting** tab, set **Alignment** of image to **Left**. Save this and see how the output now changes as shown in the following screenshot:

New from CORBA

News
HIDEOUS ART OWNERS MEETING

Lorem ipsum dolor sit amet, consectetur adipiscing elit. Phasellus quis lectus metus, at posue
Read more

News
CORBA MAGAZINE LOOKING FOR AUTHORS

Lorem ipsum dolor sit amet, consectetur adipiscing elit. Sed blandit augue vitae augue scelerisque b...
Read more

News
NEW BAD ART BOOK

Lorem ipsum dolor sit amet, consectetur adipiscing elit. Phadum. Vivamus sit amet libero turpis, non...
Read more

News
WATCH THE BAD SCULPTURE DOCUMENTARY

Lorem ipsum dolor sit amet, consectetur adipiscing elit. Phadum. Vivamus sit amet libero turpis, non...
Read more

News
NEW BAD ART GALLERY

Lorem ipsum dolor sit amet, consectetur adipiscing elit. Phasellus quis lectus metus, at posuere neq...
Read more

Reviews
CHINESE PIG SCULPTURE

Phasellus neque turpis, suscipit quis commodo a, varius eget lorem. Sed vestibulum urna nec lorem di...
Read more

The module now displays the thumbnails aligned on the left-hand side and placed above the title and intro text. Also, we've set it to display the available intro texts in two rows.

10. Let's change the layout one more time. In the **Item Layout Setting** section, set **Show Intro Text** to **No**, **Show Category Name** to **No**, and **Show Read more** to **No**. Set **Thumbnail Width** to **100** pixels to make the thumbnails a little smaller. Under **Global setting**, change **Number of Rows** back to **1**. The results on the frontend are different again.

New from CORBA

HIDEOUS ART
OWNERS
MEETING

CORBA
MAGAZINE
LOOKING FOR
AUTHORS

NEW BAD ART
BOOK

Instead of intro texts, now a scrolling row of article images and titles is shown. The visitor can click the image to read the article or navigate through the scrolling images by clicking the little dots in the upper-right corner.

What just happened?

We've deployed the **Content Slider** module to show teaser texts from a selected category on the home page. The module offers a wealth of options and presets, allowing you to create an eye-catching display of selected articles. The module navigation includes a sliding effect inviting visitors to explore different articles, much more than what a static newsflash presentation does. The module is responsive: when you resize the browser screen, you'll see how the image size and further layouts adapt to the changes.

Have a go hero – explore module options

We've only touched upon the possibilities of this module, so why don't you try out a few other options? Automatic panel animation is a popular feature, but it may be a bit too much for your sophisticated site. To switch off the automatic sliding display, under **Effect Setting** set **Auto Start** to **No**. Another powerful option is **Navigation effect**: set this to **Fade** to make the next set of available intro texts fade in (instead of sliding into view).

If you just see one or two teaser texts and no other content sliding in, chances are the category you've chosen doesn't contain enough articles. Create some new (dummy) articles to see the effect.

 It's a good idea to set **Featured Articles** to **Hide**. This will hide **Featured** articles among the selected category contents. After all, these are already set to show in the home page mainbody. If you set **Featured Articles** to **Only Show Featured Articles**, the module will display only **Featured** articles. This is useful if you want to show featured articles from particular categories through this module; you can then set the **Home** link to display featured articles from other categories.

Content Slider is a good example of the difference between Joomla's built-in extensions and the extensions that are available through third-party developers. Generally, the core extensions are lightweight, simple, and do their job just fine. However, dedicated third-party extensions are bound to have more options and features. Moreover, you usually can choose between several excellent extensions to perform the same kind of functionality. Other great extensions for displaying article teasers, for example, are News Show Pro GK4 and Mini Frontpage (both found through the Joomla extension site, `http://extensions.joomla.org`).

Showing images in a lightbox gallery

On our website we'd like to display art pictures, allowing the visitor to enjoy as much of the ugly details as possible. This means we definitely need an image gallery using a **lightbox** effect. This is a common approach on many sites: images are displayed as thumbnails, to be maximized only after the visitor has clicked them. The full-size image opens in a lightbox, greybox, slimbox, or whatever different developers like to call this technique. It looks cool and it's functional too, as it allows you to display many little thumbnails, leaving it to the visitor to pick which pictures they want to have a closer look at:

Time for action – create an image gallery

To show all images as a gallery, we'll use a plug-in from `http://www.kubik-rubik.de/`.

1. Navigate to `http://joomla-extensions.kubik-rubik.de/sige-simple-image-gallery-extended`. You can also do a web search for "Simple Image Gallery Extended", this will take you to the same page. Download the latest version; at the time of writing this file is called `plg_sige_v3-1.zip`.

2. Navigate to **Extensions | Extension Manager**. Select the plugin ZIP file you downloaded and click on **Upload & Install**. You'll see a message when the installation is finished (**Installing plugin was successful**).

3. As this is a plugin, we'll use the **Plug-in Manager** to enable the extension. Navigate to **Extensions | Plug-in Manager** and locate the **Content – Simple Image Gallery Extended** plugin. Click on the red and white cross in the **Status** column. It turns into a check mark, indicating the plugin is now active:

4. The plugin has no additional settings, so you're all set. Click on **Save & Close**.

5. Now you only have to create a new article (or edit an existing one) that will contain the gallery pictures. Navigate to **Content | Article Manager** and click on **New**. In this example, I've created an article titled **Bad Art Gallery** and assigned it to the **Bad Art | Facts** category.

6. In the article, enter the article text and add this code where you want the images to appear: `{gallery}headers{/gallery}`. This will instruct the plugin to display all image files in the images/headers folder in the article. For testing purposes, this is okay: this is the folder that contains the header images that are installed with the Joomla sample data. Of course, you can also point the module to any other subfolder of the images folder if you like.

7. Click on **Save**. You're done. On the frontend, click on the link in the **Main Menu** to navigate to the new article. It will display as follows:

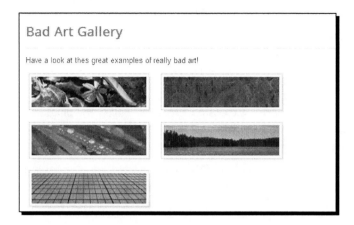

8. Click on any of the thumbnails to display it as a full-size image in a lightbox.

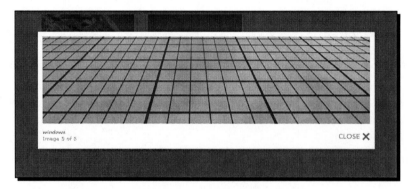

You can remove the link to the site of the Simple Image Gallery developer that's displayed below the gallery. In the plugin options, set **Show link to author** to **No**.

What just happened?

You've set up a small gallery that will impress your visitors. To do this, you only have to enter the name of the image folder in between the {gallery} and {/gallery} code in the article text. The base for this folder is the default Joomla image folder, called images. The code {gallery}headers{/gallery} indicates that image files in the images/headers folder will be displayed as thumbnails in the article. Clicking on any of the thumbnails opens a lightbox with the full-size image, allowing the user to browse through the available set of images.

Have a go hero – add your own images

In this case we've used the sample photos that are already present in the sample data of the default Joomla installation. To show your own photos, upload your photos to a new folder, for example `images/myimages`. In this case, the code needed in your article will be `{gallery} myimages{/gallery}`. If your image uploading skills are a bit rusty, please refer to *Chapter 6, Creating Killer Content: Adding and Editing Articles* again (see the *Time for action – uploading images* section).

Do you want more from your photo gallery?

The image gallery plugin is great if you've only got one or two pages where you want to display popup images. If you're looking for a more sophisticated gallery tool that allows you to manage a large number of images and show them to your visitors in a structured way, you may consider using a gallery component. A popular example is **Phoca** (`www.phoca.cz/phocagallery`). Phoca can present large image collections using categories and subcategories. Visitors can browse the photos using lightbox pop-up screens:

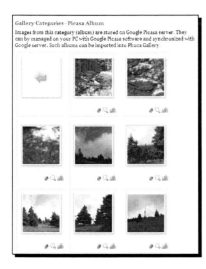

Using extensions to enhance your work space

Extensions don't just extend the functionality of the frontend of your site. There are also extensions available that enhance and extend the backend. For example, you can replace the backend article editor by a more powerful one.

Time for action – replace Joomla's default text editor

The default text editor is alright for entering text, but some of the advanced capabilities (such as adding images or inserting hyperlinks) aren't really easy and intuitive. Let's install the **Joomla Content Editor** (**JCE**), a very popular and freely available replacement for Joomla's default editor (which is called **TinyMCE**). For many Joomla users, JCE is the first thing they add after installing Joomla.

1. Go to `http://www.joomlacontenteditor.net` and download the "single installation package" for the current version of Joomla. The installation package is a compressed file.

2. Navigate to **Extensions | Extension Manager**. Click on **Browse** to locate the compressed file you just downloaded and click on **Upload & Install**. Once both are installed, you'll see the message: **Installing component was successful**.

3. Tell Joomla that you want JCE to be the default editor. Navigate to **System | Global Configuration**. On the **Site Settings** panel, set **Default Editor** to **Editor – JCE** and save your changes.

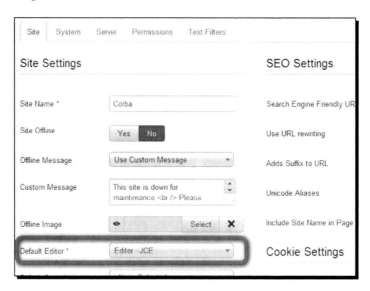

What just happened?

You've just installed the JCE editor. What's the big deal? From now on, whenever you create or edit an article, you'll see the JCE editor buttons:

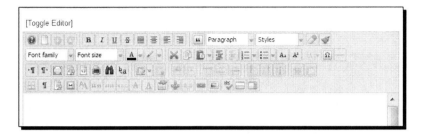

At first glance, the differences between JCE and the default editor may seem inconspicuous—but they will make a big difference in day-to-day article editing! Here are some examples of the benefits:

- You can now quickly create text links to other menu items. In *Chapter 8, Helping Your Visitors Find What They Want: Managing Menus* (see the *Creating plain text links* section) you've seen that you can create links to articles using the **Article** button, but what if you want to link to another type of page, such as a **Contact** form? In JCE, select one or more words in the article and click on the hyperlink icon (**Insert / Edit Link**) in the bottom row. JCE now lets you select any target page in a list.

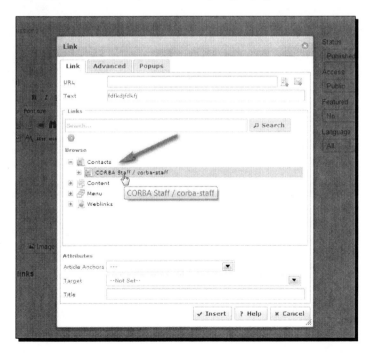

◆ In the **Attributes** section, add a link **Title** (the little pop-up text the visitor sees when hovering the mouse pointer over the actual link) and click on **Insert**. That's it.

◆ Another improvement you and your colleague content editors will appreciate is the easy way JCE handles inserting images. To add an image to an article, you no longer use the **Image** button below the editor screen. Instead, click on the **Insert / Edit Image** icon to open JCE's own **Image Manager**.

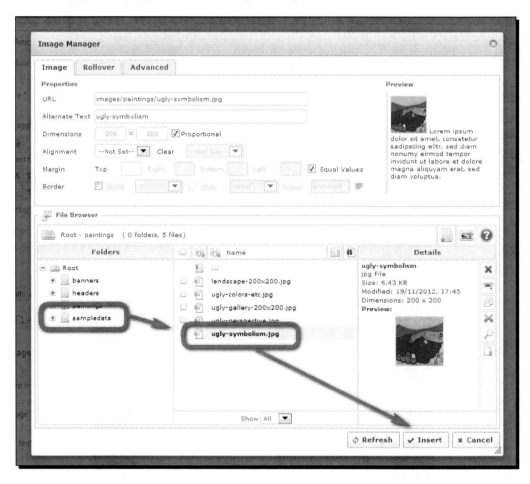

◆ To add an image, click on the desired folder, select the image file, check the preview, and click on **Insert**.

- JCE allows you to easily control the image alignment and margins. For example, set the image **Alignment** to **Left** and set the **Margin** at the **Right** and at the **Bottom** to **10** pixels to have the text flow nicely around the image. The small **Preview** window displays the desired effect as shown in the following screenshot:

- You can also set image alignment and margin preferences through the JCE component configuration options (under **Plugin Parameters | Image Manager | Default Values**).

- The **Image Manager** also makes it possible to upload more than one image simultaneously from your hard drive to the web server. You can move, remove, or rename images and preview them full-size.

You can also customize the JCE editor, to control exactly which buttons are shown to the users. See www.scribd.com/doc/82770047/Optimizing-JCE-editor-from-usability-point-of-view.

Creating a link to a PDF or Word file

Do you need to create a link to a PDF file or Word file that site visitors can download? Using JCE this is easy: in any article, select the text that should become a hyperlink, click on the **Insert/Edit link** button and click the **Browse** button (to the right-hand side of the **URL** field). Now you can browse to any PDF or Word file in the **File Browser**. If that's still on your computer, you can choose to upload it now by clicking the **Upload** icon. Next, select the file, so that the URL appears in the **URL** field. Click **Insert** and your file link is ready.

In short, JCE makes it possible to do more things with text and pictures, and it makes editing much easier. The developer also offers a set of great add-ons for JCE, which can be obtained for a reasonable fee.

> You can adjust JCE's settings via **Components | JCE Editor | Control Panel**. If you're not happy with the default editor layout and the default order of icons and buttons, you can adjust JCE to your needs via **Components | JCE Editor | Control Panel | Editor Profiles | Default | Features & Layout**. Another way to customize JCE is to use its comprehensive system of **Editor Profiles** that allow you to determine what different users (for example, editors or webmasters) may see and do in JCE. You can assign each profile to specific user groups. This functionality will come in handy if you want to limit what different types of users can do, for example if you don't want to allow editors to add images to an article.

So much more to explore

With thousands of extensions available, the best way to find the perfect addition to your site is by exploring the **Joomla Extensions database**. To whet your appetite, here's a little taste of the different types of functionality they offer:

AllVideos: Show YouTube (or other) videos inside articles.

Plugin Googlemaps: Display Google Maps within articles, modules, or components.

Virtuemart: Integrate an e-commerce shop within a Joomla site.

Kunena: A component that allows you to deploy a community forum on your site

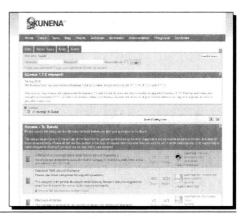

At the time you read this, the extension examples in the preceding screenshots should be ready for Joomla 3. If not, you're sure to find alternatives in the Joomla Extensions database. It's easy to find compatible extensions using advanced search (`http://extensions.joomla.org/extensions/advanced-search`). Here you can search according to specific criteria: that is, the type of extension you're looking for, whether it should be a free or commercial extension, and the Joomla version it should be compatible with.

Finding unmissable extensions

Every Joomla user probably has his own particular favorite extensions—but there sure are some great ones around that almost everybody using Joomla seems to deploy. A good way to find great extensions is to do a web search for "best Joomla extensions" or "must-have Joomla extensions". You'll get some great tips on cool extensions, both for enhancing the frontend and backend functionality of your site.

Managing the site language

In the **Extensions** menu, you'll also find the **Language Manager**. Here you can add and install languages for both the administrative interface and the frontend of the site. To install a new language pack, click on **Install Languages**. This takes you to an overview of all available language packs. Adding a language is just a matter of selecting it and clicking on the **Install** button. Once it's installed, it's available in the **Language Manager** and you can make it the new default language. Set the default language for both the frontend and backend of your website.

Changing default text strings

Any Joomla site may contain lots of built-in text strings. You see them turn up on the frontend when you display articles—just think of words and sentences such as *Read more*, *More articles*, and *Details*. These texts are part of the Joomla default package and in most cases, you won't have to bother changing them. However, sometimes the default texts don't fit your website. Luckily, it's simple to remove these texts or replace them with your own words. This is done through "language overrides".

Time for action – removing or replacing default texts

Let's say we want to remove the word *Details* that's displayed with every article. After all, it takes up valuable space on the screen and doesn't really convey useful information itself. Here's what the **Details** section of an article looks like by default:

1. In the Joomla backend, navigate to **Extensions | Language Manager** and in the menu click on **Overrides** and then click on **New**. In the **Search text you want to change** section, enter the words or words you're looking for and click on **Search**. Joomla will display all matches. In this case, the first hit is the one we're looking for:

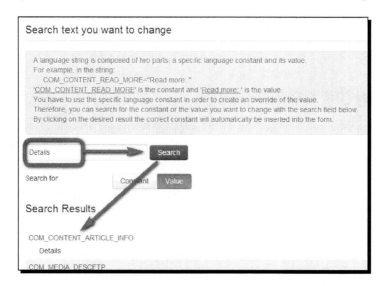

2. Click on the search result (in this case **COM_CONTENT_ARTICLE_INFO Details**). It's automatically displayed in the **Create a New Override** section on the left-hand side of the screen. In the **Text** field, enter the text you want to replace the current text with. In this case, we want to display no text at all, so keep the **Text** field empty:

Create a New Override

Language Constant *   COM_CONTENT_ARTICLE_INFO

Text

3. Click on **Save & Close**. You're done!

What just happened?

By creating a language override, you can easily delete or change the default screen text in Joomla. In this case, you've deleted the **Details:** heading that Joomla displays above the article details by emptying the **Text** field.

Have a go hero – make default texts suit your needs

In the preceding example, you've in fact deleted a text; it's equally easy to replace a text by another one. As an example, let's change the **Category:** text that's by default displayed as part of the article details. Create a new override just like you did a minute ago, enter the search string **Category:** and hit **Search**. Click on the first search result in the list. Now change the text `Category: %S` into `In: %S`. Save your override and you're done. On the frontend, you can see the output of the `%S` code you left unchanged; this is a variable that Joomla replaces by the category name.

Joomla!

Written by Joomla

In: Joomla!

01 January 2011

👁 Hits: 4

Keep in mind, however, that language overrides affect the whole site: if you change a generic word such as *Article*, this will be replaced on all pages. If you're not satisfied with the results of a language override, you can always delete it to revert to the default setup.

> It's really neat that language overrides also can be used to change the texts that are used in many extensions. This way, when an extension hasn't been translated (completely), you can easily replace the text in the original language.

Using the Language Manager to create multilingual sites

Using the **Language Manager** and a set of built-in extensions, Joomla makes it relatively easy to create a multilingual website. To find out more, please refer to *Appendix B, Creating a Multilingual Site*.

Updating extensions

Extension developers regularly release updates to solve bugs or security problems. If you have a large number of extensions, it is difficult to monitor for all those extensions when updates become available. Fortunately, Joomla features an automatic update functionality. If extensions support this feature, you can update them very easily. Go to the **Extension Manager** and click on the **Updates** link in the menu on the left-hand side. In the **Update** screen, click **Find Updates**. If updates are available, select them and install them using the **Update** button.

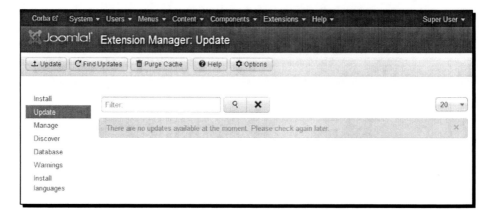

> For security reasons, it's best to completely remove extensions that you don't use any more. This way, you don't risk the code of outdated and possibly insecure extensions being exploited by hackers. To delete an extension, click the **Manage** tab in the **Extension Manager** screen. Select the extension you want to remove and then click on the **Trash** button.

Pop quiz – test your knowledge of Joomla extensions

Q1. What's the difference between components and other extensions?

    a. Components are more powerful and more complex.

    b. Components are only available to selected users.

    c. Components are shown in different module positions.

Q2. What's the use of the **Newsflash** module?

    a. To allow visitors to subscribe to newsfeeds.

    b. To show just one news item in a module position.

    c. To show one or more article intro texts in a module position.

Q3. What's the use of installing modules?

    a. Modules can make it easier entering new content.

    b. Modules can contain any kind of advanced functionality.

    c. Modules can contain lists of hyperlinks.

Summary

In this chapter, we've covered the magic of Joomla extensions:

- If you need any functionality that's not built into the basic Joomla core, you'll very likely find it in the Joomla Extension Directory (JED).
- There are three types of extensions: components (the big ones), modules (the medium ones), and plugins (the small ones). The Joomla core already contains several components, modules, and plugins. To add a third-party extension to your website, you download it from the web and install it. When it's installed, you can adjust the extension in the backend and activate it (enable it, in Joomla terms).
- Some extensions provide new ways to present content, others extend the administrative functionality.
- Using language overrides, you can replace default texts by your own texts.

Now that you've explored how extensions work and added a few to your site, it's time to focus on one special extension type: templates! In earlier chapters, you've already made some changes to the default template. However, Joomla's template capabilities are much more powerful.

In the next chapter, you'll learn how to find and install templates and apply a brand new design to your site.

11

Creating an Attractive Design: Working with Templates

You probably don't want to make websites that all look like "typical" Joomla sites. That's where templates come to the rescue. Because Joomla allows you to install a different template in a few minutes, giving your site a fresh look and feel really is a breeze. There are hundreds of templates available on the Web, making it possible to apply any style imaginable to your site. Moreover, you can easily customize templates to meet your needs. And if you're a web building wizard yourself, you can create your own template from scratch.

In this chapter, we'll explore the power of templates further. You'll learn about:

- ◆ Changing the settings of the default template
- ◆ Applying different templates to different pages
- ◆ Downloading and installing third-party templates
- ◆ Customizing templates: tweaking CSS and HTML

This is what templates do

A Joomla template is a set of files that contain the HTML and CSS code defining what your website will look like. HTML is the code used to build web pages and CSS is the code used to style them. You could say that HTML is the bricks and mortar of your site, whereas CSS provides the wallpaper and paint. Let's see how this works.

Without any CSS applied, your web browser would display a typical Joomla site as shown on the left-hand side in the next screenshot. Although the screenshots are too small for you to be able to discern the screen text, you'll notice that on the left-hand side just plain text and images are shown, with minimal styling. On the right-hand side, however, the same content is shown with CSS styles applied. Through CSS, the overall page layout and design is added:

Actually, a template contains more than pure HTML and CSS. After all, Joomla has to "know" where the dynamic content should be placed within the HTML page structure. That's why a template also contains some instructions written in the PHP language instructing Joomla where to put the main content, menus, and other modules.

All in all, templates determine just about any part of the design, from the number of columns to the position of elements, the colors, the graphics, or the choice of fonts.

And this is why templates are so much fun

Artsy, basic, flashy, grungy, playful, corporate, or clean—whatever your taste in templates may be, you're very likely to find a template that meets your needs. The following is a tiny selection of the free Joomla templates on offer on the Web—showcasing just a few of the great designs possible:

The details of these examples can be found at: `http://crosstec.de` (Prismatic template), `www.joomlashine.com` (JSN Vintage), `www.olwebdesign.com` (OL Albos), and `www.joomla-monster.com` (JM Lifestyle).

It isn't hard to find excellent (often free) templates on the Web. At the end of this chapter, you'll learn more about where to find great templates. However, first we'll have a look at the templates that come with Joomla. First, you'll activate one of the templates that ship with Joomla, after that, you'll download and customize a new one from the Web.

Changing the settings of the current template

Your starting point for managing and customizing the current templates is the **Template Manager** (**Extensions | Template Manager**). The **Template Manager** screen consists of two main screens, accessed through the menu on the left-hand side: **Styles** and **Templates**. In the **Styles** screen you select which of the available templates you want to use on the site. The current default frontend template is called Protostar. The default template for the backend of the site is called Isis. If you've followed along with the exercises in *Chapter 4, Web Building Basics: Creating a Site in an Hour*, your current default template should be called **Protostar_copy**.

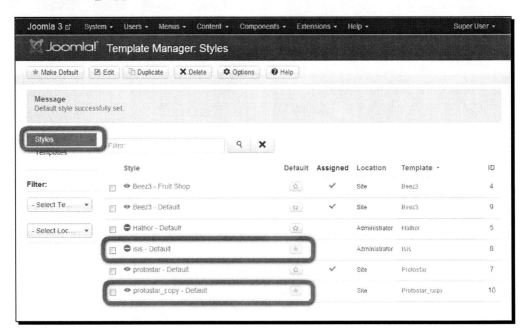

What are Template Styles?

Why is the first screen you see in the **Template Manager** called **Styles**? You might expect that this screen enables you to customize CSS styles and stylesheets that control the template design. However, this is not the case—a **Template Style** is a variation that you can create based on an existing template. Joomla allows you to save a combination of a template including its built-in settings as a **Template Style**. You can then assign this **Template Style** to one or more menu items. In other words, styles allow you to have individually styled pages or sets of pages.

One example of this is that you can set the home page to use a "green" color scheme (the first **Template Style**) and other pages in a "blue" color scheme (the second **Template Style**). We'll have a look at working with **Template Styles** in the *Applying template styles to individual pages* section.

The two meanings of the word Default

In the **Styles** screen, the word *Default* is used in two different meanings. In the top button bar, the **Make Default** button works as you would expect: it allows you to make the selected template the default one for either the frontend or the backend. However, you'll also notice templates named **Default**, such as **Protostar – Default** and **Beez3 – Default**. In this case, *default* means it's the template using its normal settings (in other words: its default, unchanged Template Style). This is to distinguish default templates from templates with a specific style applied, such as **Beez3 – Fruit Shop**. The latter template is based upon the Beez3 template, but it's saved separately as a specific Template Style for the example **Fruit Shop** site.

Customizing the current template using built-in options

Templates can include all sorts of options, allowing the site administrator to change the template width, colors, column layout, and much more without touching a single line of HTML or CSS code. Let's find out what the main options of the current template (the default style of the Protostar template) are and how they affect the look and feel of the template.

Time for action – changing the site color and layout options

We'll first have a look at some settings that affect the overall color scheme and the layout:

1. Navigate to **Extensions | Template Manager** and click the **Styles** tab. The **Template Manager: Styles** screen is displayed.

2. In the list of available templates, click on **protostar_copy – Default**:

3. You're taken to the **Edit Style** screen. Click the **Options** tab to reveal the **Advanced Options** panel, where the available settings are displayed:

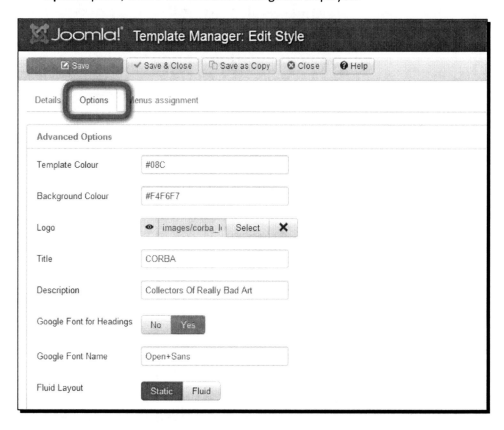

4. We'll have a look at the effects of these customization options. The **Template Colour** option allows for some quite powerful changes in the look and feel of the site. Let's try out an alternative color scheme.

5. Click **Template Colour** to select the color for accents on the website: the colored line at the top of the page, the color of menu links and headings. A color palette appears that allows you to pick a color of your choice. Click on **Select** inside the palette pop-up to confirm your choice.

6. Do the same for the **Background Colour**, the color for the background of the page (which by default is light grey).

7. Click on **Save** and then click on **View Site** to see the output:

As you can see, the **Template Colour** setting changes the colors of headings, links, and more.

8. Finally, let's find out what the effects are of the **Google Font Name** setting. By default Protostar uses the Open Sans font for all headings. Open Sans is a free font, available in the Google Fonts. You can, however, choose from hundreds of Google Fonts that you can find at `http://www.google.com/ webfonts`. Enter the font name (for example, `Bitter`). Save your changes to see the output on the frontend. All headings are now in the Bitter font:

What just happened?

Using the built-in template options you've changed the colors and fonts of the site. Every template has its own specific set of options. In this case, the template developer has added just a few basic settings that allow you to modify the site logo and colors. Other templates can contain many more options. Apart from this, you can also customize the template by changing the CSS code. We'll see an example of this later in this chapter.

Changing the site logo

It's probably one of the first things people new to Joomla do: changing the logo to put their mark on the site they've just started to build. In *Chapter 4, Web Building Basics: Creating a Site in an Hour*, you've already seen how you can add your own logo using the options panel of the Protostar template. If you don't have a logo image, the Protostar template also allows you to use a text logo instead. In the **Advanced Options** panel, locate the **Logo** option and click on the **Clear** button. The template will now display the contents of the **Title** field instead of the logo image.

Changing to a different template

Up to now, we've worked with Protostar, the default template in Joomla. However, there are a few extra templates available in the Joomla package. To see an overview, navigate to **Extensions | Template Manager** and click on the **Templates** link in the menu on the left-hand side to go to the **Templates Manager: Templates** screen:

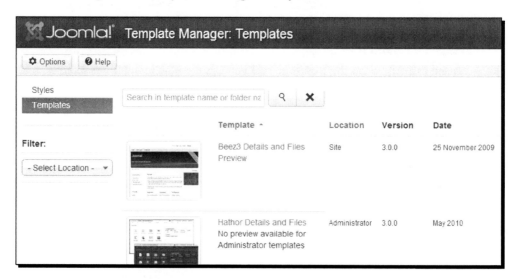

Here all available templates are displayed with thumbnail images, giving a quick impression of the page design. In the **Location** column you can see if it's a frontend or a backend template. Joomla comes with two frontend templates (**Location: Site**) and two templates that can be used in the backend (**Location: Administrator**).

Which templates come with Joomla?

A main change in Joomla 3 is the use of **Bootstrap**, a framework that's commonly used in web development. Both the frontend template and the backend template are based on Bootstrap, created by the developers of Twitter (see `http://twitter.github.com/bootstrap`). Bootstrap makes it it easier to quickly define the look and feel of websites. It contains ready-made CSS for layouts, buttons, forms, icons, table styles, and countless other design elements. The idea behind it is that web developers don't have to start from scratch—Bootstrap offers them a reliable, standards-based code library. This is great, as it offers Joomla template developers a fixed set of design elements that they can easily tap into.

One of the advantages of using Bootstrap is that all templates that come with Joomla 3 are mobile friendly. The template layout automatically adapts to the screen size of different mobile devices.

Here's an overview for the templates that come with Joomla:

Template name	What kind of template is it?
Beez3	This is the successor to Beez2, the default template in the previous version of Joomla. It's now updated for Joomla 3 and it's "powered by" Twitter Bootstrap.
Protostar	This one you know: it's the default template. In *Chapter 4, Web Building Basics: Creating a Site in an Hour*, and earlier in this chapter, you've used the built-in options to adapt Protostar to your needs.
Isis	The Isis template is the default template for the administrator backend. This is the backend template we've used throughout the book.
Hathor	There's one other administrator template available, called Hathor. It's built according to accessibility rules, allowing people using different browsers and different devices to have equal access to the site.

Previewing available templates

To get a good impression of what any of the installed templates look like, click on the template thumbnail image in the **Templates** screen. For example, clicking on the **Beez5** image opens a pop-up screen displaying a preview image:

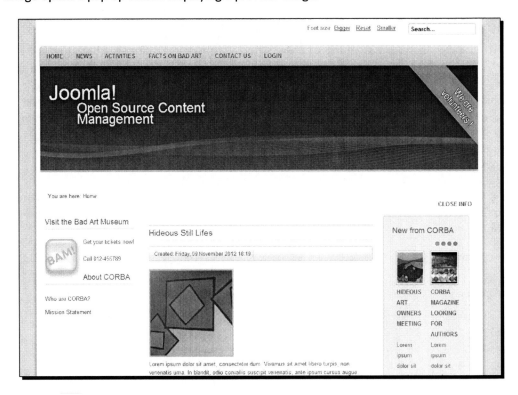

To close the preview, click on the cross in the top right-hand corner or click anywhere in the black background area.

You've just seen a template preview. However, by default the text next to the thumbnails in the **Template Manager : Templates** screen says that there's No preview available. That's because there are two ways to preview the available templates. As you've just seen, you can always click on the template thumbnail to see a bigger version of that image. To see a true preview, in the Template Manager **Options** the **Preview Module Positions** should be set to **Enabled**. This way, you can preview a template including all available module positions through the **Preview** link.

Setting a different template as the default

If you've followed along up to now, you've built an example website using Joomla's default template, Protostar. Let's assume your client has some more specific requirements. They have introduced a new visual identity and want their website to reflect this. It seems it's time for a general overhaul of the site's look and feel. As a first step, you'll explore the alternative template available in Joomla.

Time for action – activating a different template

Let's try a different template on for size. In this example, we'll choose the **Beez 3** template:

1. Navigate to **Extensions | Template Manager**.

2. Click the star in the **Default** column of the **Beez3 - Default** template. This turns Beez3 into the default template. Click on **View Site** to see the results:

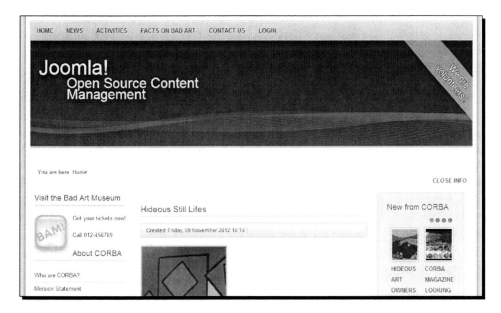

The default site name **Joomla! Open Source Content Management** is displayed in the header. Let's fix this now.

3. Click the template name in the **Template Manager: Styles** page. In **Template Manager: Edit Style** screen, click the **Options** tab to change the **Advanced Options** as desired. Select the CORBA logo image file you've used previously and enter the appropriate **Site Title** (in our example **CORBA**) and **Description** (**Collectors Of Really Bad Art**).

4. As the template's color, select **Turquoise**. This will affect the header graphic and replace it with a smooth gradient color. Save changes and take a look at the output on the frontend:

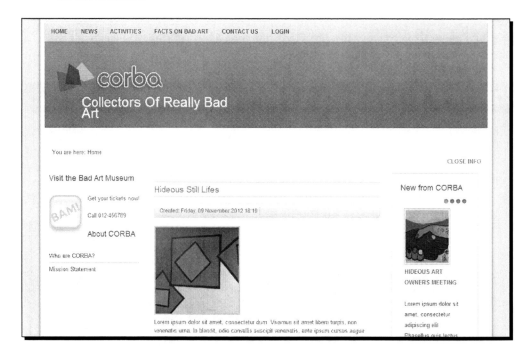

The new template looks much better now. As you can see, I've changed the Content Slider module settings to display only one column of teaser texts (**New from CORBA**, in the right column). If we were to use this template, you could also consider moving other modules to the new positions available in this template. For now, we're just trying this template on for size, so we won't bother fixing the details.

What just happened?

Same content, different design; by setting a new default template you've given the site a completely new look. The ability to change templates in a few clicks is one of the things that really makes Joomla stand out. Without needing any coding skills you can completely transform the site's appearance.

> Not every template contains this same set of options. Template builders can decide to add dozens of options—or just one or two. Having less built-in options doesn't limit your customization options though. You can still edit the template properties by looking under the hood and change the CSS or HTML code. We'll dive into this later in this chapter.

Applying Template Styles to individual pages

Most websites probably use just one template. However, in Joomla it's possible to assign specific templates to style individual pages or groups of pages. If your site is divided into five main categories, why not use the five different styles, each with their own set of options selected?

Time for action – creating a Template Style for one specific page

Let's assume your client has a few special pages on the site about a special event. They want to make this event page stand out from the rest of the site. To create this effect, we'll create and apply a Template Style. We'll create a copy of a template and use it to style only the pages that are linked to through one specific menu link.

1. First, we'll make a dummy page and a menu link pointing to it. In this example, we'll create an article page titled **Visit the Bad Art Event** and a Main Menu link of the **Single Article** type, titled **Bad Art Event**.

2. Go to **Extensions | Template Manager** to access the **Template Manager: Styles** screen.

3. We'll use the Beez 3 template we've just assigned as the default template and create a copy of it. Select **Beez3 - Default** by ticking the select box to the left-hand side of the template name. Click on the **Duplicate** button:

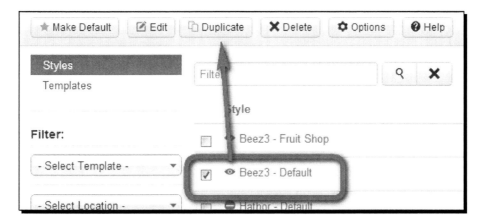

4. A copy of the template appears in the list, called **Beez3 – Default (2)**. Click on this name to edit the new style. In the **Edit Style** screen, select the settings that will distinguish this style from the default Beez template:

- ❑ In the **Style Name** field, enter `Beez3 - Bad Art Event Style`.

- ❑ Click the **Options** tab to access the **Advanced Options** panel. Click on the **Clear** button next to the **Logo** field. In the **Site Title** field, add **CORBA Bad Art Event**. Clear the **Site Description** field. This way, only the event name will be displayed instead of the default logo file.

- ❑ Select **Position of Navigation: after content**. This means the main content will be displayed on the left-hand side, before other columns.

- ❑ In the **Template colour** drop-down box, select **Red**.

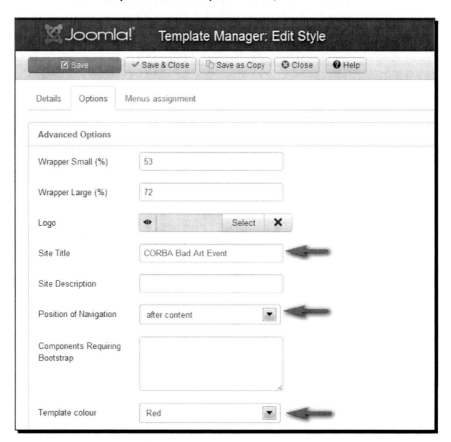

- ❑ In the **Menus Assignment** section, tick the **Bad Art Event** menu link. This will ensure the template is only applied to the one page this link points to.

5. Click on **Save**. A message is displayed, confirming that the selected menu items have been assigned to the new template style. Click on **View Site**. On the home page and on other pages of the site, nothing has changed. However, when you click the **Bad Art Event** link, you'll notice that the new Template Style is active:

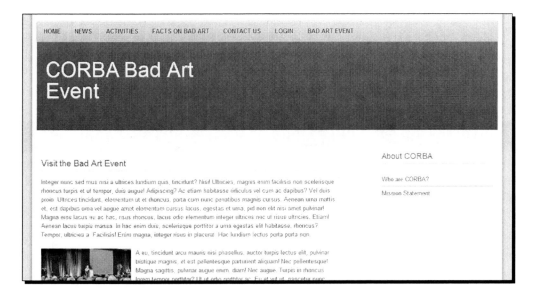

Assigning templates from the menu item itself

As templates are linked to specific menu items, you can also assign templates (or Template Styles) directly when editing a menu link. This means that you can control template assignment both from the template settings screen and the menu item screen. In the Menu Item **Details** section, use the **Template Style** drop-down box for this.

Downloading and installing a new template

Of course, the templates that ship with Joomla are just a few examples of the possible designs. Do you need a really different layout or do you want a more attractive design? There are tons of templates available on the Web. You'll download the template files as one compressed file and install this compressed template file through the Extension Manager. Once it's installed, you can activate it through the **Template Styles** screen as described earlier in this chapter.

Physically, a Joomla template is a bunch of files. When you download a template, these files are packed together in a compressed format (usually a ZIP file). Joomla provides you with a powerful one-click-method to upload and unpack the ZIP file, installing all of the required template files on the web server, ready for use.

Imagine your client wants something really different, a site with its own specific layout. In that case, you probably don't want to settle for any of the default Joomla templates. You search the Web for a template that fits the clean new logo and corporate style of your client. Let's see how you can download a free template from a professional template developer.

Time for action – downloading and activating a new template

For your site redesign, you've hit upon a great looking template on the Web. In this example, we'll use the **Future** template developed by IceTheme. It is a clean and basic template that offers enough opportunities to customize the layout and appearance.

1. Navigate to `http://www.icetheme.com/Downloads/Joomla-Templates/ Free-Joomla-Templates/Future/View-Category`.

2. Click the **Download** button. The compressed template file (`IT_Future_V.3.0.0- (unzip-first)-9544626154.zip`) is saved to your computer.

3. Navigate to the ZIP file on your computer and unzip it. The ZIP file contains several other ZIP packages: the template, an installation guide, and several free extensions that come with the template. After you've decompressed the ZIP file, the following files should be available:

Clone_Installer-(Joomla-3.0.2).zip	10.201 kB
IceCarousel_Unzip_First.zip	515 kB
IceMegaMenu_Unzip_First.zip	628 kB
Installation_Guide.pdf	1.302 kB
tpl_ice_future.zip	787 kB

4. After you've uncompressed the main ZIP file, you should also unzip the following files: `IceMegaMenu_Unzip_First.zip` and `IceCarousel_Unzip_First.zip`. Using these extensions isn't obligatory, but you can choose to deploy them to add a better menu system to your site and a home page slideshow. You can ignore the `Clone_Installer-(Joomla-3.0.2).zip` file; this is only used to create a full copy of the IceTheme demo site for this template.

5. Navigate to **Extensions | Extension Manager**. Click **Browse** and navigate to the `tpl_ice_future.zip` file on your computer. Select it and click **Upload & Install**. A notice is displayed: **Installing template was successful.**

6. To activate the new template, go to **Extensions | Template Manager**. On the **Styles** page put a check mark in the checkbox next to **ice_future**. Click the **Make Default** button in the toolbar.

7. Click **View Site**. The new template is now active:

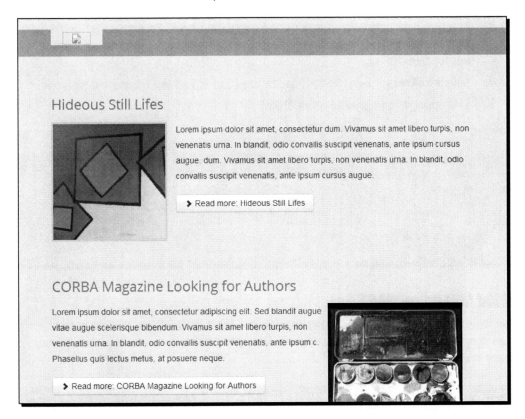

What just happened?

You've just downloaded and activated a new template. Although the new design is applied, you'll notice many elements of our original layout (such as menus) don't show up. This is common when you step over to a new template. You'll often need to change the logo, change module positions, and fix a couple of other settings.

Time for action – adding the logo file

Let's first add the CORBA logo to the new template and set a few template options.

1. Navigate to **Extensions | Templates** and open the Ice Future template. Click the **Options** tab.

2. Click **Select** next to **Site Logo** and upload and select the new graphic logo file for the CORBA website (`corbalogo_restyled.png`).

3. The template options also include the possibility to add Facebook and Twitter buttons to the site. As we won't add buttons pointing to a Facebook or Twitter account, select **No**.

4. Select **IceTheme Logo: No** to hide the logo and link to the template developer.

5. Save changes and preview the output:

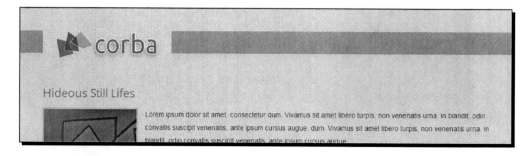

What just happened?

You've added a graphic logo file and changed a few settings. However, this is just the first step in preparing our new site design for the limelight. We'll now make sure menus and other modules are visible again.

Time for action – adding a menu module

The template we've downloaded, Ice Future, comes with a couple of free modules. You don't really need them in order to be able to use the template. However, they can add useful functionality to your site. Especially the **IceMegaMenu** module brings many advantages in comparison with the Joomla menu module and it renders a menu that blends in nicely with the template design. Let's add this module:

1. Navigate to **Extensions | Extension Manager** and click **Browse** to navigate to the downloaded menu module, `mod_icemegamenu_v.3.0.0.zip`. Install the module.

2. Next, select the `plugin plg_icemegamenu_v.3.0.0.zip` and install this plugin too.

3. Enable the plugin. Go to **Extensions | Plug-in Manager** and locate the **IceMegaMenu** plugin. Click on the red cross in the **Status** column. It changes into a check mark; the plugin is active.

4. Now we can enable the menu module and change its settings. Navigate to **Extensions| Module Manager** and open the IceMegaMenu module. Change the settings as follows:

    ❏   Change the **Status** to **Published** and change the **Position** to **Mainmenu [mainmenu]**

    ❏   Click **IceMegaMenu Parameters**. Choose **Select Menu: Main Menu**

    ❏   Click the **Menu Assignment** tab and choose **On all pages**

5. Save your changes. You're done!

What just happened?

There's now a horizontal drop-down menu that perfectly fits the blue bar at the top. In the following example, I've added a few submenu links to the **Activities** main link to illustrate the drop-down effect:

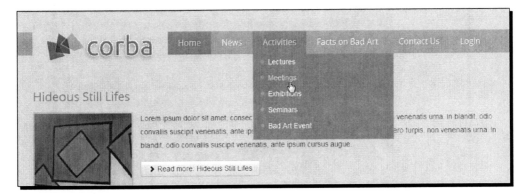

The great thing about this menu is that it's responsive, just like the template itself. You can try this out right away: if you make the browser screen smaller, the drop-down menu changes to fit the new screen size.

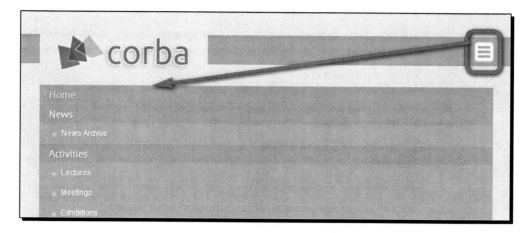

You've now changed a couple of template settings and added a better menu module. However, in the CORBA site we had a few other modules that aren't visible in the new template. Next, we'll fix this problem.

Getting the most out of the Mega Menu extension

Usually a template only contains the files that take care of the site design and layout, but the Ice Future template comes with a separate IceMegaMenu module. It's offered as a part of the free Ice Future bundle. As you've installed this extension and the accompanying plugin, you'll find a set of extra features for every menu link in the main menu.

Using a mega menu, you can add more content to the menu than just menulinks: for example, you can add descriptions and create drop-downs with two or more columns. It's even possible to add module contents to the drop-downs (for example, to display a login module in a menu drop-down).

How do you use this mega menu functionality? Open any menulink that contains submenu links and click on **Advanced Options**. Here you'll find the **IceMegaMenu Parameters**. Here you can enter a **SubTitle** (a few words of explanation that will appear below the actual menulink text) and you can set the number of columns for every drop-down submenu. The output can look as follows:

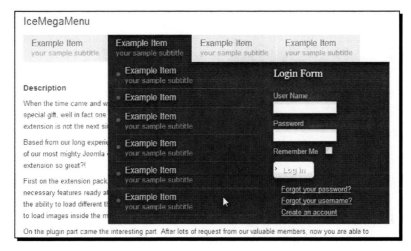

To find out more about the features of the Ice MegaMenu, have a look at the installation guide PDF that's part of the extension package.

Time for action – placing modules in new template positions

After you have installed a new template, not all module blocks will show up. This is because different templates contain different (and differently named) module positions. As you saw in a previous chapter, templates contains positions, referred to as ' left ', ' position-1 ', ' position-2 ', and so on. In this case the new template positions are different from the positions in the default template. The next step is to assign modules that we have used in the example site to their new template positions.

1. To find out what module positions are available, navigate to **Extensions | Template Manager | Templates** and click on the **Preview** link for the IceFuture template. The positions available in the current template are shown:

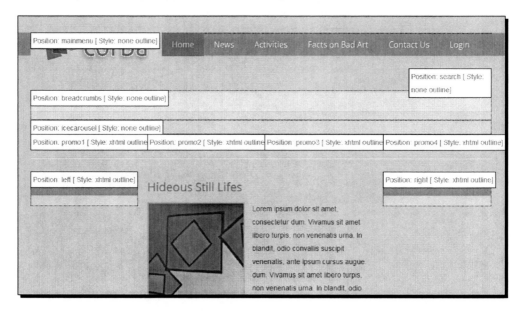

2. Navigate to **Extensions | Module Manager**. Open the following modules and assign them to the appropriate positions:

Module name	Type	New position
Visit the Bad Art Museum	Custom HTML	**footer2**
New from CORBA	BT Content Slider	**right**
Breadcrumbs	Breadcrumbs	**breadcrumbs**
Search	Search	**search**
About CORBA	Menu	**footer1**

3. Save changes and click **View Site**. The modules are displayed again:

What just happened?

You're almost done restyling your client's site. You've downloaded and installed a new template, you've changed a few settings and made sure all modules are displayed in the desired positions. The site looks pretty good now and it's quite different from your average Joomla-powered site. In the next few sections, you learn how you can tweak it further by filling more module positions and change the design by customizing the template CSS code.

Have a go hero – change page and module layout

The fun part of templates is that you can easily change the appearance of your site, not just by applying a new template, but also by playing around with template options and experimenting with moving modules to the available module positions. Here's an example of how the design and layout can change by adjusting a few options:

How can you achieve a layout like this?

- You'll notice that the Content Slider module position has changed. Instead of being displayed in the **Right** column, it's now shown in the **promotion** position of the IceFuture template. The template contains code to check if any content is assigned to this position; if it is, a big blue bar is shown in the background of the module contents. To get the module contents to fill this horizontal bar, the module properties have been set to display four teasers next to each other (in four columns).

♦ The **Home menu** link settings have been changed to display three intro texts next to each other, in three columns.

Feel free to experiment with the settings of the home page menu link, the placement of modules, and the template settings. Your choices can result in an entirely different look and feel.

Customizing a template: tweaking CSS styles

In this chapter, you've seen how to customize templates using the built-in options. However, as not all templates contain the same set of options, sometimes you'll have to dive under the hood and change a file or a few lines of code to get the template to look just the way you want. You've experienced this in *Chapter 4*, *Web Building Basics: Creating a Site in an Hour*, when you wanted to change the tagline of the Protostar template and had to change a line of CSS code.

In the beginning of this chapter you learned that Cascading Style Sheets (CSS) take care of your website's look and feel. If you want to change way the site looks, you'll edit the styles in its CSS file (or CSS files, as the template designer often splits the necessary code into different stylesheet files).

If you're not familiar with CSS and what it does, have a look at the basic explanation in the following section. After that, we'll see some examples of how tweaking CSS code of a Joomla template works. Later in this chapter you'll find some useful resources explaining CSS in more detail (see *Expanding your CSS knowledge* later in this chapter).

Understanding the very basics of CSS

If you'd like to further customize the template we've just installed, you'd have to know a thing or two about CSS—so let's have a look at the basics of CSS coding. In Joomla, HTML and CSS codes are contained in separate documents. This way, several web pages (HTML documents) can be linked to the same CSS stylesheet. That's a huge advantage in terms of customizability. By updating a few lines in just one stylesheet you change the look of several pages (without having to touch the underlying HTML).

Joomla provides a simple text editor to open up the CSS files the template uses and to modify the code. This is great for making some quick changes to the template. Luckily, the basics of CSS code aren't difficult to understand. Typically, the rules in a CSS stylesheet look like this:

```
h1 {
color: red;
font-weight: bold;
}
```

This rule applies to the h1 element (a top level heading) in the HTML document. It tells your browser to style this heading by setting the text color to red and the font-weight to bold. CSS rules always are enclosed in curly braces. The lines that are part of a CSS rule ("declarations" such as color:red;) are always separated by semicolons.

If you want to change the background color of all h1 headings to blue, you adjust the h1 style rule in the CSS file and replace the original value (that is, red):

```
h1 {
color: blue;
font-weight: bold;
}
```

Here's another example of a CSS style rule:

```
.lead {
  margin-bottom: 18px;
  font-size: 20px;
  line-height: 27px;
}
```

This style has its own class name, .lead. In this example, the properties margin-bottom, font-size, and line-height will be applied to any element in the HTML page with the .lead class. Assigning this class name to any text will make the browser render the text in a relatively big (20 pixels) font size and add some extra space between lines (line-height) and below the paragraph (margin-bottom).

That's it—this concludes your five-minute crash course in CSS. If you want to dive deeper into CSS, you'll learn more about some great web resources on this subject later on. For now, let's see what changing a few lines of CSS can do for our example site.

Time for action – customizing the background color using CSS

Customizing the CSS codes of the template can be relatively easy, especially when it comes to changing properties such as colors, font types, and images. You can edit the template stylesheets from within the Joomla backend. Here's how:

1. Navigate to **Extensions | Template Manager**. In the menu on the left-hand side, click on **Templates**.

2. Now click the link of the template you want to edit. In this example, click **Ice_future Details and Files**:

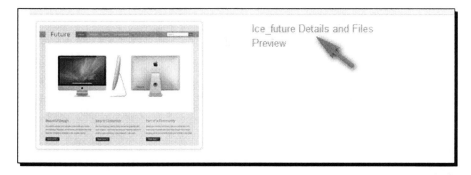

3. On the right-hand side of the screen, you'll notice a section called **Stylesheets**. Click the name of the stylesheet, `css/template.css`. This will open the source code of the stylesheet in an editor screen.

4. In the editor screen, locate the body style declaration. It should look like this:

```
body {
    background:#e5e5e5;
    line-height:26px;}
```

5. Change the highlighted line as follows:

```
    background:#ffffff;
```

This will change the background color of the site to white (the color code for white is `#ffffff`).

6. The site logo also has a grey background. We'll change this in a similar way. Locate the the `#logo` style. It should look like this:

```
#logo {
    float:left;
    background:#e5e5e5;
    display:inline-block;
    padding:0 20px;
    font-size:18px;}
```

7. Change the highlighted line as follows:

```
    background:#ffffff;
```

8. Save your changes and have a look at the frontend of the site.

What just happened?

You'll notice the site now has a fresh, white background color:

(If you don't see any changes, press *F5* or **Refresh** to force your browser to reload the page.) Of course, you can change the color to any value you like: just do a web search for "css colour codes" to find an overview of the codes to apply.

Analyzing Joomla CSS using web developer tools

In the previous section, you've changed a few lines of CSS code in the Joomla editor—but how do you find out which particular CSS styles you have to edit in order to get the desired effect? How can you find out, for example, that the logo background is styled through the `#logo` style?

In Joomla, your best chance would be to go to the Template Editor and try to figure out what's the appropriate style by analyzing the CSS stylesheet. However, template and extension developers are likely to add several CSS files containing any amount of styles. Luckily, there's a much more effective solution. Using the **Inspect element** feature of the Chrome browser (or using Firefox along with the Firebug web development plugin) you can inspect any web page and analyze the current HTML and relevant CSS styles, shown in separate sections of the browser window.

Let's take a look at an example, using the Chrome browser. Suppose you want to find out what CSS code you need to change to customize the logo background color in the current template. Open your Joomla-powered website in Chrome, right-click anywhere in the window and select **Inspect element**. In the bottom half of the browser window, two screens will display the HTML and the CSS code of the current web page. Now you can start inspecting page elements, just by clicking the little lens icon at the bottom of the browser screen and hovering your mouse over the web page. Select any part of the web page to see all related code, as shown in the following screenshot:

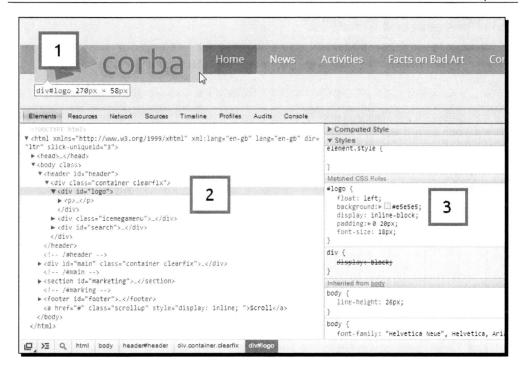

By clicking the logo area on the web page (1), we see that the logo background is styled through the **div#logo** style. In bottom-left screen (2) you can see the HTML code of this DIV element, in the bottom right screen (3) you can see the relevant CSS. In this case, the background color is set to #e5e5e5.

Now here's the fun part: you can even edit the CSS and type another color code (such as **#ffffff** for white) and immediately see the effects. This is a great way to test code changes. Your edits aren't stored, as the browser doesn't have access to your Joomla files. To commit changes, you edit the original CSS files using the Joomla CSS editor or any other text editor, and save the CSS file. The inspector tool even tells you exactly what CSS file contains the current code.

To find out more about using the Chrome developer tools, have a look at this tutorial at http://webdesign.tutsplus.com/tutorials/workflow-tutorials/faster-htmlcss-workflow-with-chrome-developer-tools. A very similar tool for Firefox is the Firebug plugin; see http://www.w3resource.com/web-development-tools/firebug-tutorials.php.

Expanding your CSS knowledge

Do you want to get deeper into the fine art of creating and editing stylesheets? You'll find plenty of helpful resources on the Web. Just search for "CSS tutorial" or take a look at:

- The basic tutorial article, CSS from the Ground Up: `www.wpdfd.com/issues/70/css_from_the_ground_up`.

- The CSS Tutorial site: `http://www.csstutorial.net/introductionCSS.php`.

- W3Schools' CSS tutorials, examples, and demo's: `http://www.w3schools.com/css/css_intro.asp`.

Editing the template HTML

If you want to make more fundamental changes to a template, Joomla also allows you to edit the template HTML. There's an HTML editor available in the Joomla backend, much like the CSS editor screen. If you want, you can change any template code. You can add, change, delete, or move any existing page element—columns, header, and footer, whatever you like. Of course, you should only do this if you know your way around in HTML; don't risk messing up the site layout.

Even if you're not aiming to immerse yourself in the nitty gritty of HTML, being able to change the template HTML directly in Joomla is still useful. It allows you to change or remove unwanted items that are sometimes "hardcoded" (that is, a fixed part of the HTML code) into the template, such as a footer text or copyright notice. To access the HTML editor, navigate to **Extensions | Template Manager**. On the **Templates** page, click on **[template name] Details and Files**. In the next screen, click on the **Edit Main Page** link. You're taken to the HTML editor screen. This works similar to the CSS editor screen; you can change code and store your changes immediately in the original file.

Backing up and restoring a customized template

Editing a template directly in Joomla is a great way to tweak the layout as you go. You're able to apply changes in the backend and immediately preview the effects of every adjustment you've made. However, there is a drawback: all changes in the template files are only stored on the web server. If for some reason you were to re-install the template, these changes would be lost.

To prevent this from happening, back up the template as soon as you've finished customizing it. This is how:

- Start up your FTP program and browse to the folder that contains the template you want to backup. In the case of the **ice_future** template, this would be something like `/httpdocs/templates/ice_future`. Here `httpdocs` is the root folder of the Joomla installation on the web server; in your situation the root folder might have another name, such as `www` or `htdocs`.

- Download the template folder (including subfolders and their contents) to your computer.

This folder contains all template files. If you want to re-install the template later, just upload this folder to the same location on the web server again—the `templates` folder in the root directory of the Joomla installation.

A different approach: customizing a template offline

In this chapter, you've customized a template by editing the template files in the Joomla template editor screen. Another option would be to download the template files first, open them for editing in the web editing program of your choice, and uploading them again after you've finished customization. This can be a good idea if you know your way around in (and like working with) web editing tools such as Notepad++ or Adobe Dreamweaver. The template building resources mentioned in the next section should help you on your way if you like to explore this method.

Where can you get a new template for your site?

If you search the Web for "Joomla 3.0 template", you'll get a dazzling number of results. It can take hours to find the one template that's just right for your goals. Instead, you might want to start your template search in dedicated Joomla template gallery sites.

- Good starting places are template sites such as `www.joomla24.com`, `www.bestofjoomla.com`, and `www.cmslounge.com`. These sites offer hundreds of templates. Browse the collections and check out live previews of the templates you like.

- Check the collections of professional Joomla template developers, such as `www.rockettheme.com`, `www.joomlashack.com`, `www.gavick.com`, `www.yootheme.com`, and `www.joomlabamboo.com`.

How do you find the perfect template, with the quality and the design approach that suits your needs? It's good to be picky—after all, the default template Protostar is already pretty versatile. It's suitable for smartphones and tablets, you can customize colors and fonts, and it contains many module positions that give you a lot of freedom to determine the page layout. Here are a few more things to keep in mind when you're looking for a template:

- The template shouldn't be too complicated. Some developers add more and more options to their templates. Although that may seem advantageous, it also means that it takes time to get the template to work just the way you want it to. Beware of "heavy" templates with a lot of code, scripts, and large images, as they can slow down your website.

- You'll be able to find quality templates that are completely free. There are also many templates offered by commercial developers. Note that makers of free templates sometimes require you to keep a copyright-link in the footer, pointing to the developer website. Often, it's a matter of trying out the template and checking its license restrictions.

- Should the template be suitable for all screen sizes and all devices? In that case, check if the template is "responsive". This way, it will automatically adjust the layout for different devices.

- Make sure that the template you download is suited for the Joomla 3. Joomla 1.5 and 2.5 templates won't work in newer releases.

Creating your own template

Using an existing template (and customizing it) will help you get great results while saving lots of time, compared to creating your own template from scratch. However, if you want full control or need a unique layout you can make a Joomla template all by yourself. It isn't complicated, but it does require a good deal of HTML and CSS coding skills. If you know how to build a website using HTML and CSS, then you won't experience any problems converting your design into a Joomla template. Most of your time and effort will go into creating a page design from the ground up, rather than into the adjustments needed to adapt that design for Joomla.

As it is mainly a question of HTML and CSS coding, we won't cover template creation in full detail here. To get you started, here are a few pointers. These are the five main steps it takes to create your own template:

- **Sketching**: Design an overall layout for your website. Where do you want the main content, the navigation, and the other page elements? Think blocks, just like Joomla does. Divide the page into blocks containing menus, articles, and images. The result is a schematic representation of the page.

- **Designing**: Create a layout in a graphic editor, such as Photoshop or the GIMP. The result is a mockup of the site design. You'll only use bits and pieces of that image in the final template, such as the logo image or some image parts containing shadow effects.

- **Coding**: Turn your design into real web page code using HMTL and CSS. You can use a web development tool such as Dreamweaver that allows you to immediately see the results of your coding.

- **Customizing the code for Joomla**: Adapt the CSS and HTML code to create Joomla template files. In the main template file you'll insert codes telling Joomla where it should place its dynamic content (such as modules).

- **Putting your template together**: Any template consists of a set of required files, such as a file containing information about the template (author name, copyright, and so on). Finally, you'll include all of these files in a compressed file (a ZIP file). Now your template is ready to be uploaded and installed via **Extensions | Install & Uninstall**.

Template building resources

There are many tutorials on the Web that can help you on your way when you want to create Joomla templates. A web search for "Joomla template tutorial" will surely help you on your way. However, since Joomla 3 the technique behind templates has changed substantially. The main change is the integration of the Twitter Bootstrap web development framework you read about earlier in this chapter.

- **Building a Basic Joomla 3.0 Template with Bootstrap**: `http://www.inmotionhosting.com/support/edu/joomla-3/create-template`

- **Tutorial: Make a Joomla 3.5 Template [blank template included]**: `http://www.barryflood.com/create-a-template-for-joomla-35.php`

- **Blank Template and Twitter Bootstrap Tutorial for Joomla!**: A guide to creating your own Joomla template based upon a free empty template. `http://blank.vc/de/blog/6-blank-template-and-twitter-bootstrap-tutorial-for-joomla.html`

Using template generator software

What if you want to create your own template from scratch, but don't feel confident using coding languages? You could consider using a special Windows-based software program to create Joomla templates for Joomla, called **Artisteer**. It's a very user-friendly program that allows you to use example templates or design suggestions, but you can also choose full manual control over the layout and appearance of the site. You can export your design as a Joomla template and install it in the usual way. There are a few caveats: the program isn't free (it costs about $100) and the code it generates is less optimized than custom-made HTML and CSS. However, it can be a great solution if you're creative and want to have full control over the site design. You can download a trial version at www.artisteer.com.

Using a template framework as a base for your own template

Instead of downloading a ready-made template or creating your own template from the ground up, there's also a third option—using a template framework. A framework is basically a template with a huge amount of built-in options, allowing you to define the layout, module positions, menu styles, colors, fonts and sometimes much more straight away from the template control panel. Although template frameworks come packed with features and give you a great deal of control , they do require you to spend some time getting to know your way around and learning how to customize them (as different framework developers follow their own specific design strategies).

If you are interested in template frameworks for Joomla, this is a good introduction on the subject: 'Using a Joomla Template Framework to Design your Site', http://magazine. joomla.org/issues/issue-oct-2012/item/891-using-a-joomla-template-framework-to-design-your-site. For a comparision of frameworks, have a look at www.joomlashine.com/blog/9-joomla-framework-solutions-for-developers. html.

Pop quiz – test your knowledge of Joomla templates

Q1. What does a Joomla template actually do?

    a.   It changes the colors and the header graphic.

    b.   It determines the overall layout and design.

    c.   It allows you to set all sorts of layout options.

Q2. After installing a new template, you notice some empty spaces in your site layout. What does this mean?

    a.   Something went wrong and you should re-install the template.

    b.   You have to assign modules to the available (empty) positions.

    c.   You have to add content to some (empty) modules.

Q3. What are the benefits of using web developer tools, such as the the Inspect element feature of the Chrome browser?

    a.   You can preview CSS edits and automatically save changes to your template.

    b.   You can edit CSS in the backend of your Joomla site.

    c.   You can analyze and edit CSS styles of any website, and you can preview the effects of any changes you make.

Summary

In this chapter, you've learned much about the power of Joomla templates:

- A Joomla template is a set of files containing the HTML and CSS code that defines what your web page looks like. Joomla comes with a few different templates. Most templates have built-in options that allow you to tweak the look and behavior.

- If you want a different layout, there are tons of templates you can download from the Web, and a good many of them are available for free. Customizing an existing template is a great way to personalize the look and feel of the website. Joomla's Template Manager allows you to change the CSS styles the template uses—for example, when you want to change the color scheme or replace the default logo image.

- If you need a customized template for your site, you can consider either building your own template from the ground up, or using a template framework as a base for your own design.

As far as content, functionality, and looks are concerned, your site is about finished; but there are still a few important things to take care of. In the next chapter, you'll learn what measures you can take to attract visitors and get search engines to pick up your site.

12

Attracting Search Engine Traffic: SEO Tips and Techniques

You've created a great site—now it's time to get the world to discover that it's there! Up to now, your attention has gone towards the site's content, navigation, its extra features, and its design. In this chapter, let's see what you can do to attract more visitors (or site traffic, as it's usually called). You'll deploy some essential techniques and basic settings in Joomla that can influence your search engine rankings. This is called **Search Engine Optimization** *(SEO).*

In this chapter, you'll learn about:

- ◆ Optimizing articles
- ◆ Adding metadata to your content
- ◆ Using search engine friendly (SEF) URLs
- ◆ Creating internal hyperlinks
- ◆ Redirecting visitors to updated URLs

SEO is a subject surrounded with many secrets and myths—and with gurus claiming they have the definite answer to all questions. As search engines obviously won't reveal the secret algorithms they use to calculate their search results rankings, these definite answers do not exist. There's no SEO technique or mix of SEO techniques that will bring you overnight success. However, there are some common-sense techniques you can apply in your Joomla-powered site to optimize your visibility for search engines and to get them to pick up your content.

The first and foremost SEO rule is to make sure you offer great content. If you don't have a site that's regularly updated with quality content, people won't bother to visit (and they certainly won't bother to come back). Only if your site offers relevant content, is it worth optimizing that content for best search engine results.

Why do you need to accommodate for search engines?

Search engines are probably the main tool people will use to get to your site. To add your site to their database, search engines use software to scan the World Wide Web looking for relevant content. Of course, search engines can't see your site. They'll analyze the source code text of the site (shown in the following screenshot) and try to understand what your site is about, and what data in it could be important to search engine users:

```
140                    <div class="items-row cols-3 row-0 row-fluid">
141                            <div class="item column-1 span4">
142                                    <h2 class="item-title">
143                            <a href="/index.php/news/107-join-the-bad-art-course"> Bad Art Course
       </a>
144                    </h2>
145
146                                    <p><img style="margin: 0px 10px 10px 0px; float: left;"
       src="/images/hideous-abstract-200x200.jpg" alt="" width="200" height="200" />Lorem ipsum dolor sit amet,
       consectetur adipiscing elit. Sed blandit augue vitae augue scelerisque bibendum. </p>
147                            <a class="btn" href="/index.php/news/107-join-the-bad-art-course"> <i class="icon-
       chevron-right"></i>
148            Read more: Bad Art Course    </a>
149                                    </div>
150
151
152
153                            <div class="item column-2 span4">
154                                    <h2 class="item-title">
155                            <a href="/index.php/news/109-magazine-out-now"> Magazine Out Now</a>
156                    </h2>
157
158                                    <p><img style="margin: 0px 10px 10px 0px; float: left;"
       src="/images/ugly-colors.jpg" alt="" width="200" height="200" />Lorem ipsum dolor sit amet, consectetur
       adipiscing elit. Sed blandit augue vitae augue scelerisque bibendum. Vivamus sit amet libero turpis, non
       venenatis urna. In blandit, odio convallis suscipit venenatis, ante ipsum c. Phasellus quis lectus metus
```

All SEO techniques really boil down to increasing the visibility of your content to the search engines. How can you make it as easy as possible for search engine robots to interpret your web pages' source code and to find, understand, and index your content? We'll explore a few different techniques, starting with the stuff it's all about: articles.

Optimizing articles for findability

When writing or editing articles in Joomla's article editor, what can you do to optimize your content for search engine visibility? Let's start with some simple good practices.

1. The article title – make it meaningful

The first thing to think about carefully is the article title, the very first piece of data you enter in the article editor. In Joomla, the title entered in the article **Title** field will be displayed on two key positions. It's of course shown above the article itself, but it's also displayed in the browser title bar or in the current browser tab:

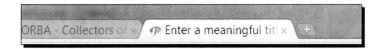

It's a good idea to use strong, meaningful, descriptive, and specific titles. Don't use a similar title for different articles. Make sure you know what people are looking for on your site; if possible, use relevant keywords in your article titles. If you're aiming at amateur painters, it's good to have clear titles carrying keywords that appeal to your readers, such as *Ten tips to create better paintings*, *How to paint like the pros*, or *Painting techniques tutorial*. Being as specific as you can means it's better to have a title such as *Ugly Paintings Society Annual Meeting* than just some general title such as *This Year's Meeting*. In the example site, we've used a few randomly picked titles. You'll notice there's room for improvement there. A title such as *The Art of Bob Ross* doesn't make it clear that the article is about a lecture on this subject. Something more specific would be: *Art Lecture on Bob Ross Paintings*.

Although it's good to be specific, you should also aim to keep things short. Bear in mind the page title will usually be shown as the first line in the site description on the search engine's results page (and might be truncated). Google, for example, will only display the first 66 characters.

2. The article structure – use clear formatting

Don't use headings that are just plain text styled as bold type. Your visitors may recognize those lines as headings, but search engines won't. Search engines scan HTML documents for headings that follow a hierarchical structure. The main page heading should be formatted with a `Heading 1` (or `H1`) style, the secondary level headings should have a `Heading 2` (`H2`) style, and so on.

In Joomla's article editor, you apply **Heading 1** through **Heading 6** using the article editor **Format** drop-down box. As search engines give headings more weight than regular article text, it's a good idea to use keywords in your page headings. Instead of generic headings ("Lesson Two" or "Improve your art skills") use specific heading texts ("How to Paint Great Landscapes").

Adding H1 headings

Joomla uses the H1 tag for page headings. These headings are only displayed if you select this in the options of the menu link pointing to this page: under **Page Display Options**, select **Show Page Heading: Yes**.

Instead of using the **Menu Title** text as the page header, you can also choose to write an alternative H1 page heading. This is also done through the menu link settings: whatever menu link you create, in the **New Menu Item/Edit Menu Item** screen, you'll find a field where you can enter a specific **Page Heading** under the **Page Display Options**:

Using this option, you can customize the H1 heading for any article that's directly linked to through a menu item. On the frontend of the site, the new **Page Heading** is displayed just above the (first) article title:

Page Heading and Page Title – what's the difference?

Don't be confused by the **Page Display Options** panel: the **Page Heading** is the text in the H1 element, the **Browser Page Title** is the text contained in the HTML title element. In other words, you can set both the H1 element and the title element for any menu item. You'll learn more about the HTML title in the *Configuring HTML page titles section* later in this chapter.

Adding H2 headings

The second heading level, H2, is used for the main content headings. On a Joomla article page, H2 is the article title.

Adding H3 through H6 headings

The article editor **Format** drop-down box allows you to apply any heading tag from H1 to H6. As H1 is already used for the page heading and H2 is used for the article title, you should use only H3, H4, H5, and H6 headings within the article text:

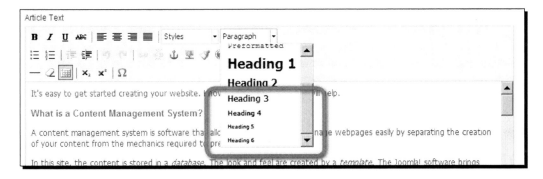

Optimizing the use of H1 headings

Using the approach described above, you can have a page structure like this:

- ◆ H1: Main page heading set though **Menu Title** (for example, **Web Design Trends**)
- ◆ H2: Article heading set through **Article Title** (for example, **An Overview of Current Web Layouts**)
- ◆ H3 − H6: Article subheadings set in the article text itself

This default setup means that you can end up with pages without an H1 heading, if you don't add page headings. In those cases, it would be better to use the H1 element for the article heading, as it is the only remaining page heading. Unfortunately, Joomla doesn't allow you to display the article title using H1 tags instead of H2 tags.

However, if you want more control over heading tags in your site, there's a great free plugin available called **Header Tags**. This changes existing heading tags according to your specifications. After installation, it checks if there is an H1 tag in the output. If there isn't, the first H2 tag will be changed into an H1 tag. Problem solved! See http://extensions.joomla.org/extensions/site-management/seo-a-metadata/meta-data/14835.

3. The article body text – use relevant keywords

It's a good idea to use relevant keywords in your article body text. When writing or editing your text, ask yourself what words your visitors would use when searching for the content you offer? Try to anticipate the different search terms, synonyms, and abbreviations that different types of visitors would use.

If you're stuck for keyword inspiration, you should definitely consider using one of the many online tools available. The **Google Adwords Keyword Tool** is an excellent example; you'll find it at `https://adwords.google.com/select/KeywordToolExternal`.

Make sure you use keywords and synonyms throughout the article, but don't stuff your article with keywords just to get search engines to pick up your article—their robots won't be amused, and neither will your flesh-and-blood visitors.

Updating articles regularly

Try to regularly add quality content to your site. Search engine spiders visit your site regularly; aim to have some new content added when they come around. This doesn't mean that the bigger the site is, the better your search results will be; it's a good practice to delete or archive outdated content.

4. The images – explain what they're about

To search engine spiders, an image is just a meaningless data file. This means you can help search engines by using distinct filenames for any image you use. Moreover, when inserting an image in the Joomla article editor, add a specific alternate text.

This **Alternate Text** (or `alt` text) is the short description that is shown when the image itself isn't displayed for some reason. You may also want to add a similar description to the **Title** field (under the **Advanced** tab). This title text pops up when the visitor's mouse pointer hovers over the image:

More on SEO-aware writing

Of course, creating great content isn't a Joomla-specific art. If you want to read more on SEO-aware writing, there are many resources on the Web. To get a clear overview of the basics, download Google's *Search Engine Optimization Starter Guide* from `www.google.com`. Sites such as `Copyblogger.com` offer numerous tips on writing effective copy for the Web.

Configuring HTML page titles

It's considered good SEO practice to not only add a specific page heading (contained in the `H1` element), but to also make sure that each page has a descriptive HTML page title (the `title` element). Page titles are one of the most important ranking factors for search engines, so it's important to make sure they contain relevant information about the content.

The contents of the `title` element aren't displayed on the web page itself, but they're shown in the browser title bar. The following screenshot shows how the page title **Using Joomla!** is displayed in Mozilla Firefox:

In most browsers, the page title is also displayed in the current browser tab.

Time for action – setting the HTML page title

By default, Joomla bases the HTML page title upon the menu link text (the menu item's **Menu Title**). However, you can also control the page title text manually. If you want the HTML page title to be different from the menu item title, you can set a specific HTML **Page Title** in the **Menu Link** details. Let's find out how this works:

1. Navigate to **Menus | Menu Manager** and select the menu containing the link you want to edit. In this example, let's select the **About Joomla!** menu.

2. Click on the **Using Joomla** link to edit it. In the **Page Display Options** panel, enter the desired **Browser Page Title** text. For testing purposes, you can enter something like **Browser Page Title Set in Menu Item**:

3. Click on **Save & Close** and then click on **View Site** to see the output on the frontend. Navigate to the menu item that you've changed to see the new title in the browser title bar (and in the current browser tab):

What just happened?

You've seen how to control the **Browser Page Title** by editing the Menu Item details. However, you can't change the **Page Title** for an article that isn't directly linked to through a menu link. If, for example, an article is displayed through a link on a **Category Blog** page, Joomla will base the **Browser Page Title** on the article title (set in the article edit screen details).

Adding the Site Name to the page title

Another way to configure the HTML page title is to append the **Site Name** to it. This is the name you've entered when installing Joomla and that you can also enter or change in the **Site Name** field found through **Site | Global Configuration | Site Settings**.

The benefit of having the option to add the site name is that all the pages will display both information about the site *and* about the current page contents. If your organization feels that having its brand in the title is important, now you can add it through a site-wide option in the **Global Configuration** settings.

To try this out, navigate to **System | Global Configuration**. In the **SEO settings** section, the option **Include Site Name in Page Titles** is set to **No**. This indicates that the page title will be taken from the current article heading or page heading. For example, the page title for the **Getting Started** page in the sample data is **Getting Started**, as shown in the following screenshot:

If you choose **Before** or **After** in the **Include Site Name in Page Titles** option, the site name will be added. For example, if you had entered **Your Site Name** as the site name, the page title would change as follows:

In this example, the text **Your Site Name** is added to the beginning of the HTML page title.

 Should you choose to put the brand name or site name before the page topic in the HTML title? For search engines, the first word in the title tag is most relevant. When you expect people to search for your brand name, putting it in the HTML title can boost your ranking. But if people search specifically for the topics of your pages—and your site name or brand name isn't well known or doesn't describe the topic—you might want to add the site name at the end of page titles.

Adding meaningful metadata

Up to now, we've focused on actual content. You've seen how you can optimize articles to present their content in a clear and well-structured way. However, web pages also contain information that's not shown to site visitors, but is aimed specifically at search engine robots: metadata.

Metadata is information about the contents of the HTML document hidden in the document's source code. Browsers (and search engines) will read it; humans won't know it's there (unless they specifically look for it by selecting the **View Source** option in their web browser). Search engines may present the content of the meta description tag in the search results page. Although meta keywords aren't of importance for many search engines anymore, it won't hurt to add meaningful metadata to your site.

In Joomla, you can enter metadata on four levels:

- ◆ Site-wide, through **Global Configuration**
- ◆ For individual menu links
- ◆ For individual categories
- ◆ For individual articles

By default, your Joomla-powered site will only contain some dummy metadata, consisting of a short description and a few Joomla-related content keywords. Let's change these to something more appropriate.

Time for action – personalize the site metadata

You'll find the controls for optimizing your site for search engine traffic in the backend **Configuration Panel**. First, let's add some global keywords that characterize the site's content:

1. Navigate to **System | Global Configuration**. On the **Site** tab, there's a section called **Metadata Settings**.

2. Change the **Global Site Metadata Description** default text to a short summary of the content of your website. In our example, we'll enter **CORBA is an international club of Collectors Of Really Bad Art**.

3. In the **Global Site Meta Keyword** textbox, enter a few keywords that match the content of your website. Make sure to use the words and synonyms the visitor might use to search for your site's contents. You'll probably use a few words that are also part of the site description. In our example, we'll enter these keywords: **bad art**, **ugly art**, **bad paintings**. The **Metadata Settings** should now look similar to the following screenshot:

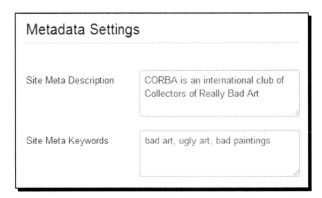

4. Click on **Save & Close**.

What just happened?

You've added some keywords and a descriptive text to your site. This information will be included in every page of your Joomla-powered site. Although search engines don't give much weight to meta keywords any more, the site description is still very important (and will show up when your site appears on a search results page).

 It's a good idea to keep your meta description as concise as possible. Google will only use the first 155 characters.

Choosing what metadata to set

You can override the global metadata description and keywords on three sublevels. Which of these meta tags are used on the actual web page? The principle is that metadata set on more specific levels override other metadata. In other words:

- Global metadata are used if you haven't set other meta information.
- You can override the global data by entering metadata for specific menu items. Entering these metadata is done in the **Metadata Options** panel in the **Edit Menu Item (or New Menu Item)** screen.
- Metadata for a category override global metadata or menu item metadata. You can enter metadata for articles categories, but also for categories in other components, such as **Contacts** categories.
- Finally, you can set metadata on the level of individual articles. These override global, menu item, or category metadata.

Now that you can set metadata on four levels, do you need to use them all? It's a good idea to set global metadata, as this provides search engines with general information on the nature of your site. You can choose to set metadata for specific menu items, categories, and individual pages if these are important from a SEO point of view. But there will probably be many pages that you don't have to bother adding metadata for; for example, a **Site Policy** page or a **Disclaimer** article are probably much less important than specific pages describing the services or products you want to sell.

Have a go hero – find metadata to fit your site

All that bad art business is okay for the example site, but what particular metadata description and keywords would fit your particular site best? First, do a little research and use the Google keyword tool mentioned before (or a similar tool) to get a few keyword ideas. Another way to get going is to have a look at how others do it—what kind of keywords and descriptions do similar sites use? Of course you won't copy that text (as that will be of little use in making your site a unique source of information), but it may inspire you.

To explore metadata, point your browser to a site you'd like to explore and select the option to look under the hood of the current website—it's probably called something like **View Page Source**. A new browser window or tab will open showing the HTML source code of the current page. You'll find the meta tags in the `<head>` section of the document.

Don't forget to choose the perfect site name

One of the first things you do when you set up a new site is entering a name for it. You'll be prompted to enter a name when installing Joomla; after that, you can change this text from the **Global Configuration** screen. It's a good idea to think very carefully about the **Site Name** as this will appear in the browser title bar of the home page.

Using search engine friendly URLs

Up to now, we've focused on SEO techniques you can apply when writing and formatting articles, and on adding metadata. Another technique that can make search engines pick up the contents of your site more easily is to make your URLs clear and readable.

You don't have to do anything to make this happen: by default, **Search Engine Friendly URLs** are turned on. In **SEO Settings** (found via the **System | Global Configuration | Site** tab), the **Search Engine Friendly URLs** option is set to **Yes**:

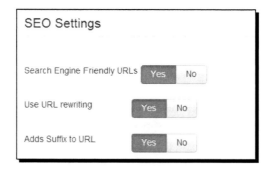

The resulting URLs are readable and easy to understand:

`http://www.example.com/index.php/getting-started.`

This is good news for site administrators, as they don't have to change any settings here. The default URLs are fine for search engines.

There's still some room for improvement: all default Joomla URLs still share the `index.php` bit. You can get rid of this part of the URLs using the **Use URL rewriting** option, found in the **SEO Settings** section. However, this requires a bit more work than just setting this option to **Yes**. If your site is hosted on an Apache-powered web server (which is very common), you'll also have to rename the `htaccess.txt` file in the Joomla root folder on the web server to `.htaccess` (with a leading dot). Not all hosting providers allow you to use `.htaccess` files or have the necessary Apache module installed. If you're not sure whether your account supports this, check with your hosting provider.

If your web host runs IIS web server software, consult `http://docs.joomla.org/ Enabling_Search_Engine_Friendly_(SEF)_URLs_on_IIS`.

By setting **Adds Suffix to URL**, the **html** suffix is added to **URLs**. This is recommended because this makes the Joomla output look like pages in static sites. Search engines tend to prefer static pages to dynamic output, which is likely to change all the time.

 And what if the pretty URLs function doesn't work? First check if you've renamed `htaccess.txt` properly to `.htaccess` (mind the leading dot!). If you still get error messages when checking out the frontend of the site, it's possible your web server doesn't support the advanced requirements of the second option (using `mod_rewrite`). To check this, go to **System | System Information** and click the **PHP Information** tab. Search that page for **mod_rewrite**; it should be mentioned under **Loaded Modules**. If it's not, you should try if setting only the **SEO Settings** option **Search Engine Friendly URLs** to **Yes** does the trick.

Adding extra links to site content

Search engines rate your site higher if it's an active part of the World Wide Web community. That means it's good to create links to other sites (outbound links) that offer relevant quality content on related subject matter.

Of course, it's great if other quality sites contain links to your site. One way to get the world to notice your site is to notify Google, Bing, and others that they're welcome to index your content; all search engines have a service that allows you to submit your site. Another way to get others to link to your site is by submitting your site to several useful directories. Other sites or blogs might want to link to your site if you offer good and relevant content. You can also consider writing articles for related sites, providing these allow you to link back to your site.

It's also worth adding *internal* links (that is links within your site). By adding these, you'll make it easier for both visitors and search engines to find your content. You can manually create links in your articles, but Joomla also allows you to automatically create internal hyperlinks. It allows you to set all article titles to be hyperlinks to the main article text and it enables you to dynamically create lists of hyperlinks.

 By default, the titles of articles displayed with intro texts (on the home page, or on overview pages) are hyperlinks to the full articles. It's best to leave this setting unchanged, as it provides an extra link to the article contents (apart from Read more links).

Creating an automatically generated list of hyperlinks

Another way to easily create internal hyperlinks in Joomla is by adding link lists. Joomla contains a few modules allowing you to add different hyperlink lists, for example a list of links to the most popular articles on the site or to the articles that have been added most recently.

Time for action – adding a list of links to popular articles

Let's add a list of links to popular articles on the example site:

1. Navigate to **Extensions | Module Manager**. Click on **New**.

2. Select the **Most Read Content** module. In the **Module Most Read Content** screen, enter the details for this module. In the **Title** field enter **Popular Articles**.

3. In the **Position** field, select **footer3** to show this module at the bottom-right position of the Ice Future template (covered in the previous chapter):

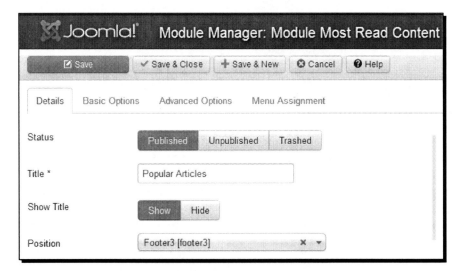

4. Leave the other settings as they are. By default, the **Menu Assignment** settings will make the module display on all pages. The **Basic Options** are set to show a list of five hyperlinks from all articles.

5. Click on **Save** and click on **View Site** to see the output on the frontend of the site:

> ## Popular Articles
>
> - Hideous Still Lifes
> - Mission Statement
> - Just What is Ugly Art?
> - CORBA Magazine Looking for Authors
> - An Overview of Bad Art Musea

What just happened?

You've added the **Most Read Content** module to your site to display a list of popular articles. These are the articles that have the highest number of page views. Having lists like this on your site is again good for both your real visitors (who'll be able to find out what other visitors like to read) and for your robot visitors who appreciate regularly updated links to different articles within the site.

Have a go hero – add link lists

Have a look at the other link list modules that Joomla contains, such as the **Latest News** module (displaying recently added articles) and the **Articles - Related Articles** module, showing a list of articles related to the current article the visitor sees. Articles are considered to be related if they share at least one keyword in the article's metadata information. If you've got lots of content on your site, it's a good idea to offer visitors several ways to find popular, related, or recently added articles.

Using a site map

A site map is a one-page overview of your site's contents containing links to all pages. Adding a site map will automatically create internal links to all pages, and both real visitors and search engine robots will benefit from it as it presents a clear overview of the site's contents. In small sites with a simple basic structure (such as our example site) a site map doesn't add much value. However, when you've got lots of categories and lots of contents, displaying a clickable tree structure of the site contents can be useful. You may want to experiment with Joomla's built-in basic site map capabilities: there's a **Menu Item Type** available called **List All Categories**. It displays a list of hyperlinks to all articles categories. However, it doesn't display content other than just plain articles. If you need a more powerful sitemap, try out the Xmap extension found through `http://extensions.joomla.org`.

Redirecting visitors to pages that have been moved

Joomla features a component called **Redirect Manager**. It works in conjunction with a plugin called **Redirect**, which is enabled by default. The **Redirect Manager** and plugin keep track of any "page not found" errors that occur when visitors are trying to visit pages in the current domain that have been removed or deleted. In the **Redirect Manager** screen, these URL errors are listed. This way, you can keep an eye on the old URLs that still attract visitors, but just generate "page not found" errors. For each of these URLs, you can choose to redirect future visitors to the right pages.

This feature can be quite useful, especially if you're migrating to a new site. URLs from your old site are bound to change, resulting in broken links from other sites that still point to expired URLs. Using URL redirection will also help search engine spiders to detect valuable content, instead of just hitting a dead-end error page.

Time for action – creating page redirects

Let's assume you've replaced your old site with a brand new one. We'll try out how the **Redirect Manager** component works by entering a non-existing old URL and tell the **Redirect Manager** what new page it should show instead:

1. Go to **Components | Redirect** to open the **Redirect Manager: Links** screen:

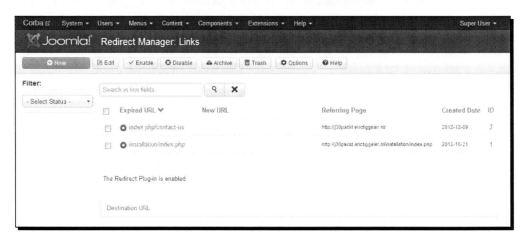

In the course of time, the **Expired URL** column in the **Redirect Manager: Links** screen will automatically be populated with broken links. These are URLs that visitors have entered or clicked on in their browser and that have generated an error page. Clicking an **Expired URL** will allow you to enter a redirect URL. However, if you've just installed Joomla or if your site isn't live yet, the **Redirect Manager: Links** screen won't contain any expired URLs.

1. Click on **New** to open the **Redirect Manager: Link** screen.

2. In the **Source URL** field, enter the outdated URL. Make sure to enter not just any wrong URL; it should contain the domain name from the current site. Replace www. example.com in the following example by your own domain name:

3. To find the URL you want to redirect visitors to, navigate to the new page to copy the URL from the browser address field. To do this, click on **View Site** to open the website in a new browser tab. Navigate to the page you want to redirect visitors to. Don't copy the following example URL—navigate to an existing page on your site:

4. Copy the URL in the browser URL field using *Ctrl + C*. The URL data is now stored in the clipboard.

5. Click on the browser tab that takes you back to the backend of your site, displaying the **Redirect Manager: Link** screen again.

6. In the **Destination URL** field, paste the copied URL using *Ctrl + V*:

7. In the **Comment** field, you can enter a short note about the nature of this redirect—for example, **redirecting from old About Us page**.

8. You can leave the **Options** unchanged. Actually, there's just one option available: you can either enable or disable this redirect. The redirect is turned on by default, so that's OK.

9. Click **Save & Close**. You're done. To test the redirect, navigate to the frontend of the site and enter the expired URL. You shouldn't get any error messages now; you're immediately taken to the new URL.

Getting to know more about your site traffic

In this chapter, you've focused on optimizing your site to get search engines to notice its contents and to entice people to explore it and to visit your site regularly. However, the best way to improve your sites visibility is to get to know your visitors really well. Where do they come from? What search words do they use to end up on your site? What are the articles they favor? A great (free) tool to help you discover all there is to know on your site traffic is **Google Analytics**.

Using Google Analytics will help you understand what makes your visitors tick, and can make it easier to effectively adapt your content, the language, the keywords you use, and even your choice of subjects to what your visitors care for. It's easy to use Analytics to analyze Joomla sites. It's free. These are the steps involved: make sure to get an account at www. google.com, go to www.google.com/analytics and sign up for this service. Add the domain you want to keep track of. Google will verify you're the domain owner (you'll have to upload a specific file to your site). In Joomla, add a code provided by Google to your template's HTML file, enabling Google to start analyzing and keeping track of your site traffic. To get a quick overview of the possibilities of Google Analytics, visit http://www.google.com/analytics/tour.html.

More SEO resources

Using your favorite search engine to do a web search for "Joomla SEO" will help you on your way when you want to know more about optimization techniques. If you want to delve a little deeper into the principles of SEO for your website, make sure to have a look at the Google starter guide on SEO (http://www.google.com/webmasters/docs/search-engine-optimization-starter-guide.pdf).

You might also want to have a look at these sites:

- ◆ SEO tips for Joomla on the JoomlaBlogger site: `http://www.joomlablogger.net/seo`.

- ◆ The Joomla community magazine on SEO: `http://magazine.joomla.org/issues/issue-feb-2012/item/675-5-great-SEO-Resources-Be-Your-Very-Own-SEO-Expert-for-Free`.

- ◆ Browse the SEO and Metadata and SEF categories of the Joomla extensions directory (`http://extensions.joomla.org`) to get an idea of the many extensions available to assist you in optimizing your site's search engine visibility.

Pop quiz – test your knowledge of Joomla search engine optimization

Q1. What's the use of adding metadata descriptions to the articles of your website?

- a. Site visitors can quickly find out what your site is all about.

- b. Search engines can display the descriptions in their search output.

- c. They're not really useful, because search engines ignore descriptions.

Q2. To optimize Search Engine Friendly URLs in Joomla:

- a. You have to rename Joomla files on the web server.

- b. Check the appropriate SEO Settings in the **Global Configuration** (and maybe rename a file on the web server).

- c. You have to install a special SEO extension.

Q3. What kind of links are important for SEO?

- a. Links from other sites to your site, and links from your site to other sites.

- b. Links within your site.

- c. Links to, from, and within your site.

Q4. What's the SEO benefit of the Joomla Redirect component?

- a. It allows you to redirect visitors and search engines that visit your site through links to outdated URLs.

- b. It allows you to analyze traffic (visits) on your site.

- c. It allows you to direct visitors to the most popular pages.

Summary

In this chapter, we've covered some Search Engine Optimization techniques that will help in getting your site's contents picked up by search engines.

◆ First of all, making sure your site contains valuable and relevant content is the best way to optimize search engine visibility.

◆ It's important to use the appropriate heading elements to organize the article text (such as H3, H4, H5, and H6). Another way to tell search engines what your site is about is by adding metadata.

◆ Joomla generates Search Engine Friendly URLs: the browser address bar displays readable URLs that match the content of the page.

◆ Linking is very important; it's good to link to other sites, it's great if other sites link to your site, and it's also useful to create links within *your* site. Joomla allows you to automatically create internal hyperlinks: lists of links to popular or recently updated articles.

◆ The **Redirect Manager** in Joomla helps you to direct visitors and search engine spiders from expired URLs to new URLs.

Keeping the Site Secure

You've created a great site, customized its design, and added valuable content. That's an investment worth protecting. Rest assured, most Joomla sites will run for years without any hiccups. However, it's a good idea to take some precautions to minimize the risk of your website getting broken. A few simple measures can make it a lot harder for malicious hackers to get access to your site and mess up its contents. Backing up regularly can get you out of trouble fast if you run into hardware disasters (think crashing hard drives) or software trouble (installing extensions that somehow mess up your existing site). Fortunately, these problems are rare, but it's definitely worth the little extra time investment needed to minimize risks.

How can you protect your site and how do you get your site up and running again when something has gone wrong? This appendix contains some essential tips and best practices to keep your site in perfect health (and save yourself some headaches too).

Choosing a web host that meets security requirements

In this appendix, you'll learn what you, as the site administrator, can do to keep your site safe. However, there are also some basic but critical security measures that your web hosting company should take. You'll probably have a shared hosting account, where multiple sites are hosted on one computer server, each site having access to their part of the available disk space and resources. Although this is much cheaper than hiring a dedicated server to host your site, it does involve some security risks. Good web hosting companies take precautions to minimize these risks. When selecting your web host, it's worth checking if they have a good reputation for keeping their security up to standards. The official Joomla resources site (`http://resources.joomla.org/directory/support-services/hosting.html`) features hosting companies that fully meet the security requirements of a typical Joomla-powered site.

Tip 1: Download from reliable sources

To avoid installing corrupted versions, it's a good idea to download the Joomla software itself only from the official website (`www.joomla.org`) or from reliable local Joomla community sites. The same holds for downloading third-party extensions. Use only extensions that have a good reputation; check the reviews on `http://extensions.joomla.org`. Preferably download extensions only from the original developer's website or from Joomla community websites with a good reputation.

Tip 2: Update regularly

The Joomla development team regularly releases updates to fix bugs and security issues. Fortunately, Joomla makes keeping your site up-to-date effortless. In the backend Control Panel you'll find two Quick Icons displaying the current status of both the Joomla software itself and of installed extensions. If updates are found, the Quick Icon text will prompt you to update. Here's what it looks like when a Joomla update is available:

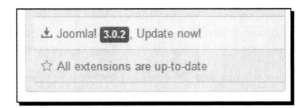

Clicking the **Update now!** link takes you to the **Joomla Update** component (also found via **Components | Joomla Update**) **Extensions | Extension Manager**. Here you'll see the details of the update. Just click on **Install the update** –the process is fully automated.

If updates for installed extensions are available, you'll also see a notice in the Quick Icon list in the Control Panel. It's also possible to manually check for updates: in the backend, navigate to **Extensions | Extension Manager** and click **Update** in the menu on the left-hand side. Click **Find Updates** to search for updates.

After you've clicked the **Find Updates** button, you'll see a notice telling you whether updates are available. Select the update you want to install and click the **Update** button. Be patient, you may not see much happening for a while. After completion, a message is displayed that the available updates have been installed successfully.

The **Update** functionality only works for extensions that support it. It's to be expected that this feature will be widely supported by extension developers, but for other extensions you'll still have to manually check for updates by visiting the extension developer's website.

Before you upgrade Joomla to an updated version, it's a good idea to create a backup of your current site. If anything goes wrong, you can quickly have it up and running again. See *Tip 6: Use extensions to secure your site* in this appendix for more information on creating backups.

> The Joomla update packages are stored in your website's tmp directory before installing the update on your site. After installation you can remove these files in the tmp directory to avoid running into disc space problems.

Tip 3: Choose a safe Administrator username

When you install Joomla, you also choose and enter a username for your login account (the critical account of the almighty **Super User**). Although you can enter any administrator username when installing Joomla, many people don't bother to change the default administrator username, **admin**. However, this generic username is a security risk—hackers only have to guess your password to access to the site.

If you haven't come up with something different during the installation process, you can change the administrator username later on. This is how you do it:

1. In the backend of the site, navigate to **Users | User Manager**.
2. Select the **Super User** user record.

3.   In the **Edit Profile** screen, enter a new **Login Name**. Be creative!

4.   Click on **Save & Close** to apply changes.

Log out and log in to the backend with the new username.

Tip 4: Pick a strong password

Pick an administrator password that isn't easy to guess. It's best to have a password that's not too short; eight or more characters is fine. Use a combination of uppercase letters, lowercase letters, numbers, and special characters—this should guarantee a strong password.

Don't use the same username and password you use for other online accounts, and regularly change your password. You can create a new password anytime in the backend User Manager in the same way you enter or change a username (see *Tip 2: Update regularly*).

Tip 5: Protect files and directories

Obviously, you don't want everybody to be able to access the Joomla files and folders on the web server. You can protect files and folders by setting access permissions using the CHMOD (Change Mode) command. Basically, CHMOD settings tell the web server who has access to a file or folder, who is allowed to read it, write to it, or to execute a file (run it as a program).

Once your Joomla site is set up and everything works OK, you can use CHMOD to change permissions. You don't use Joomla to change CHMOD settings; these are set with FTP software (for more information on FTP programs, see *Chapter 2, Installation: Getting Joomla Up and Running*). This is how it works:

1.   In your FTP program, right-click on the name of the file or directory you want to protect. In this example, we'll use the open source FTP program FileZilla.

2.   In the right-click menu select **File Permissions**.

3.   You'll be presented with a pop-up screen. Here, you can check permissions and change them by selecting the appropriate options as shown in the following screenshot:

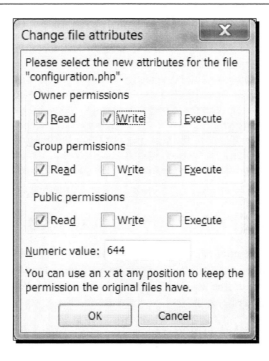

As you can see, it's possible to set permissions for the file **Owner** (that's you), for **Group** members (that's likely to be only you too), and for the **Public** (everyone else). This last one is the tricky part; you should restrict public permissions as much as possible.

When changing the permission settings, the file permissions number (the value in the **Numeric value:** box in the previous screenshot) will change accordingly. Every combination of settings has its particular number. In the previous example, this number is **644**.

4. Click on **OK** to execute the CHMOD command and set file permissions.

Setting File Permissions

What files should you protect and what CHMOD settings should you choose? Here are a few pointers:

- By default, permissions for files are set to 644. Don't change this; it's a safe value.
- For directories a safe setting is 750 (which doesn't allow any public access). However, some extensions may need access to certain directories; the 750 setting may result in error messages. In this case, set permissions to 755.

♦ Never leave permissions for a file or directory set to `777`: this allows everybody to write data to it.

 You can also block direct access to critical directories using a `.htaccess` file. This is a special file containing instructions for the Apache web server—among other things, it tells the web server who's allowed access to the directory's contents. You can add a `.htaccess` file to any folder on the server using specific instructions. This is another way to instruct the web server to restrict access. See the Joomla security documentation on `www.joomla.org` for instructions.

Tip 6: Use extensions to secure your site

There are many things you yourself can do to keep your site safe, but there's also dedicated security software available. Just like you've probably installed a firewall and antivirus software on your computer, you can install security extensions to add a layer of protection to your site and prevent intrusions and hacker attacks.

The Joomla extensions site has a special security category, found at `http://extensions.joomla.org/extensions/access-a-security`. Just a few examples to give you an idea of what's available:

♦ A relatively simple plugin is **AdminExile**, which prevents hackers from gaining access to the backend of your site by blocking the possibility of using the `www.mysite.com/administrator` login page. Users can only get to the login page using a secret key.

♦ A much more elaborate system (a combination of a component and plugin) is **Securitycheck**, which functions as a web firewall, performs security vulnerabilities checks for components, and much more.

It's a good idea to browse the **Access & Security** section now and then to see what's available and to read user reviews. It's best not to use too many extensions on your site. Potentially, every piece of code added to your site creates an extra security risk. If you've tried an extension and decide not to use it, uninstall it though **Extensions | Extension Manager | Manage | Uninstall**.

Using the Joomla Captcha plugin to avoid spam

To prevent spam bots from using site forms (such as the contact form and the login and registration forms), consider using the new **ReCaptcha** extension that comes with Joomla. This plugin requires anyone filling out a form to copy a few words which are displayed in an image of distorted text, before they are allowed to actually send the form data.

To enable ReCaptcha spam control in Joomla, you need a Google account.

1. Go to `www.google.com/recaptcha` to sign up and get two unique codes, the ReCaptcha keys. These keys are restricted to the domain name you specify.

2. Copy these codes to Joomla: in the backend, navigate to **Extensions** | **Plug-in Manager** | **Captcha – ReCaptcha** and enter both codes.

3. Finally, activate the captcha system via **System** | **Global Configuration** | **Captcha Settings** and select **Captcha - ReCaptcha**. From now on Joomla will display a ReCaptcha field on every form that you add through the Contacts component.

Tip 7: Have a backup ready

Whatever precautions you take, be prepared for catastrophes. Always have a backup ready to restore your site to its most current healthy state.

There are a few great Joomla extensions that automate the backup process. A very popular one is **Akeeba Backup**. It will back up all necessary files (all Joomla files and the database contents) to recover your site. Akeeba will allow you to restore the backup file to any location (not just to its original location).

Creating a Backup with Akeeba Backup

This is how you install Akeeba and create a backup:

1. Go to `https://www.akeebabackup.com` to download the Akeeba Backup Core extension file.

2. Navigate to **Extensions** | **Extension Manager** to install the extension.

3. Navigate to **Components** | **Akeeba Backup**. In the **Post-installation configuration** screen, click **Apply these preferences** to confirm the default settings. The Akeeba **Configuration Wizard** will now run a series of test to optimize the server configuration. This may take several minutes, but it's something that needs to be done only once. Finally, the **Finished Benchmarking** screen is displayed.

4. Click on **Backup Now** to make a backup using the default settings. In the next screen, Start a new backup, again click on the **Backup now!** button. The backup starts immediately and the **Backup Progress** screen is displayed:

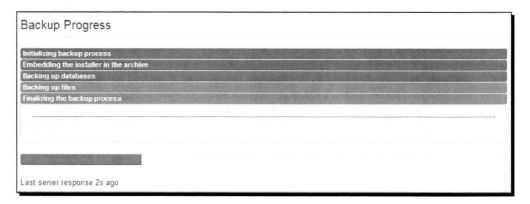

5. Backing up your site may take a while (depending on the size of the website and the speed of the web server). Although a progress bar is displayed, you may not see anything happen on the screen for several seconds. Don't close the browser screen before you see a completion message.

6. When the backup is complete, you'll see a message: **Backup Completed Succesfully**.

7. To save the backup file on your computer, click on **Administer Backup Files**. Select the backup file and click on the **Part 00** button in the **Manage & Download** column. A file with a JPA extension will be downloaded to your computer. A JoomlaPack Archive (JPA) file is a compressed file in the special archive format used by Akeeba Backup.

If you have any problems downloading the backup file in your browser, you can also use your FTP program. This is a more reliable method to transfer large files to your computer. Navigate using your FTP program to the root folder of the website. You'll find the backup file in the `administrator/components/com_akeeba/backup` folder.

Restoring a backup

This is how you restore a backup file:

1. To decompress the backup file on the web server, you need a special Akeeba utility called **Akeeba Kickstart**. Download it from `https://www.akeebabackup.com`. Extract the ZIP file containing `kickstart.php` and several other files in a folder on your computer.

2. Using an FTP program, upload the following files to the original location:
   - ❑ The JPA file (the backup created by Akeeba)
   - ❑ The decompressed files of Akeeba Kickstart.

   Upload these to the web server directory where you want to restore Joomla. If you want to restore the site to another location, upload the files there.

3. When all files have finished uploading, point your browser to the URL of the original site (or the new location), followed by `kickstart.php`. For example, `www.yoursitename.com/kickstart.php`.

4. Akeeba Kickstart will start with a warning screen. Close this pop-up screen.

5. Click **Start** to run Kickstart and begin decompressing the backup file. This may take some time.

6. As soon as this is done, click **Run the installer**. The **Akeeba Backup Installer** screen will appear. Follow the instructions of the installer.

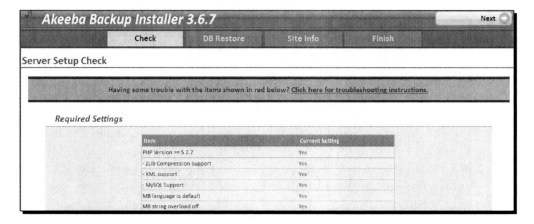

7. When you're installing to a different location than the one you backed up from, Akeeba will display a warning and allow you to enter the new database details. When done, click **Next** to see the database restoration progress.

8. Click **OK** to proceed to the next step. In the **Site Setup** screen, check if the site details (such as the **Site Name**) are okay. Click **Next**. In the **Finish** screen, click the **remove the installation directory** link. You'll see a notice confirming the deletion. Click **OK**. This will take you to the restored site.

You're done! To enter the administrative interface, as usual add /administrator to the site URL.

There are other ways to restore websites using Akeeba Backup; whether these are useful in your situation, depends on the web server configuration. Not all web servers support Akeeba's more advanced features. To find out more, have a look at the step-by-step tutorial and extensive documentation on at `https://www.akeebabackup.com/documentation.html`.

Tip 8: Stay informed!

Obviously, there's much more to learn about keeping your site secure. For more tips, have a look at:

- Joomla Administrators Security Checklist:
  `http://docs.joomla.org/Category:Security_Checklist`

- The official Joomla security forum at:
  `http://forum.joomla.org/viewforum.php?f=714`

To keep up-to-date with the latest news on Joomla security issues, visit `http://developer.joomla.org/security/news.html`.

If you use news reader software, you can subscribe to Joomla Security Announcements there.

B

Creating a Multilingual Site

One of the advantages of Joomla 3 is that is makes it relatively easy for you to create a multilingual website, without having to install extensions. In this appendix you'll find a short walkthrough explaining the general process of creating multilingual sites.

This appendix gives you an idea of the steps involved in creating multilingual sites in Joomla. If you want to make a multilingual site yourself, you'll find a full step-by-step tutorial including detailed instructions and all the necessary screenshots on the website accompanying this book, www.joomm.net.

Let's assume you want to have a bilingual site. In this example, the default site should be in English and we'll use Dutch as the second site language.

1. Adding a new language

After you've installed Joomla, there's one language available. First, you need to install the language files for the second language on the site. In the **Language Manager**, install a Site Language pack for the Dutch language. This contains the translated versions of all texts that come with Joomla (such as Read more).

Moreover, you need to add what Joomla calls a **Content Language**—a language profile, containing the details needed for Joomla to be able to use the English or the Dutch language as "switchable" content languages.

2. Enabling Joomla to switch between languages

The next step is to enable Joomla's **Language Filter** plugin, which enables the CMS to recognize the different installed languages and display only the content relevant to the current language. This plugin will try to detect the language settings of the site visitor's browser and display the site in this language (if this is present).

3. Adding multilingual content

To organize the actual content on your site, you need to create top-level categories holding (in this case) English and Dutch content. Moreover, you'll need to tell Joomla what language the content belongs to: assign the appropriate Language setting (English or Dutch) to both the categories and the articles they contain.

4. Creating menus for the multilingual content

Next, you need to create a menu pointing to the English articles, and a separate menu pointing to the Dutch articles. Again, when adding menu links, you'll need to tell Joomla what language the menu link belongs to. Finally, you'll select one menu link to be the default link—the home page to be displayed for either the English site or the Dutch site.

5. Connect menu links to their translated counterparts

The next step is to "draw lines between menu links" in different languages. In other words, you need to tell Joomla what Dutch article should serve as the translated alternative of a particular English menu item. For each menu link (for example, the Dutch Article 1 menu link), you can create an association with the English counterpart (for example, the English Article 1 menu link).

6. Finalizing the site menus

As is the case with every new menu created in Joomla, you have to add a menu module in order to be able to display the menu on the site. Again, you should assign these modules to the appropriate languages.

Apart from the new menus, Joomla will still need the default Main Menu (and the Home link it contains) to function. However, as the Main Menu doesn't need to be displayed any more, you can unpublish the menu module associated with the Main Menu.

7. Enabling the visitor to select a language

Just one step to go before your multilingual site is finished. When the user visits the site using a browser which is set to use the English language, Joomla will display the English content—all articles and modules that have English as their content language. However, we also want the visitor to be able to actively switch to the translated content in another language.

To add this functionality, you install the **Language Switcher** module that comes with Joomla. Should visitors wish to see the Dutch version of the site contents, they can now click the Dutch flag icon in the **Language Switcher**, as shown here:

After the visitor has clicked the Dutch flag, Joomla will serve the Dutch articles and the Dutch menu.

Read the step-by-step tutorial on multilingual sites

This appendix gives you a general overview of the steps involved in creating a multilingual site. If you want to create a multilingual site for yourself, you'll find a full step-by-step walkthrough of all steps on the website accompanying this book: `http://www.joomm. net/index.php/joomla-tips-and-tutorials/creating-a-multilingual- site-in-joomla-3`.

C

Pop Quiz Answers

Chapter 2, Installation: Getting Joomla Up and Running

Pop quiz – test your knowledge of installing Joomla

Q1. Why do you need FTP software before you can install Joomla?

    a. To unzip the installation package.

    b. To upload files from your computer to the web server.

    c. To back up your site.

Answer: b

Q2. What are the main steps in installing Joomla?

    a. First upload the Joomla files and then run the web installer.

    b. Download Joomla, unpack and upload the files, create a database, then run the web installer.

    c. Download Joomla, unpack and upload the files, run the Web installer, and create a database.

Answer: b

Q3. Which username and password do you have to enter in the Joomla web installation wizard?

    a. The username and password needed to log in to the Joomla backend.

    b. The username and password needed to access the MySQL database.

    c. The username and password needed to access the MySQL database, and the username and password needed to log in to the Joomla backend.

Answer: c

Chapter 3, First Step: Getting to Know Joomla

Pop quiz – test your knowledge of Joomla basics

Q1. What's makes a CMS-based website different from a traditional, static website?

    a. A CMS consists of an unlimited database of web pages.

    b. A CMS doesn't use traditional coding languages, such as HTML.

    c. A CMS dynamically builds web pages by gathering content blocks from a database.

Answer: c

Q2. What's the backend of a Joomla-powered website?

    a. It's the interface where administrators log in to change site configuration settings.

    b. It's the interface where administrators log in to build and maintain the site.

    c. It's the part of the site that's only accessible for registered users.

Answer: b

Q3. How can you rearrange the page layout of your site and move about content blocks?

    a. By moving and deleting articles.

    b. By using the **Module Manager** to change the position and visibility of modules.

    c. By using the **Article Manager** to change the position and visibility of articles.

Answer: b

Chapter 4, Web Building Basics: Creating a Site in an Hour

Pop quiz – test your basic Joomla knowledge

Q1. What can you use the built-in Joomla CSS editor for?

    a. To add some content containers.

    b. To change the appearance of your site.

    c. To change menu settings.

Answer: b

Q2. In what order do you add articles and menu links?

    a. Create menu links first, then add articles.

    b. Add articles first, then create menu links.

    c. You can choose whatever order you like.

Answer: b

Q3. How can you insert images in articles?

    a. You can add images in fixed positions through the **Images and links** feature in the article editor.

    b. You can add images anywhere you like in the article text by using the Image button below the article editor text field.

    c. You can choose between a) and b), whatever is more appropriate for your goals.

Answer: c

Q4. What do you use **Components** and **Extensions** for?

    a. Adding extras, such as newsletters or contact forms.

    b. Adding content that only registered users can see.

    c. To quickly add new content.

Answer: a

Chapter 5, Small Sites, Big Sites: Organizing your Content Effectively

Pop quiz – test your site organization knowledge

Q1. What's the best order in which to build Joomla-based sites?

    a. Start with extensions, add content, add menu links, add content containers.

    b. Start with menu links, add content containers, add content, add extensions.

    c. Start with content containers, add content, add menu links, add extensions.

Answer: c

Q2. What can you use uncategorized articles for?

    a. To display articles that have not yet been authorized.

    b. To display articles that do not belong to categories.

    c. To display articles that are displayed on the homepage

Answer: b

Q3. How can you get categories to display in the frontend?

    a. Categories are backend stuff; they're only displayed in the **Category Manager**.

    b. A category can be displayed by adding a specific menu link that points to a category overview page.

    c. Categories are automatically displayed on overview pages when added to the **Category Manager**.

Answer: b

Chapter 6, Creating Killer Content: Adding and Editing Articles

Q1. The article editor screen in Joomla allows you to do which of these three things?

a. Formatting article text.

b. Inserting images.

c. Controlling the start and end date of publishing.

Answer: all three are correct

Q2. What's the use of the Joomla Media Manager?

a. It allows you to manage all sorts of media (images, movie files, and MP3 files).

b. It allows you to upload images and insert them into an article.

c. It allows you to insert images that come with the default Joomla installation.

Answer: b

Q3. You open an existing article in the Joomla article editor and see a red dotted line. What does that mean?

a. Text below the line will not be displayed.

b. The article text has exceeded the maximum number of characters allowed.

c. If needed, Joomla can separately display the intro text and the full article text.

Answer: c

Q4. How can you break a long article into a series of short ones?

a. By manually creating several individual articles.

b. By entering page breaks in an article.

c. By entering **Read more** links in an article.

Answer: b

Q5. What's the function of archiving articles?

    a. Archived articles cannot be edited any more.

    b. Archived articles aren't displayed in the frontend.

    c. Archived articles are displayed in a special **Archive** part of the frontend.

Answer: c

Chapter 7, Welcoming your Visitors: Creating Attractive Home Pages and Overview Pages

Pop quiz – test your knowledge of home pages and overview pages

Q1. How can you change the arrangement of items on your home page?

    a. By adding new content in the **Featured Articles** list.

    b. By changing the **Main Menu Home** link settings.

    c. By selecting **Status: Featured** in the **Article** editor.

Answer: b

Q2. How do you create a category overview page?

    a. By adding a new article in the **Article Manager**.

    b. By adding a new category.

    c. By adding a new menu link to point to category.

Answer: c

Q3. In what cases would you choose to present content in a **Category Blog** layout?

    a. **Category Blog** layouts are used strictly for web logs.

    b. **Category Blog** layouts are used to show a row of article titles.

    c. You use **Blog** layout to show teaser texts or full articles.

Answer: c

Chapter 8, Helping your Visitors Find What they Want: Managing Menus

Pop quiz – test your knowledge on menus

Q1. How many menus can you add to your website?

    a. Six Menus (the Main Menu and five other menus).

    b. As many as you want.

    c. You can only have one Main Menu.

Answer: b

Q2. How can you add submenu items to a menu?

    a. By creating *parent links* and *child links*.

    b. By assigning a different Parent Item to a menu link than the default (Home).

    c. By creating a new menu.

Answer: b

Q3. When you create a new menu link, why does Joomla show such a big list of Menu Item Types?

    a. To enhance navigation.

    b. To enable you to create new menus.

    c. To enable you to create different types of target pages.

Answer: c

Chapter 9, Opening up the Site: Enabling Users to Log in and Contribute

Pop quiz – test your knowledge of Joomla user management

Q1. What's the difference between registered users and ordinary site visitors?

    a. Registered users can add content to the site.

    b. Registered users are able to view *registered* content.

    c. Registered users are team members.

Answer: b

Q2. What's the use of displaying a login form on your website?

    a. To allow users to log in or to register.

    b. To allow anyone to log in to the backend.

    c. To allow users to activate their account.

Answer: a

Q3. What's the advantage of using the **Register to read more** links?

    a. Site visitors will feel encouraged to add content.

    b. Site visitors will feel encouraged to register to read partly hidden content.

    c. Site visitors won't be able to know what content is hidden.

Answer: b

Q4. On which levels of the site can you set permissions for user groups?

    a. Only for the whole site, through **Global Configuration**.

    b. For components, for categories or for individual articles.

    c. Site-wide, for components, for categories, or for individual articles.

Answer: c

Chapter 10, Getting the Most out of your Site: Extending Joomla

Pop quiz – test your knowledge of Joomla extensions

Q1. What's the difference between components and other extensions?

    a. Components are more powerful and more complex.

    b. Components are only available to selected users.

    c. Components are shown in different module positions.

Answer: a

Q2. What's the use of the **Newsflash** module?

    a. To allow visitors to subscribe to newsfeeds.

    b. To show just one news item in a module position.

    c. To show one or more article intro texts in a module position.

Answer: c

Q3. What's the use of installing modules?

    a. Modules can make it easier entering new content.

    b. Modules can contain any kind of advanced functionality.

    c. Modules can contain lists of hyperlinks.

Answer: b

Chapter 11, Creating an Attractive Design: Working with Templates

Pop quiz – test your knowledge of Joomla templates

Q1. What does a Joomla template actually do?

    a. It changes the colors and the header graphic.

    b. It determines the overall layout and design.

    c. It allows you to set all sorts of layout options.

Answer: b

Q2. After installing a new template, you notice some empty spaces in your site layout. What does this mean?

    a. Something went wrong and you should re-install the template.

    b. You have to assign modules to the available (empty) positions.

    c. You have to add content to some (empty) modules.

Answer: b

Q3. What are the benefits of using web developer tools, such as the the Inspect element feature of the Chrome browser?

    a. You can preview CSS edits and automatically save changes to your template.

    b. You can edit CSS in the backend of your Joomla site.

    c. You can analyze and edit CSS styles of any website, and you can preview the effects of any changes you make.

Answer: c

Chapter 12, Attracting Search Engine Traffic: Tips and Techniques

Pop quiz – test your knowledge of Joomla search engine optimization

Q1. What's the use of adding metadata descriptions to the articles of your website?

    a. Site visitors can quickly find out what your site is all about.

    b. Search engines can display the descriptions in their search output.

    c. They're not really useful, because search engines ignore descriptions.

Answer: b

Q2. To optimize search engine friendly URLs in Joomla:

    a. You have to rename Joomla files on the web server.

    b. Check the appropriate SEO Settings in the **Global Configuration** (and maybe rename a file on the web server).

    c. You have to install a special SEO extension.

Answer: b

Q3. What kind of links are important for SEO?

    a. Links from other sites to your site, and links from your site to other sites.

    b. Links within your site.

    c. Links to, from, and within your site.

Answer: c

Q4. What's the SEO benefit of the Joomla Redirect component?

    a. It allows you to redirect visitors and search engines that visit your site through links to outdated URLs.

    b. It allows you to analyze traffic (visits) on your site.

    c. It allows you to direct visitors to the most popular pages.

Answer: a

Index

Thank you for buying
Joomla! 3 Beginner's Guide

About Packt Publishing

Packt, pronounced 'packed', published its first book "*Mastering phpMyAdmin for Effective MySQL Management*" in April 2004 and subsequently continued to specialize in publishing highly focused books on specific technologies and solutions.

Our books and publications share the experiences of your fellow IT professionals in adapting and customizing today's systems, applications, and frameworks. Our solution based books give you the knowledge and power to customize the software and technologies you're using to get the job done. Packt books are more specific and less general than the IT books you have seen in the past. Our unique business model allows us to bring you more focused information, giving you more of what you need to know, and less of what you don't.

Packt is a modern, yet unique publishing company, which focuses on producing quality, cutting-edge books for communities of developers, administrators, and newbies alike. For more information, please visit our website: www.packtpub.com.

About Packt Open Source

In 2010, Packt launched two new brands, Packt Open Source and Packt Enterprise, in order to continue its focus on specialization. This book is part of the Packt Open Source brand, home to books published on software built around Open Source licences, and offering information to anybody from advanced developers to budding web designers. The Open Source brand also runs Packt's Open Source Royalty Scheme, by which Packt gives a royalty to each Open Source project about whose software a book is sold.

Writing for Packt

We welcome all inquiries from people who are interested in authoring. Book proposals should be sent to author@packtpub.com. If your book idea is still at an early stage and you would like to discuss it first before writing a formal book proposal, contact us; one of our commissioning editors will get in touch with you.

We're not just looking for published authors; if you have strong technical skills but no writing experience, our experienced editors can help you develop a writing career, or simply get some additional reward for your expertise.

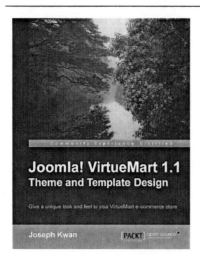

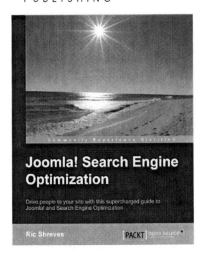

Joomla! Search Engine Optimization

ISBN: 978-1-84951-876-5   Paperback: 116 pages

Drive people to your site with this supercharged guide to Joomla! and Search Engine Optimization

1. Learn how to create a search engine-optimized Joomla! website.

2. Packed full of tips to help you develop an appropriate SEO strategy.

3. Discover the right configurations and extensions for SEO purposes.

Git: Version Control for Everyone

ISBN: 978-1-84951-752-2   Paperback: 180 pages

The non-coder's guide to everyday version control for increased efficiency and productivity

1. A complete beginner's workflow for version control of common documents and content.

2. Examples used are from non-techie, day-to-day computing activities we all engage in.

3. Learn through multiple modes – readers learn theory to understand the concept and reinforce it by practical tutorials.

Please check **www.PacktPub.com** for information on our titles

CPSIA information can be obtained at www.ICGtesting.com
Printed in the USA
BVOW06s1708090913

330704BV00003B/90/P

OCT - - 2013